PRINCIPLES
OF
CATHOLIC
SOCIAL
TEACHING

PRINCIPLES
OF
CATHOLIC
SOCIAL
TEACHING

David A. Boileau

Editor

MARQUETTE
UNIVERSITY

PRESS

MARQUETTE STUDIES IN THEOLOGY
No. 14

ANDREW TALLON, SERIES EDITOR

Library of Congress Cataloging-in-Publication Data

Principles of Catholic social teaching / David A. Boileau, editor.
    p. cm. — (Marquette studies in theology ; no. 14)
    Includes bibliographcal references and index.
    ISBN 0-87462-638-2
    1. Sociology, Christian (Catholic) 2. Catholic Church—Doctrines
I. Boileau, David A, 1930– . II. Series: Marquette studies in
theology ; #14.
    BX1753.P754 1998
    261.8'088'22—dc21

First published in Dutch by Acco
Tiensestraat 134-136, B-3000 Leuven, 1994

MARQUETTE UNIVERSITY PRESS
MILWAUKEE

The Association of Jesuit University Presses

DEDICATION

In Memoriam

Professor Eugene De Jonghe

(1922-1996)

Professor, Mentor, Friend

Contents

Introduction

The goal of this study, entitled *Principles of Catholic Social Teaching*, is to call attention to the contemporary significance of this teaching and, at the same time, to investigate what is meant by a number of central ideas that surface again and again in these essays. The reader will quickly note that these essays have a geographical focus centering on Dutch and German speaking communities. However, this focus should not blind us to a larger applicability to other countries. It was Professor De Jonghe's wish that I give it some American focus. So, with respect for his wish, I asked Professor Fred Crosson to do that for us.

However, before we begin we should correct what seems to be a common historical inaccuracy. Catholic social teaching began long before the last century. Professor Michael J. Schuck has shown[1] that the social teaching of the Papal Encyclicals began in 1740 under the pontificate of Benedict XIV (1740-58). What Professor Schuck calls the pre-Leonine period (1740-1877) will show that by a "textually inclusive and topically broad-gauged approach,"[2] a previously unacknowledged body of papal social teaching emerges. Primarily aimed against the Enlightenment and, of course, the French Revolution and its aftermath.

Nine Popes from 1740 to 1877 made negative judgments regarding the erosion of communal unity in traditionally Roman Catholic countries and regions. This erosion is significant in religious, political, family, economic and cultural life. And the Popes believe that all of this erosion is due to false ideas which were rampant in the 18th and 19th century, all a product of the Enlightenment.

Also, the Popes offer what Schuck[3] calls a "territorial" communitarian ethic. This ethic is based on the papal understanding of the self and society. That self is embedded in the tradition of a territorial community. This embeddedness provides a person's sense of identity and purpose and defines one's function and obligation. The Popes also understand this social ethic as "theological." The source is God's will mediated through Scripture, patristics, and Church tradition which is primarily handed down from the top to the bottom. The metaphor is of a shepherd and a flock.

Professor Schuck also corrects a historical misunderstanding by establishing a coherence between the pre-Leonine period and all subsequent periods (Leonine 1878-1888) (post-Leonine 1959-89).[4] To avoid distorting the understanding of encyclical teaching, Professor Schuck proposes a new method, which is now appearing in encyclical commentaries, which calls for an inclusive, holistic reading of a given pope's total encyclical corpus.

Secondly, his method will show that the encyclicals demonstrate serious interest in social relations involving not only economic affairs, but also political, religious, family and cultural affairs. He also claims that the pope's encyclicals contain several critical judgments of Enlightenment premises which become constituent of encyclical social teaching. These criticisms are not simply "historical artifacts."[5] And because the method employed by Professor Schuck shows the methods employed in arriving at the social teachings by the popes are eclectic, substantive contradictions occur in encyclical social thought. No single source nor method molds encyclical thought as a whole. Thus, to base them all on natural law thinking or on Thomistic, neo-Scholastic theology is, in Professor Schuck's opinion, inaccurate.[6]

Yet, because the encyclicals from 1740 until today share several common recommendations on God, the world, humanity, and issues of religion, politics, family, economic and culture, these recommendations are communitarian in nature and combined with the persistent negative judgments made by the popes, form and constitute a coherence of encyclical social teaching.

The interesting results of the methodological approach made by Professor Schuck opens papal teaching to European political thought and third world liberation theology. And with the decentering of natural law theory and the passing of neo-Thomism as the sole philosophical approach, the way is open between papal thought and Protestant social ethics in North America and Europe. There is also a development of new links between the critiques of Western liberalism, child of the Enlightenment, and papal social teaching so interpreted. We are in Professor Schuck's debt.

These essays contribute in no small way to the universal Church's attempt to celebrate, reevaluate and bring forward the tradition of Catholic social teaching for our own time and in our place. Looking over the entire papal social teaching from Benedict XIV's time to our own, Leo XIII stands out as a giant. He is, for sure, the keenest pope of the last three centuries. He, more than any, stands at the forefront of a tradition which emphasizes the radical primacy of human dignity and human solidarity as correctives to mere technocratic understandings of any economy or politics.

Basing themselves on the life and words of the Lord Jesus, the popes in the 18th and 19th centuries have, as we have seen and as John Coleman[7] points out, spoke a loud no to an excessive individualism; a decided no to attempts to privatize religion; a no to an espousal of a liberty of rights with no corresponding duties; a no to positivism in law, in politics, and in economics which renders it unaccountable to moral scrutiny or humanity; and finally, a no to civil rights without moral obligations. What the popes consistently did was insist upon the fact that no realm whatsoever could be outside the dominion of God. Nothing is a law unto itself. Positivism and agnosticism, two orphans of the Enlightenment, were singled out for criticism. God's ubiquitous presence must be admitted. This presence finds itself incarnate in the words, life, and death of Jesus, and not in any political or ideological agenda. There is a constant call, occasioned by new situations, which forces us to rethink what the dignity of man will mean in our century and in the large organizational structures of our society. The past is prologue and dated. It is especially in the world of work where human dignity is at risk, and so we must think anew the challenge of Jesus in the sermon on the mount as to what it means to be "poor in spirit" in the industrial, technological and consumer society in which we now live. The present pope, John Paul II, called work the central problem of our time.[8]

It is the present pope, John Paul II, who offered a definition of the concept "social teaching of the church" when in *Sollicitudo Rei Socialis* (Dec 30, 1987) he stated that it is a "doctrinal corpus" edited by the magisterium of the Roman Pontiff, beginning with the encyclical *Rerum Novarum* (May 15, 1891). He became more explicit in paragraph 44 when he says:

The Church's social doctrine is *not* a "third way" between *liberal capitalism* and *Marxist collectivism*, nor even a possible alternative to other solutions less radically opposed to one another: rather, it constitutes a *category of its own.* Nor is it an *ideology,* but rather the *accurate formulation* of the results of a careful reflection on the complex realities of human existence, in society and in the international order, in the light of faith and of the Church's tradition. Its main aim is to *interpret* these realities, determining their conformity with or divergency from the lines of the Gospel teaching on man and his vocation, a vocation which is at once earthly and transcendent; its aim is thus to *guide* Christian behavior. It therefore belongs to the field, not of *ideology,* but of *theology* and particularly of moral theology.[9]

He follows closely here the definition given in *Gaudium et Spes* of "the duty of scrutinizing the sign of the times and of interpreting them in the light of the Gospel."

We can nuance the Pope's definition by pointing out that Pope Leo's encyclical *Rerum Novarum* was not only a starting point but it was also a point of arrival. The social tradition of the Church, as we saw above, was much older and *Rerum Novarum* cannot be understood apart from the "social Catholicism" movement.

Nor can the social teaching of the Church be limited to the texts of papal encyclicals alone. As a permanent "learning process," the social teaching of the Church should be considered as the result of a dialogue between the magisterium of the pope, the bishops (including their general and regional synods and the texts made in the context of bishops conferences), the specialists in social ethics and social sciences and the people of God.

Paul VI in *Octogesimo Adveniens* (nr 4) expressed a methodological option to this "learning process" when he said:

> In the face of such widely varying situations it is difficult for us to utter a unified message and to put forward a solution which has universal validity. Such is not our ambition, nor is it our mission. It is up to the Christian communities to analyze with objectivity the situation which is proper to their own country, to shed on it the light of the gospel's unalterable words and to draw principles of the church (...) It is up to these Christian communities, with the help of the Holy Spirit, in communion with the bishops who hold responsibility and in dialogue with other Christian brethren and all men of good will, to discern the options and commitments which are called for in order to bring about the social, political and economic changes seen in many cases to be urgently needed.

We must also make some distinctions as to the several types of texts which make up the social teaching of the Church. There are three with seven parts:
1) Texts from an ecumenical council.

The pastoral constitution *Gaudium et Spes*, in the form of a hermeneutical point of view, is the most important document, not only because it is a constitution of an ecumenical council, but also because of its elaboration of the anthropological-ethical foundations.
2) Texts from the magisterium of the Roman Pontiff and from the Curia. There are seven types:

2.1) Social encyclicals.

Among the most important are Leo XIII's *Rerum Novarum* (1891); Pius XI's *Quadragesimo Anno* (1931); John XXIII's *Mater et Magistra* (1961); *Pacem in Terris* (1963); Paul VI's *Populorum Progressio* (1967); John Paul II's *Laborum Exercens* (1981), *Sollicitudo Rei Socialis* (1987), *Centesimus Annus* (1991). For a better understanding of John Paul II's ethical and anthropological presuppositions see also: *Redemptor Hominis* (1979), *Dives in Misericordia* (1980) and *Veritatis Splendor* (1993).

2.2) Apostolic Exhortations.

Since the general synod of bishops of 1974, the final text is not written by the bishops but officially by (or in the name of) the Pope. For the development of Catholic social teaching, the most important apostolic exhortations are: *Evangelii Nuntiandi* (1975) and *Christifedeles Laici* (1988).

2.3) Occasional texts and messages.

Pius XII used the radio in June of 1941, December of 1942, and September of 1944, to express his social vision. These radio messages are famous. For a most constituent text, see Paul VI's *Octogesimo Adveniens* which was an apostolic letter to Cardinal Roy on the 80th anniversary of *Rerum Novarum*.

2.4) Instructions from the Congregation for the Doctrine of the Faith.

Two are of especial interest: *Libertatis Nuntius* (1984), "on certain aspects of liberation theology," and *Libertatis Conscientia* (1986), on "Christian freedom and liberation."

2.5) Texts from the Pontifical Commission.

Justitia et Pax: here we should make note of: *The Church and Human Rights* (1974), *The Universal Distribution of Goods* (1977), *In Service of the International Community: An Ethical Approach on the International Debt* (1986).

2.6) Documents from the Congregation for Catholic Education.

It is here we find the very interesting and informative document: *Guidelines for the Study and Teaching of the Church's Social Doctrine in the Formation of Priests* (1988). We will see later on in our text how Professor De Jonghe makes use of this document.

2.7) Finally, there are official statements of the Holy See.

Of note here is Cardinal Casaroli's address to the United Nations on November 18, 1983. He addressed a special session on disarmament.

3) And then there are documents from Bishops. The South American Bishops (CELAM) in their Conferences of Medellin (1968),

Puebla (1979) and in Santo Domingo. Add to these texts from the Conferences of Bishops in Africa and Asia[10] and two very influential documents from the American National Conference of Bishops (NCCB) entitled: *The Challenge of Peace* (1983) and *Economic Justice for All* (1986).

All of these texts need to be interpreted. To do that at least six steps are needed: (a) We must understand the complexity of the text; (b) We must understand the author(s). Who wrote these texts for the pope's signature? What was their education? From what schools of thought did they come? What ideologies are operative? What defensive interests are manifest or hidden? Real tensions are obvious when one seeks out the ghost author; (c) We must then understand the "schools" to which the author(s) belong; (d) We must understand the social context of both text and author. Don't get the texts out of context, which means to (e) understand the "world of the text," and finally (f) we must understand the "wirkungsgeschichte" of the the texts.

If we start our celebration of one hundred years of Catholic social thought with the publication of *Rerum Novarum* (May 1891) and not forgetting the period before (1740-1877) we can pinpoint stages of development in the social teaching of the Church. The pastoral metaphor of flock and shepherd which characterized the pre-Leonine period changes during the Leonine period (1878-1958) to a communal character of self and society grounded not in the exigencies of living in a localized sheepfold but to a place in nature of universal design (natural law). This is the period of "social doctrine" following Leo XIII with Pius XI and Pius XII. All is natural law based, and the Magisterium of the Pope is the only legitimate interpretation. The method is deductive with emphasis on the continuing importance of the principle of subsidiarity as enunciated in *Quadragesimo Anno* (1931).

It is with John XXIII and Vatican II that a turning point takes place by becoming more personalistic and concrete than by the former abstract natural law approach. An inductive method of see, judge, act is used in scrutinizing the signs of the times and interpreting them in the light of the Gospels. Thus, more biblical elements enter into the social teaching of the Church.

Paul VI will continue this development by a recognition of the role of the local church as we saw above.[11] A long development and discussion now takes place centering on development and liberation. The reader should see: *Populorum Progressio* (1967), Medellin (1968), Synod on Justice (1971) and *Evangelii Nuntiandi* (1975).

It is with John Paul II that the main concern again shifts to the emphasis on the unity and consistency of the principles of the social thought of the Church in light of which the complex social unity should be judged. The core of his doctrine is the meaning of the human person in the light of the Mystery of Jesus Christ. As we saw above, John Paul II theologizes the social teaching of the Church. We could call it a Christocentric personalism. Any yet despite his criticism of liberation theology, he remains in dialogue with it. He retains the option for the poor; the correlation between the history of salvation and the history of emancipation; a recognition of social conflict and the introduction of the notion of the "structures of sin."

It is with the popes of the last one hundred years that we find an immediate background to our series of essays. Leo XIII's *Rerum Novarum* (1891) surfaced the role of social Catholicism and exposed the first tension between a European Corperatistic view and the more open Anglo-Saxon view of Cardinals Manning and Gibbons. Leo's encyclical was a reformist and not a radical document. Leo was a Centrist. He condemned both socialism and laissez-faire liberalism. He put the church on the side of the workers by offering the positive responsibility of the state to intervene on the side of the poor and uphold the claim in justice to decent wages, safe working conditions and the establishment of workers unions. We must not forget that Leo had previously established a philosophical basis for this position by his encyclical *Æterni Patris* (1879), which restored the study and doctrine of St. Thomas Aquinas as the official philosophy of the Church. His most trusted agent in this effort was Désiré Cardinal Mercier who established the Higher Institute of Philosophy at the Catholic University of Louvain.[12]

And, as Professor O'Brien points out,[13] *Rerum Novarum* was the document of the Ultramontaine Church. Everything was to be done under the direction of the hierarchy. Independent lay action was strongly discouraged. Using the balanced rationalism of Thomism, the Church could restore both the social order and bring about distributive justice.

The document surely is prophetic with its implied option for the poor. It is a criticism of socialism with its defense of private property. It struck at laissez-faire liberalism with its recognition of the social task of the state and of the public right of workers to form and join unions. Yet an ambiguity exists in it with its mix of social concern and its nostalgia for traditionalism.

Forty years later, the signs of the times were different. The optimism of the end of the 19th century died early in the 20th century.

The first world war was its graveyard. Capitalism faltered in the war and in the great depression. Fascism and Communism arose. So *Quadragesimo Anno* was radical. It called for reconstruction, not reform. Its keynote was social justice. This justice is, as Calvez and Perrin point out:[14]

> [Thus,] the statements of the ecclesiastical magisterium furnish us with a precise description of the extent of social justice as the general norm of the life of the entire social body. It is not to be reduced to particular forms of justice, which have to do with the direct relationships between individuals, nor with those which concern the political activities of governors. It includes these different forms: it concerns the dealings of men with one another, inasmuch as they are related to the whole society and its common good, and also the dealings of rulers with ruled, inasmuch as the ruled receive from society their part of the common good. The concept of the common good is at the center of its definition, and the idea of a social body, of a social universal, really existing by itself, contrary to all nominalist or individualist theory, is implicit in the descriptions which the popes give of social justice.

Although Pius XII made changes influenced by the fundamental changes in economic theory initiated by Keynes, it was not until John XXIII with *Mater et Magistra* (1961) that a new methodology and the discovery of the problem of "development" called for substantial changes in the social teaching of the Church. His encyclical is *Pacem in Terris* (1963).

The Second Vatican Council, with its Pastoral Constitution *Gaudium et Spes*, (1965) moved the Church from a "liberal agenda" to third world concerns. Its underlying anthropology of social personalism radicalized property ethics.

Paul VI will follow up on these themes by making a transition from "development" to "liberation." His encyclical, *Populorum Progressio* (1967), shows the influence of new theories of liberation and a sharp criticism of capitalism. Paragraph 31 spells out the problem of the justification of revolution:

> We know, however, that a revolutionary uprising—save where there is manifest, longstanding tyranny which would do great damage to fundamental personal rights and dangerous harm to the common good of the country—produces new injustices, throws more elements out of balance and brings on new disasters. A real evil should not be fought against at the cost of greater misery.

It was during Pope Paul VI's pontificate that the synod of Bishops took place. During the second general assembly (Nov 30, 1971) the Bishops made the definitive statement that action on behalf of justice and participation in the transformation of the world fully appears as a constituent dimension of the preaching of the Gospel. It was in the third assembly (Oct 26, 1974) that evangelization is once again proclaimed as the essential mission of the Church. Liberation through evangelization is not limited to political or social elements but leads towards liberation in all forms—liberation from sin, from individual or collective selfishness, and to full communion with God and with man who are like brothers. In 1975, the synod gave special attention to the mutual relationship between evangelization and integral salvation or the complete liberation of man and peoples. The pope, in his concluding remarks, made note of liberation rightly emphasized, thus not just on a temporal level, but also spiritual. This was the first official recognition by a pope of the theme of "liberation."

Finally, it is with our present pope, John Paul II, that a dialectical relation to liberation theology takes place. A theologization of the Church's social teaching is stressed. But it is especially his radicalization of the theme of work and his ethic of private property which is interesting. Gregory Baum[15] maintains that in treating the theme of work in *Laborum Exercens* (1981), Pope John Paul II has lifted Catholic social teaching to a new height. This encyclical, by emphasizing the priority of labor over capital with the belief that capital is meant to serve labor and those who make up the labor force, becomes a significant new development in the Church's social teaching. The papal document argues that the present capitalist system in the Western world can no longer provide people with the basic requirements of their existence. What is needed, the encyclical claims, is a planned economy based on Christian socialist principles and international cooperation.

Pope John Paul II radicalizes the theory of work in five different ways. First, he makes man the subject of labor. This means that man's work is more important than the object his work produces. The encyclical's originality resides in placing emphasis on the subjective meaning of work over the objective. It is man's engagement which counts, his fidelity to his call, his increasing sense of responsibility, his self realization. This is how man becomes a person. And no matter how alienated man is, he is always a person. Human subjectivity becomes the guiding norm for all society.

Secondly, the notion of work is radicalized by placing labor prior to capital. Economics everywhere forms the basis of human life. And in our world, the conflict between capital and labor is definitive. The encyclical claims that the conflict between labor and capital stands at the center of modern history, and the other conflicts and structures of oppression must be understood in the light of the economic infrastructure.

Capital is labor and labor piled upon labor. Yet, labor produces capital and, at present, is controlled by it. The Pope radicalizes capital by emphasizing its "use" not its "ownership." This "use" the Pope finds abused in history by the greed and stupidity of "owners." So the responsibility for history is ultimately people who think and choose. There is nothing inevitable about it. The oppressed, the "used" by reflecting on their situation constitute a moral reality which accounts for the struggle of the "used" against the "users" and thus transforms society into the direction of greater justice. The Pope theologizes this by claiming that since freedom (reflection on your situation) is a divine gift, the dynamics of history is presented in the encyclical as the locus of God's presence. Justice then comes to mean that capital is made to serve labor. So one must expect a new and constant burst of solidarity and organized action among those who are "used." This struggle is always a struggle for justice within limits defined by justice. This struggle or call for the solidarity "of" the poor "with" the poor is truly a radical Christian principle. Again a theologizing point comes into play. Why should we feel responsible for everyone? Because, for the Pope, we are responsible for one another before God.

The fourth radicalization of work is the question of the priority of use over ownership. "The only legitimate title to the possession (of the means of production), whether this be in the form of private ownership or in the form of collective ownership, is that they should serve labor" (n 14).[16] The problem which results as a turning of these priorities around (capital over labor) can only be solved by remuneration for labor. That's why the Pope makes the strong case for labor unions: "the experience of history teaches that organizations of this type are an indispensable element of social life, especially in modern industrial societies" (n 20). So to correct the misplaced priorities of capital over labor, the encyclical calls for two things: labor unions and labor involvement in the political process to obtain the kind of government needed to involve society in the planning of the economy.

Finally, work is radicalized by insisting technology be an ally. A great moral wrong happened, the Pope says, in history by the early capitalists who decided to organize their capital against the workers who had produced it. These very structures which are created for his benefit, after an historical development, became a source of oppression.

The Pope distinguishes economic labor from social labor. The former includes production, the organization of labor, the distribution of resources and goods. The latter, social labor, includes language, family, peoplehood and religion. The Pope assigns priority to economic labor and understands social labor as serving the laboring society. Whenever these priorities are mixed-up there is both a structural and moral failing.

So the encyclical concentrates on a twofold direction to bring about justice, namely, the introduction of democracy at the workplace and the creation of a political system that allows for the rational planning of the economy. Gregory Baum[17] is right for if American Catholics made a radical reading of this encyclical they would be overwhelmed by the judgment of the encyclical on their societies. The existing economic and political system in North America is profoundly at odds with papal teaching, nor is there a nationwide, worker-based socialized organization that struggles for the primacy of labor over capital.

We seem to be where Studs Terkel found us, when in 1972 he wrote his monumental book on *Working, or How People Talk About What They Do All Day and How They Feel About What They Do*. His first paragraph frames the Pope's insight on work:

> This book, being about work, is, by its very nature, about violence—to the spirit as well as to the body. It is about ulcers as well as accidents, about shouting matches as well as fistfights, about nervous breakdowns as well as kicking the dog around. It is, above all (or beneath all), about daily humiliations. To survive the day is triumph enough for the walking wounded among the great many of us.[18]

The social teachings of the Church have not gone without criticism. Contemporary social Catholicism is influenced by the teaching of the Church. Contemporary social Catholicism is influended by the Magisterium which also promotes it. Contemporary social Catholicism is also influenced by the welfare state. It assumes not only a priority in meeting the basic needs in determining the direction of the economy, but also the teaching justifies cases of nationalization.

It hardly justifies capitalism as we know and experience it. Father Philip Land, S.J., a shrewd observer of the scene, lists for us nine axioms, drawn from the teachings, for judging any economy:

> 1) The economy is for people; 2) The economy is for being, not having; 3) The economic system ought to be needs-based; 4) The economy is an act of stewardship; 5) The economy must be a participatory society; 5) There must be fair sharing; 7) The system must permit self-reliance; 8) The economy must be ecologically sustainable; 9) The economy must be productive.[19]

Criticism should point out the limitations of the social teaching. John H. Coleman, S.J., does just that with four insights. First, the economic thought of the social doctrine, which stressing the need for just distribution, pays too little attention to the necessity of production. You can't distribute what you don't have.

Secondly, is society as harmonious as the social teaching presupposes? Are not the fundamental social values pluralistic? Pluralism is not sufficiently thought out.

Thirdly, what kind of society does the social teaching recommend? What social model do they envision ? They seem to lack an institutional organization. Playing only a critical and not a constructive role condemns me to share responsibility for any and all outcomes.

Fourth, you can't really separate politics from the social question. You'll either take too narrow a view of politics or you'll trivialize the social question.[20]

Moral theologians are not uncritical of the social doctrine of the Church. They are concerned about how issues are approached. What has primacy? Scripture or natural law? After all, what is natural law? And how is one using human reason: inductively or deductively? How does one move from the time and place in which Scripture was written to our time and place and construe a meaning from Scripture for it? Should we employ an ascending (low) Christology or a descending (high) Christology? Does Christian faith add anything or any unique material content to morality, the moral order or the moral life?

Reason appeals to intrinsic necessity for verification. If we base the social teaching on redemption, in, by and with Christ, then we are basing human rights and dignity found in redemption. Is humanity's true identify found only in faith? Are we not escaping the problem of verification? If the social teaching is not philosophy, nor sociology

and only theology, cannot ideologies be hidden? Can we not transcend our human situation by thought? Is our link with Divine Reality broken and do we need revelation to understand the social teaching of the Church? Is the social doctrine of the Church not addressed
to all people of good will to work together toward the common good?
If so, then reason is requiring that we overcome the lack of fundamental questioning and rise to the demands and possibilities of
thought itself.

If we broaden the range of reason we can move toward a consistent
ethical method. We find, at the moment, that some of the teachings
on social morality simply reflect the characteristics of sound moral
reasoning: biblical, communal, dynamic, personal. Thus, the teachings are empirically oriented, tentative, open to change, collaborative and so on. By contrast, matters of personal morality are deductive, nontentative, authoritative, noncollaborative, heavily reliant on
past sentiments. So, a kind of double standard prevails. When this
latter happens, no one is taught. No eyes are opened. No sensitivities
shaped. No minds enlightened.[21]

How do we account for the fact that the social teaching of the
Church is, as Henriot says, "our best kept secret"?[22] Most Catholics
are apathetic to the issues of problems pointed out by the social teaching of the Church. Apathy is overcome by learning to *feel* badly about
injustice and to *feel* right about justice. Most Catholics are ignorant
about the social teaching. They need to be educated. Above all, the
social teaching hardly ever tells us *what* to do, so we feel inadequate.
We must learn to *act* right.

It was Bishop F. Wiertz, the Bishop of Roermond, who welcomed
the writers of the first eight papers with words of congratulations for
the eminently successful effects that have come from the Catholic
social teaching over the last one hundred years. The symposium which
was held in Rolduc (Kerhade, Holland, 6-7 November 1993) and it
was there that Bishop Wiertz pointed out that according to *Centesimus
Annus* the social doctrine is an aid for evangelization, yet nevertheless, because of the great shifts in the social and spiritual life of the
last decades, a crisis in the understanding of the social teaching has
occurred. The Bishop pointed out that progressive secularization also
raises the question whether a social teaching of the Church, even if it
has one, can be understood any longer, and whether Christians have
a right to convey their own views about social life.

In the past, the social doctrine of the Church was based on philosophical foundations that entailed a valid vision for all people of good
will. But, with a conceptual shift having taken place inside the Church

for the last thirty years that the present Pope John Paul II speaks of the social teaching as theological discipline, one must search for the reasons for this change in the notion that the social mission of the church lies within the domain of theology and is pastoral in nature. From revealed doctrine, the church must hold forth that which can lead people to their true and ultimate goal. Another reason for this shift in stress is the general conviction adopted by many that there is no clear philosophy anymore, but rather only a multiplicity of views (K. Rahner). A definite social doctrine based on philosophical foundations is no longer possible. In Catholic circles, the question whether or not one must speak about a new foundation of the ecclesiastical social doctrine, has intensified in two critical areas: first, the place that John Paul II confers to natural law, or in other words, the attitude of the Pope against philosophy and the social sciences and against the tradition of the ecclesiastical social doctrine influenced by natural law; second, the actual role of theology in the development of the ecclesiastical social doctrine, and its relation to philosophy and the social sciences. One has spoken about a "duplex ordo cognitionis."[23]

The encyclicals of John Paul II and important ecclesiastical documents published over the last few years nevertheless imply that while the ecclesiastical social doctrine is situated in moral theology, it nevertheless uses a great deal of philosophical materials, and that in order to grasp certain problems it has to make an appeal to the contribution of the social sciences There are moreover a number of important insights concerning the social life of humans that also can be recognized and accepted by non-Christians. In this way, the philosophical substructure of the social doctrine that can be reached through natural reasoning plays a large role in the collaborative dialogue with people of other convictions. Believers and non-believers can also agree about the importance of the contribution of certain social sciences. This is, then, all brought out by the church to the level of Christian life and taken up in a general Christian reflection, so that it becomes subservient to evangelization. Naturally the Christian vision and *caritas* give a whole new inspiration to the social life.

The different authors contributing to this volume have handled the given issue, in ten articles, according to their own specializations. M. Spieker gives and overview of the actuality of Catholic social doctrine through an analysis of the demand for its teaching. At the same time he points out its presence in a number of important and actual social, economic and political debates. In the study of E. De Jonghe, some aspects of discussion about the nature and method of this doctrine are treated. L. Roos treats the theme of human dignity, the most important starting point of the Christian social doctrine from a theological perspective. At the same time he points out the factors that present a threat to Christian humanism in modern culture. Family, private property, and the state are continually regarded as the fundamental institutions of the society in the upbuilding of the ecclesiastical social doctrine. A. Rauscher puts these institutions in the general framework of a united social vision. B. Kettern investigates how the concept of social justice was introduced in the development of the ecclesiastical social doctrine and how it has its roots in antiquity and the philosophical tradition of the Middle Ages. L. J. Elders treats the common good as the goal and principle of organization in social life. He examines in detail how the concept of "bonum commune" that occurs many times in the work of Thomas Aquinas must be understood in an adequate manner and how the discussions on this subject have developed in the last half century. E. De Jonghe investigates the use of the term "common good" in the encyclicals and in a few other ecclesiastical texts.[24] At the same time, as well, a summary is given of the developing conception of "the common good" up to the *Catechism of the Catholic Church* (1992). In the study of J. Verstraeten, the evolution of the use of the terms "solidarity" and "subsidiarity" is pointed out. Herewith a distinction is made between the period before John XXIII and the period from John XXIII to John Paul II. He maintains that these concepts have undergone an important theologizing process through the interpretations of John Paul II. Finally, the participation principle is pointed out in political, economic, and business economic areas according to the developmental level of the society where it can be applied.

It is in Professor Verstraeten's article that we find the heart of the book. Catholic social teaching is a permanent process of learning in which the continuity of the fundamental principles are always paired with new insights. Analyzing interpersonal relations in terms of duty, subsidiarity becomes the vertical perspective while solidarity is the horizontal perspective. Solidarity means we are responsible for everybody. Everybody must be respected as another self and an injustice against one is against all and against oneself. No man is an island. Professor Verstraeten points out, as do other writers in this book, that in the last analysis it is the *actions* of Christian people that make the Catholic social teaching credible, not the internal logic.

Professor Crosson situates the peculiarities of the American scene as a locus for the application of the social teaching of the Church. American constitutional traditions and the nature of justice (natural law) became the place and occasion for the social teaching of the

Church to find its place. Besides that, he points out how the social doctrine of the Church was always taught in the multiple Catholic colleges, universities and seminaries.

What Professor Crosson points out as most significant is in the area of religious liberty. It is here that the experience of Americans makes its most decisive contribution to Catholic social teaching.

Professor Crosson has, I am sure, fulfilled Professor De Jonghe's last wish to me when he requested an American perspective be added to these essays. The readers, as I, are indebted both to Professor De Jonghe's insight and to Professor Crosson's accomplishment.

The abbey of Rolduc, where the aforementioned symposium took place, has always played an important role in the cultural life of Limburg and also far outside of it. In the years before the war (1940-1945) the yearly social studyweeks that were organized by Msgr. H. A. Poels (1868-1948) were quite famous. In the current difficult situation the participants of the symposium attempted to come to a "status quaestionis" with regard to the basics. Perhaps later this can be further developed. A word of thanks is due to the abbey of Rolduc, to the speakers and participants, and to the institutions and the General Christian Workers Union of Flanders which made the meeting of the symposium and the publishing of the lectures possible. Our thanks goes also to Drs. H. M. G. Kretzers, who made the necessary translation from German of a number of texts and who made a consensus with respect to the language sentiments of North and South Belgium possible.

A great deal of thanks goes to David A. Wilson and Anne Marie Anselmo of New Orleans, who translated the texts from the Dutch into English. Nor must I forget my secretary Sharon Harbin who edited and typed the manuscript with such care. Permission has been obtained by Professor De Jonghe for me to translate the texts into English and publish. Many thanks to Marquette University Press and its Director, Dr. Andrew Tallon, for publishing.

Finally, to the memory of my professor, mentor and friend, Dr. Eugene De Jonghe, heartfelt thanks not only for these manuscripts but for some thirty-five years of treasured friendship.

David A. Boileau
New Orleans, Louisiana
1998

1

The Actuality of Catholic Social Doctrine

Professor Dr. M. Spieker

The social doctrine of the Church has found resonance today more than ever before in our century. Both geographically and thematically, qualitatively and quantitatively, the need for this doctrine has grown enormously. Anyone concerned with the social doctrine of the Church, regardless of occupation, has to be more concerned with satisfying this need than with determining how a demand can be created in order to be "supplied" by a social-ethical theory of the Church. The social-ethicist resembles certainly not the Old Testament Joseph, who managed corn-lofts and could satisfy every demand, even from abroad, and subsequently ruled as viceroy over Egypt. Rather, he resembles the apostle, who to Jesus' question about how the crowd could be fed, somewhat evasively answered: "we have only seven loaves of bread and two fish."

In the first place from an undoubtedly subjective and therefore limited perspective the market-situation of the social doctrine of the Church should be investigated. By whom, where, and why is there any demand for the social doctrine of the Church? In what measure can the Church satisfy the demand? What does it have to offer? In the first place it does not concern social questions, the answer to which Catholic social doctrine, according to the convictions of its representatives, could supply any help and thus could play an actual role and could apply. It rather concerns the actual demand and the actual supply in the form of new ecclesiastical documents. In the second place the demand is established for intrinsic developments, subjects, problems, paradigms, and conflicts that characterize the current discussion within Christian social sciences. Are there new main points, new dialogs, new shortcomings?

1 Supply and demand

By whom, where, and why is there demand for Christian social doctrine? The Catholic social doctrine should provide an orientation with the completion of the European integration, the bringing under control of the post-communist transformation processes, the conquering of the integral or even fundamentalist tendencies in Islamic states, and for the stabilization of the welfare state based on achievement and for the challenging of the general economical and business-economical changes. The actual conjuncture of the subsidiary principle can illustrate the rising demand as a first example. In the treaty concerning the formation of the European Union of Feb. 7, 1992, the Treaty of Maastricht, the subsidiarity principle was proclaimed a guideline for further European integration. The heads of state and government of the European Community swore to this during their summit conferences in Lisbon, Birmingham and Edinburgh. In Edinburgh, the European Council issued important guidelines concerning the introduction of the subsidiarity principle. The European Parliament spoke out as well in its debate of Nov. 18, 1992, without distinction of parties, in favor of the subsidiarity principle. The European Commission, under instructions from the council of ministers, kept itself busy with the actualization and the judicial formulization of this principle. It also underlined this principle in its memorandum of Nov. 5, 1991, concerning the development of higher education in the European Union and then again in its communiqué of Oct. 27, 1992, to the council of ministers and the European Parliament concerning the application of the subsidiarity principle.

The Federal Government published on Sept. 18, 1992, a memorandum about the subsidiarity principle. In its debate of Dec. 18, 1992, about the Treaty of Maastricht, the federal council referred repeatedly to the subsidiarity principle and the Lower House of the German Parliament on Dec. 2, 1992, finally accepted the new article 23 of the Constitution, the Europe-article. In the first paragraph of this article, the subsidiarity principle found for the first time, *expressis verbis*, entrance into the German constitution. In the first paragraph, line one, reads as follows: "*For the realization of a unified Europe the German constitution grants its cooperation for the development of the European Union, that knows itself to be bound to the principles of democracy and the constitutional state, to social and federative principles, as well as the fundamental principle of subsidiarity... .*" In 1992 a discussion of the subsidiarity principle that overshadowed all previous debates was reflected in the German daily and weekly papers in main articles, editorials, letters from readers, and reports of gatherings.

European politics is not the only thing to contribute to the modern-day "economic climate" of the subsidiarity principle. It is reflected also in social politics, developmental politics, and in the business economy, especially in the discussion concerning "lean management" and in governmental psychology.[25]

Now one could make the objection that the demand for the subsidiarity principle is not a demand yet for Catholic social doctrine. The subsidiarity principle is, of course, not an exclusive possession of Catholic social doctrine and is definitely not a doctrinal rule. It is an organization principle that is anthropologically founded and that can be made rationally insightful. This far, it is possible to be made understandably approachable also for non-Catholics and even for non-Christians and unbelievers.[26] However, right in the discussion about the European integration it is sworn in the sense of *Quadragesimo anno* of 1931: "What individual small units inside of the European Economic Community, such as regions and member states, can rule and realize independently, cannot be taken from them and assigned to the European Economic Community?" The most controversial discussions that are also being carried out on the European level about the subsidiarity principle—it is sometimes not put into perspective by an adequate efficiency criteria or even defined as an efficiency rule—are, according to me, only to be won by referring to its anthropological suppositions.[27]

In the post-communist transformation processes, especially in Poland, Catholic social doctrine plays an important role. Almost all the chosen parties in the 1991 "Parliament" have made reference to this. The one exception to this resulted in the coalition of post-communist alliance between the democratic (left) party and the nationalistic leaning Coalition of Independent Poland. The reference of almost all political parties to Catholic social doctrine quite resembled a ritual. All knew themselves to be bound in their programs to Catholic social doctrine, but no one knew the doctrine. In the elections of 1993, these parties, with an exception of the democratic union, were quite split by differences, and were all "stuck" by the minimum vote stipulation (they have to get a five or eight percent plurality vote).[28] It is true that in the political development of the Islamic states Catholic social doctrine is institutionally as good as not being there at all, but a symposium about economic ethics, and especially the influence of religions on economic organization, that the Konrad-Adenauer Institution and the Arab Thought Forum (end of October 1993) organized in Amman and that brought together Christians and Muslims from 10 Arab countries, shows the actuality of it. The Christian-Islamic dialogue quickly changed into an inter-Islamic controversy between democratic and secular forces on one side and the fundamental forces that wanted to put the order of the state and the order of the economy under the "sharia" on the other side. But right here Catholic social doctrine should have made clear that one can let the values and norms of an extremely religiously founded ethics be valid as well, when church and state, religion and politics are separated, and that the subordination of political institutions and economic order is not the condition for religion for letting these values and norms apply, but rather the evidence of beliefs of competent laymen in economics and politics.

These three examples can satisfy to illustrate the contemporary demand for Catholic social doctrine and consequently its actuality. How is it related to supply? Will Catholic social teaching solve the problems that are hidden behind the question?

The supply of the social doctrine of the Church may certainly be seen, if we look first to pontifical proclamations. Three social encyclicals and three magnificent documents with the Vatican congregation's mark of identification up to now during the pontificate of John Paul II: *Laborem exercens* (1981), *Sollicitudo rei socialis* (1987) and *Centesimus annus* (1991), the two instructions of the Congregation of Faith about the liberation theology *Libertatis nuntius* (1984) and *Libertatis conscientia* (1986), as well as the Guidelines of the Congregation for Catholic Education for the studying of and the instruction of Catholic social doctrine in the education of priests (1988). Also, in his apostolic exhortation of *Christifideles laici* (1988), the pope underlines the importance of Catholic social doctrine for the Church and world, and especially for the lay apostolate. This is of essential importance for the discussion with fundamentalism. Here can be added a number of addresses that the pope held on his trips to hotspots of social duress or political conflicts, as in September 1992, in the Baltic states, and each time he returned to the social doctrine as a way of humanizing social, economic, and political relations on one side and, also, as an instrument for proclaiming belief on the other hand. These trips and speeches contributed, I believe, to the collapsing of the oppressive systems in the 1980's in many countries of our world, e.g. in Chili and in Korea, in Benin and in the Phillippines, and last but not least in Poland, and instead of these oppressive systems democracies began to develop. They have also strengthened the demand for Catholic social teaching world-wide.

Supply and demand is reflected in a number of pastoral letters and regional bishop conferences about social problems, as well as in the celebrations of the hundred-year anniversary of *Rerum novarum*. The pastoral letters in the 1980's, have made clear to numerous episcopates in the industrialized countries, as well as in the developing countries, that it is not only the right, but the duty of the Church to involve itself in questions concerning the preservation of peace, in areas concerning political, social, and economic order, and concerning the developing of the third world or the respecting of human rights. Besides, in many countries and on many continents, texts of a high standard have appeared, and in this the episcopates did not overstep the boundaries of their competence. This applies especially to the pastoral document of the German bishops of 1983 about the guaranteeing of the peace, *Gerechtigkeit schafft Frieden*, the pastoral document of the American bishops about Catholic social doctrine and the American economy in 1986, and the pastoral document of the Austrian bishops *Der Mensch ist der Weg der Kirche* (1990). Also the great documents of the Latin-American bishops of Puebla (1979) and Santo Domingo (1992) must be mentioned here; and in Africa the national bishop conferences, e.g. in Nigeria, Benin, the Ivory Coast, Cameroon, and Zaire, time and time again have supported with expert documents the efforts regarding democratization.[29]

Concerning the celebrations surrounding the 100-year anniversary of *Rerum novarum*, first and foremost what is of value are the social-ethical contributions of Leo XIII, his speeches about just wages, property, the freedom of unionization among workers, the role of the state, and the necessary simultaneity of changes in structure and mentality—speeches that were in part revolutionary and have not amounted to anything of actuality in many regions of the world. However, these celebrations were not the area of concern to the historians. They did not check the historical roots of Catholic social doctrine, but rather they came face-to-face with new challenges. They concentrate on the present-day potential of the solutions offered by *Rerum novarum*, its self-image and often also the actual questions concerning the political, social, and economic order of the country celebrating the 100-year anniversary.[30] The world-wide demand is reflected finally, as well, in the activities and contacts of the "International Federation for Christian Social Teaching" founded in 1986. This independent establishment with a small office in Geneva, whose financial and personal means resemble very particularly the five loaves of bread and two fish, began in 1989, a cooperation with scientific establishments—that consider the Catholic social doctrine to be important—not only in Moscow, but also in other states of Eastern Europe, India, and Africa. It established, in 1990, a center for postgraduate studies for Catholic social doctrine for students from Eastern Europe.

However, the reviving of the demand for Catholic social doctrine is not only of a quantitative, but also of a qualitative nature. In different areas it has been confronted in the 1980s with new challenges and has been able to enjoy new interest. Economic ethics came even before the collapse of communism into a "boom-phase." The relation between profit and the common good, the ethos of the entrepreneur, the culture of the entrepreneurs, problems of the economic order, and the functions of the marketplace and the state are often-posed questions, that have led not only to a true flood of symposia and publications, but also to new chairs and interdisciplinary research projects. The interest of the economists for Catholic social doctrine is in theory and in practice often much greater than that of the theologians for the economy. Catholic social doctrine has until now met this challenge. Its traditional connection with the economic sciences is beneficient to it.

The demand for Catholic social doctrine and its orientation has not in the last place expanded through the ecumenic junction of "justice, peace, and care for creation" without which it has reacted to its supply as in the area of economic ethics. Also the economic dimension of this process entails new challenges, that force the social doctrine to take into account its theological and philosophical starting-points and to intensify the dialogue with the social sciences. The development of modern technology, the problems of energy supply, the solving of traffic and trash problems, research in biology and pharmaceutics, as well as changes in the climate, contain a whole series of challenges of a social-ethical nature; however, challenges that are not sufficiently acknowledged and taken up.

We have already mentioned that the development in Middle-Eastern Europe and Eastern Europe stimulated the demand for Catholic social doctrine. The collapse of communism left behind a vacuum for Catholic social doctrine, less in the political and economic fields but more in the social and cultural regards, that creates a powerful challenge, as *Centesimus Annus* also stresses. The problems of the transformation process in all former socialist states—not only in Europe, but also in Africa and Asia—are without precedent. The establishment of "civil societies"—of free, democratic, self-conscious societies—in which citizens govern themselves is the condition for stabilizing economic and political change. Catholic social teaching, with its vision of humanity, with its organizational principles, and with its two-pronged starting point which connects changes of structures and mentality (which are also attacked by political and social scientists) could contribute to the success of these changes, but has not reacted sufficiently to the challenge.

2. Themes and Problems, Paradigms and Conflicts

Which intrinsic main points, which themes, problems and conflicts characterize the development of Catholic social doctrine in the 1980's? The number of treated themes can be divided into three areas: 1) the problems of the third world, 2) the individual problems of a dignified arrangement of work and economy, society and state in industrialized countries, 3) the relation between Catholic social doctrine and theology, the mission of the Church and the related disciplines of the social sciences.

2.1 The misery of the developing countries and the tense relation between rich and poor countries—already a subject of papal, conciliar and episcopal speeches—in the 1960's, for example, in *Mater et magistra, Gaudium et spes, Populorum progressio* and in the document of Medellin—became, in the 1980's, ever more a theme of Catholic social doctrine. The documents of Puebla and Santo Domingo, the instructions of the Congregation of the Faith concerning liberation theology and especially *Sollicitudo rei socialis*, but also *Centesimus annus*, reflect this development.

From the beginning of the 1970s, Catholic social doctrine, with the treating of these problems, had to see to the challenge of liberation theology, which was oriented to Marx. This theology, which not only wanted to awaken interest in the problems of the third world, but also wanted to place the whole theology under the paradigm of liberation, entailed the most fundamental critique of Catholic social doctrine since *Rerum novarum*.

Moreover, liberation theology usually undervalued history, the starting-points of Catholic social doctrine, and what it had brought into being. It conceived liberation as an alternative to development, made use of the theory of dependence and Marxism, whereby it thought it could separate the criticism of religion, anthropology, and philosophy from methodology, it obfuscated the difference between human well-being and Christian salvation, and worked with an integralistic, and on occasion Manicheistic, concept of economics and politics. Politics was, according to Leonardo Boff, a choosing between liberation and slavery, between grace and sin, between light and darkness.[31] Such a conception about politics made politics inefficient. In this manner the choice for the poor, according to many representatives of this, became not only a priority, but also an exclusive and even naive defense for socialism. The readiness to subject socialism to a critique was substantially greater, for example, with Gorbachev than with Leonardo Boff.

Catholic social doctrine has responded to the challenge of liberation theology, in German, Spanish, and Portuguese language regions. It judged itself not to be in a state to adopt the starting points, the perspectives, and the goals of liberation theology. It even dismissed liberation theology in a large way as counterproductive, which means it neither was useful for liberation in any respect, nor was useful as a choice for the poor. Also, one can read the stated ecclesiastical documents of the 1980s as a partially implicit (Puebla, *Sollicitudo rei socialis*) and partially explicit (*Libertatis nuntius* and *Libertatis conscientia*), critical confrontation with liberation theology.

Even before the collapse of socialism, an end came soon to the boom of liberation theology after *Libertatis conscientia*. There are many different fundamental reasons for this. On the one hand, numerous dictatorial systems in the third world, and practically all in Latin-America, have been replaced by democratic and market-based economic systems. This development has been made difficult by many uncertainties and problems, but it confounded all expectations of liberation theology and because of this, liberation theology was barely achieved or even supported. On the other hand, important representatives of liberation theology further developed their points of view—some like Gustavo Guttierez corrected [their ideas] and others like Leonardo Boff radicalized [their theories]. The collapse of socialism in Central and Eastern Europe and the problems of the transformation processes force liberation theology—if it has not been struck completely silent—to further corrections. Possibly these will lead to a replacement of the paradigm "liberation" with that of "reconciliation," a paradigm that is beginning to play an important role in the social-ethical and theological starting points in Latin-America. A rather sectarian radicalization is found in Leonardo Boff and Hugo Assmann, who reproach the market-based economy for elevating the market to a death-bringing idol.[32] *Centesimus annus*, when it at least takes papal encyclicals into consideration, becomes reduced to a critique of communism.

The end of the conflict between East and West can promote the acceptance of the view that is defended in Catholic social doctrine from *Pacem in Terris*, namely that for the developing countries the most important task that is needed is the development of their countries.[33] The acceptance of this view is again the condition that Catholic social doctrine searches on the scene for the necessary dialogue with the social sciences of the country concerned and the cooperation of the social forces that want to use it. The Catholic doctrine—until now the best-hidden secret of the Church in most countries of the third world, but definitely also in Europe—has been able to gain a foothold in the past years in Africa, Asia, and Latin-America. In this manner (e.g., international initiatives for French-speaking as well as in English-speaking countries in trans-Sahara, symposia, unions like the "African Association for the Advancemant of Catholic Social Teaching," institutes, and publications) arises the hope that with the planned bishop synod, by its analysis of the problems of trans-Sahara, and with the suggestion of an enlightenment from this, Catholic social doctrine shall establish its future place. In the preparation document social doctrine plays an important role and, during his last African trip, Pope John Paul II recommended it many times at various occasions to his ecclesiastical listeners.

In the countries characterized by Islam, from Morocco via the Near East to Pakistan, it shall be more difficult to let Catholic social doctrine take root. It is necessary, nevertheless. Its values, norms, and governmental principles are also suitable to contribute to a humanizing of social relations in these societies formed by Islam. The wealth of communal values and norms in social ethics is considerable. Catholic social doctrine at this time can make use of these communal values and norms in secular states.

2.2 Individual problems of a just and decent organization of economy, state and society inside the industrialized countries continually challenge Catholic social doctrine to keep itself occupied with actual economic, social, and political developments. It must analyze the signs of the time and search for solutions that guarantee that the human remains origin, carrier, and goal of all social institutions with help of the governing principles of solidarity, subsidiarity and the common good. In the German-speaking area problems with relation to the labor market, social politics, the economic system, and ecology seem to have more weight than problems concerning the state, constitution, or police culture. Unemployment, just wages, family politics, protection of Sunday, employee participation, wealth-forming, national debt, and expansion of social public services were repeatedly the subject of social-ethical discussions and of episcopal views. Also, the social pastoral letter planned for 1995 appears to want to concentrate on these fields of attention.

In the most recent period, favored by the fact that the former socialistic states of Central and Eastern Europe are turning to the free-market economy, there is a heated discussion to determine the relation of Catholic social doctrine to the social market. The view that the social market economy is for the most part compatible with Catholic social doctrine, and that it is a successful substitution and even is the option for poor people, wins ground in spite of the verdicts of leaders of liberation theology. The plea of John Paul II in *Centesimus annus* for a market economy protected by the state and flanked by a system of social obligations would exert a good influence on this discussion.[34]

Also, the efforts in political ethics, which have increased in recent times, should be able to get another stimulus through *Centesimus annus*, since this encyclical as no other ecclesiastical document has worked out the underlying dependence between economic, political, and social organization. This also could do well for the acceptance of the social-scientific paradigm of the civil society.[35] Pope John Paul II picked up this paradigm for the first time in the spring of 1993, in Agrigento, for a gathering of Sicilian employers. To solve the problems of the "mezzogiorno" there would have to be a need for a "culture of initiatives," the rediscovery of the "desire for creativity in all areas," and a "new dominating role in society.... A strong and independent organization of the citizen-society is a decisive and indispensable factor for the development of the south."[36]

For the upbuilding of a civil society, Catholic unions and the unions of employees, entrepreneurs, artisans, and assistants have much to contribute. With the translation of Catholic doctrine into a juridical, social, and economic order in Germany in the twentieth century, they play an important role. They confront academic social ethics and the ecclesiastical proclamations with the actual problems of work-life and politics. With their demands they force Catholic social doctrine to become continually more concrete. The rebuilding of the civil society in the post-communistic transformation processes seems, in this area, to be still more difficult than expected.

The development of a just and dignified economic, social, and political order also demands from Catholic social doctrine that it continually enters in its discussions with actual political theories. This happens nevertheless within the frame of the German social ethics only in a very unpretentious manner.[37]

2.3 Within Christian social doctrine, as within every scientific discipline, the discussion about the scientific theoretical sense of identity has acquired a principal place. In the past years one could perceive an increasing effort to express the theological dimension of Catholic social doctrine. One can distinguish two trends. One trend strives to an ethics of Catholic social doctrine based on natural law and to connect more narrowly the person-directed anthropology with the message of the New Testament, especially with Christology and Soteriology. It wants to reiterate that the origin of humans is the binding theological foundation of the social movement of Christians. John Paul II gave, since *Redemptor hominis*, many impulses to this trend and repeatedly categorized Catholic social doctrine as a subject area within theology (lastly within *Centesimus annus*, number 55).

However, the philosophy of the natural law remains, for this trend, the valid and necessary second origin of knowledge, which makes the dialogue between Catholic social doctrine and the world possible.[38] The facts of a postmetaphyisical period can make the passing-on of the doctrine of the natural law difficult, but it was never easy and unchallenged. Because humans, due to their nature as people, nevertheless, always strive to achieve fulfillment of their lives and in every society there remains a context that makes this striving easy or difficult; and natural law will also continually experience a new return. Fundamental rights and human rights, their expansion and their threat will be the way along which natural law will become manifest.

The second direction, which reflects the scientific position of Catholic social doctrine, regards the contemplated theological foundation of Catholic social doctrine as an alternative for a foundation on natural law. It expresses a critique of the development of Christian social doctrine from *Rerum novarum* until the Second Vatican Council, and categorized it as apologetic and directed against the Enlightenment. The encyclicals after *Mater et magistra*, especially those of John Paul II, are still valid as emendations. Whether or not this trend works now with the paradigm of a society of contrasts, in which it wants to change the church in the middle of a corrupt civilian society, or with political theology, ethics of social movements or ecological social ethics, it rejects in each instance the social doctrine that searches its arguments in natural law, and on occasion also the autonomy of politics. It pleads for an integral consciousness in which politics is conceived as an intrinsic moment of the faith. One can distinguish tendancies of a new integralism and fundamentalism, which are related to the tendencies of the liberation theology.[39]

For the clarification of the sense of a personal identity, new efforts must also be pointed out to bring Catholic social doctrine and the scientific consciousness of the *caritas*, which until now hardly anyone examined, in contact with each other. This contact could bear fruit for both parties. Catholic social doctrine could be helped to

integrate the concrete terrains of human need in its research projects
and by these means to diminish the danger of flying on sheer abstract
theories. The scientific consciousness of the *caritas* could be helped
to take into account with the social and political context of grief and
need on one side and of ecclesiastical assistance on the other side,
and in this manner reduce the danger of an ideological equation with
social work.[40]

For Catholic social doctrine, contact with the social sciences remains an essential important condition. On this point there exists a
considerable shortage, which is increasing, in proportion to the separation between theology and the universities. The continual dialogue,
not only with the economic sciences, but also the political sciences,
judiciary science, sociology, social psychology, and philosophy is not
only useful for the concerned parties, but also useful for the humanizing of social relations. The development of church and society in
Germany in the last hundred years offers many an impressive example of this.

However, the integration of theology in the public universities is
no guarantee that this dialogue is taking place. Also, in Germany
there is definitely a lack of good will, perhaps also the ability, to see
how to carry out this discussion. This shortage affects the social-ethi-
cists in first place, but also priests, bishops, and students of theology.
These last-mentioned have otherwise trouble not only with this dialogue, but also with Catholic social doctrine itself. The spiritual trend
among the students does not want to hear very much about the duty
of Christians in the world. This trend is not favorable for Christian
social doctrine, which is in contrast to the existing social trends.

The contribution of the current pope to the social doctrine of the
Church is outstanding. Whether it is in encyclical letters, in addresses
during his trips, or in *ad limina*-visits, John Paul II rarely lets an
opportunity go by to point out its meaning or even to give it new
tasks. Recently, in the beginning of September 1993, in Vilnius, he
urged bishops, priests, monks, seminarians, and laypeople to study
Catholic social doctrine and to apply it in the post-communist transformation processes. In *Centesimus annus* 59 he underlined again the
meaning of the dialogue with the social sciences.

However, if this dialogue were to lead anyone to believe that Catholic social doctrine be made dependent on certain central theoretical
and ethical starting points under the pretense that it otherwise would
be only a self-referential system, or that it characterizes itself as dis-
cursive-ethical, system-theoretical, transcendental-pragmatic, anti-
idealistic or feministic, then this dialogue would have missed its goal.

This dialogue then would hardly make the balance possible that Hans Maier formulated in the rhetorical question in the symposium of the papal commission *Justitia et Pax* on the occasion of the hundred-year anniversary celebration of *Rerum novarum* on May 15, 1991, in Rome: "Why was the church in its social doctrine much happier, laborious, and successful than in so many other summonings of the people for the past hundred years?"[41]

Whoever wants to answer this question must point out two things: on one hand the great popes, bishops, and the impressive teachers of Catholic social doctrine, and the practical establishments, for example the "Katholische Sozialwissenschaftliche Zentralstelle" in Moenchengladbach, that have contributed to its deepening and spreading. He must point to their readiness and their capability to enter into the signs of the time, the plausibility of their arguments, as well as the truth of their regulative principles and of their human image. On the other hand, he must point out the evidence of the works that the church and especially engaged laypeople, from Mother Theresa and her sisters to the great assistance organizations, such as Adveniat, "Church in Need" (Kerk in Nood), Missio, and Misereor have always given[42] and to which, according to John Paul II, in *Centesimus annus* (nr. 57) often more importance should be attached than to the logic of the doctrine.

2
Nature and Method of Catholic Social Doctrine

Professor Emeritus Dr. E. De Jonghe

Specifications concerning the *nature* of Catholic social doctrine have been given by the highest teaching authority in some documents which cannot be ignored. However, we are aware of the frequently repeated critique concerning *methodology* that Catholic social doctrine is based upon abstract natural law principles and that a theological point of departure would give it a larger dynamic. Together with this critique, there is a necessity to examine the facts, to use an empirical method, and then to judge the facts in the light of revelation.

We shall first treat the nature of Catholic social doctrine according to a few ecclesiastical documents that have appeared in the last four years.

Secondly, we shall investigate the critique that maintains that Catholic social doctrine is based on an abstract natural law and, furthermore, that it has a socially conservative character, a critique that we encounter in representative texts of the three American theologians, John Coleman, Richard McCormick, and Charles Curran (texts written around 1980). These very texts plead for a broader use of theology and also of the inductive method in the development and application of Catholic social doctrine.

It is our intention to answer this critique by pointing out that the knowledge of empirical reality by the authors of the encyclicals was never lacking, that a theological foundation has always been present where demanded by demonstration, and finally, that the use of the natural law or social philosophy was introduced where the transition from a theological statement to concrete social reality demanded different intermediate stages or levels of concretization.[43]

Finally, we draw from an important historical example the objection to that which sometimes led to great problems for theological arguments in political matters.

1. According to the *Guidelines* of the Congregation for Catholic Education concerning the study of Catholic social doctrine in the educational institutes for priests, the origin and development of this doctrine can be traced to the encounter of the message of the Gospels and its ethical demands with the problem of social life. This doctrine is built up by appealing to theology and philosophy, which give it a foundation and which must supply an adequate vision on the social reality with the help of social and human sciences. According to these *Guidelines*, an integrating component of Christian social doctrine about humans is, nevertheless, a pronounced theological profile. This is confirmed in *Veritatis splendor* (1993) with the words adopted from *Sollicitudo rei socialis*: "The social teaching of the church lies in the area of theology and more specifically in that of the moral theology." Catholic social doctrine proposes norms which entail an organization of the social, political, and economic life. These norms not only have a connection to, but also concern with concrete behavior and actions. *Veritatis splendor* refers here to the *Catechism of the Catholic Church*, where in relation to the social doctrine of the Church, social justice, solidarity of the peoples, and the love for the poor are given a number of clarifications.[44] The origins of Catholic social doctrine are the Holy Scriptures, the teachings of the Church fathers and of the great theologians, and the ecclesiastical teaching function itself. With respect to content, it contains a vision about humans and society in which the integral Christian anthropology stands out and each one-sided worldly humanism is rejected or at least deemed incomplete.

"The theological root of Catholic social doctrine expresses itself likewise in its pastoral definition of its purpose in service to human development and the humanization of the world, namely, through the practice of Christian liberation, both in its worldly and in its transcendental meaning."[45] It is thus about a theoretical-practical knowledge, with a theological foundation in service for all people.

What is then the relation between Catholic social doctrine, understood as moral theology (*Veritatis splendor*, 1993), and natural law or social philosophy? The point of departure is "an anthropology received from the Gospel, in which a human as image of God never can be converted into a simple part of nature or an anonymous element of the human society."[46] Still, human thinking leads one likewise to the knowledge of one's own nature and the demands that it makes, so that one would come to a real human development, in oneself and in the fundamental relations in which one finds oneself: it is about the minimum demands of what is necessary to bring about personal perfection and, above that minimum, everything that is necessary to maintain and encourage moral order. Natural reasoning expresses the demands of the natural law. This is the way in which God invites the person to share in His providence, to commit humans as rational and responsible beings, not only in the world, but also in human society. This natural law, says *Veritatis splendor* with St. Thomas, is the human expression of the eternal law of God. "The thought of man," wrote Pius XII in his Christmas message of 1955, "can discover a natural order that, even when the historical forms change, stays the same in its essential characteristics: the family, property as a basis for personal security, with as complementary elements of security the local communities, professional organizations, and the state."

Concerning the relation between the two [natural law and Catholic social doctrine as moral theology], Pius XII pointed out that the principles of natural law and revealed truths travel along different paths, but as two converging streams come forth from the same source.[47] The *Guidelines* refer in this metaphor explicitly to the passage in *Gaudium et spes*, where it is said that the church worked out the beginnings of justice and fairness —demanded by the *recta ratio* and especially brought forth in our time—in the light of the Gospels.[48]

2. The *Guidelines* point out that, at a certain moment, doubt and mistrust of Catholic social doctrine was expressed as if it "was a social doctrine, abstract, deductive and static and uncharacterized moreover by a total deficiency of critical sense."[49] Already before and during the Council (Dec. 1963 - Dec. 1965), objections were brought forth against the "abstract natural law as foundation for Catholic social doctrine." In fact, because of the term "natural law," the whole scholastic philosophy was intentionally present as the background in a number of systematic exposés of the Catholic social doctrine. One found that this social philosophy had an a-historical character and allowed no dynamic vision of the development of society (it was the time when neo-marxism with its utopian "projects" was in fashion, for example, in the works of R. Garaudy and E. Bloch, and existentialism and situation ethics underminded the meaning of immutable moral norms).[50]

3. Growing preference for a theological foundation? The opinion that Catholic social doctrine now should give preference to and emphasize its theological foundations has penetrated into some manuals. In this manner, one gives more publicity to complaints against its natu-

ral law foundations and its shortage of dynamism. We ought now to investigate how, in reality, this critique was expressed by the three North American theologians mentioned above. Their studies were published in a collection of *Readings* about "Official Catholic Social Teaching."[51] My questions with this will be: how they have expressed this critique, if it was justly expressed, and if the history of Catholic social doctrine teaches in an ample enough way that a theologizing of certain questions or controversial points always was a guarantee for a better vision.

3.1 According to John Coleman, the social-philosophers of the "solidarity school" before the Second Vatican Council stood reluctantly against every attempt to let their syntheses be influenced by theological concepts. He clearly meant by this that a few continental authors, such as, H. Pesch, J. Messner, and others, who although they never disputed the importance and the fundamental value of theology for Catholic social doctrine, nevertheless principally developed its social-philosophical foundations. Oswald von Nell-Breuning, who published in 1947, in the *Wörterbuch der Politik*, a short synthesis of a neo-scholastic social philosophy, was still convinced, in 1962, that Catholic social doctrine clearly existed from social-philosophical knowledge, which is limited by a negative norm of revelation and, which for the most part, was neither present in the *depositum fidei* nor could be derived naturally from it. According to him, social doctrine was theology only in a limited way. In the same sense Gustave Gundlach, in 1958 - 1959, and Johannes Messner, in 1960, expressed themselves.[52] Coleman says that the central concepts of Catholic social doctrine, such as, "the value of the human," "solidarity," "subsidiarity," "participation," and "the subordination of the economy and politics to the higher goals of the human," must be interpreted in light of the Holy Scriptures and be inspired by it. Theological notions such as "liberation" and "grace" should have come on the agenda in the development of Catholic social doctrine.[53]

3.2 Richard A. McCormick introduced, in this context, the importance of distinguishing Catholic social doctrine before and after the Second Vatican Council, a distinction which has since then (1982) often been adopted. He writes that he is supported by an article that was published in 1981 in the *Civiltà Cattolica*, which is summarized as follows:

- In the first place, that of Leo XIII and *Rerum novarum*, Catholic social doctrine would have been dominated by a "rigid deductive method" which did not give any room for the social sciences, sociology, political science, and economy.
- The second period, in which McCormick places the writings of Pius XI and Pius XII, is that of the "social doctrine" of a social image supported by an organic conception of the society, in the frame of a deductively constructed social philosophy. The author thinks that, in this period, the popes possibly made more of a reference to competent "co-workers" (?).
- A third period begins with the writings of John XXIII: we are to understand that this pope changed from the deductive to the inductive method. His point of departure was the historic moment interpreted in the light of the Gospel. What is new in the text of John XXIII was, according to McCormick, that Catholic social doctrine no longer referred to an unchangeable dogmatic whole. Even the term "doctrine" would now deteriorate and be reserved for the period that preceded John XXIII.[54] With John XXIII, the Church would have transferred from a deductive to an inductive method in the development of its social doctrine and would, from then on, clearly receive a more scriptural foundation.

3.3 The third American theologian, Charles Curran, agrees with McCormick's chronology and mainly discusses the last period. One has now come, according to him, to a conception in which the social doctrine of the Church formulates options and makes proposals from a certain situation, with a limited bearing, while taking the faith and the data of the empirical sciences into consideration. It is from this perspective, he says, that one must read *Gaudium et spes* (July 12, 1965), which begins with "the signs of the time" and thus, an end is made to any derivative from an unchangeable divine plan. In *Octogesima adveniens* (1971), Paul VI would, according to Curran, likewise have left the deductive method. The stress is on the role of Christian community, which with the help of the Holy Spirit, in a dialogue with the responsible bishops, with the other Christian brothers and all humans of good will, must formulate options resulting in social and economic changes. With Paul VI, the Church would no longer refer to unchangeable social doctrines and an unchangeable divine plan. The stress would come to lie now on freedom and the responsibility of the Christian community in the light of the Holy Scriptures.[55]

4. In this manner we come to the fourth part of our exposé: what to think about the arguments of these theologians, who while they say that they do not want to reject the tradition of Catholic social doctrine, do indeed go on a completely different path. Let us first remark, without going deeper into this, that Catholic social doctrine has never ceased to call Catholics to experience responsibility in the social, political, and economic life—each from the position where Providence has placed that person in society. However, with Curran, it is about a choosing and acting without further reference to Catholic social doctrine, but with a knowledge reached through the social sciences and in the "light of the Gospels." From that, three questions:

• Is there truly a radical break in the method that should appear since *Mater et Magistra* (1961), followed by the systematic emergence of theological premises?
• Is it true what Curran writes, that Catholic social doctrine, until the Second Vatican Council, has held up a static social doctrine? Was this, in fact, deducted from unchangeable natural law principles and without any empirical reference?[56]
• How should one view the coming together of data from the empirical social sciences and Catholic social doctrine?

4.1 Concerning the first question, namely whether *Mater et Magistra* means a radical turn to an exclusively or principally theologically founded argument, we want to investigate a not unimportant example. It is about the reception of the "human rights" in Catholic social doctrine. Historical and cultural circumstances have made it such that these rights—the demand for these was initially refused the Church—were recognized only late in Catholic social doctrine. The first ecclesiastical formulation of these rights is found in the pope's Christmas Message of 1942. A few of these rights were enumerated by and connected with "human dignity, from the beginning granted by God to humans." They were introduced by this very pope in his vision of democracy, developed in the Christmas Message of 1944. The pope wrote that it belongs also to the tasks of the Church to point out that democracy must respect not only freedom, but also human dignity and a human's supernatural goal. The actual theological argument is rather limited here.

About twenty years later, in 1963, *Pacem in terris* of John XXIII appeared, an encyclical that is placed clearly after the "break" in the so-called chronology. Therefore, one would expect here an important theological introduction. It is true that here human rights is mentioned with a few biblical references, but mainly it addresses the conceptual apparatus and the terminology of social philosophy: "Both," we read in the text, "derive their origin, both rights and duties, their substinence and their indestructible force, to the natural law, which gives as a gift and imposes" (*Pacem in terris*, nr. 28).

Nevertheless, it is just, and even very remarkable, that John Paul II, once again sixteen years later in *Redemptor hominis*, strongly supports human dignity and this, for him, means the introduction of the theme of "human rights." When the pope concerns himself with these rights, he refers to the *Clarification of Human Rights* which was proclaimed by the Organization of the United Nations. His exposé must be understood within the semantic field of this clarification. The pope confirms and clarifies here expressly that the Church wants to contribute its part to help promote the respecting of these rights.[57]

The recognition of human rights and the support of these rights by a theological argumentation was a slow, historical process in which the Church, for important reasons in the 18th century, did not take part. Concerns, facts, principles, legal traditions, revolutions, and compromises all played a role in the development that led to the Clarifiation of 1789 [sic]. Still, the French Revolution introduced the cult of the goddess Reason, and the Church was robbed by her of goods that formed the basis for an effective and wide social action, the priests remaining faithful to Rome were persecuted, the influence of the Church was banned from public life, and the teaching and the education of youth were taken from it. *Mutatis mutandis*, the entire western world would come under the influence of the French Revolution and its range of ideas remained, even until now, perpetuated in a part of liberal thought. The Church has then condemned, as well, the so-called liberal freedoms, especially in their philosophical foundations.[58]

We find in *Pacem in terris*, the now usual arrangement: first the treating of "rights" and then afterwards, the duties with yet a strong reference to natural law: "Both rights as well as duties take their origins to be the natural law," as we already stated. J. Maritain pointed out a long time ago that human rights cannot be understood from a Christian perspective without the notion of natural law and the duties that this holds before us. The substantiation of individual human rights from a theological perspective is a long process. Between the theological confirmation of human dignity and individual human rights there needs to be quite a few intermediary stages.[59]

4.2 It is right that Catholic social doctrine, until the Second Vatican Council, without a single empirical reference, derived and held before us a static social image from the "eternal unchangeable natural law"?

We shall not go into the so-called "static" character of natural law. Maritain and others have comprehensively pointed out how in the application of the first principles of the natural law, as they were formulated by St. Thomas, there have been a number of developments that have taken place and can take place that are historically and culturally determined. In the acknowledgement of human rights, periods of stagnation, progress, and regression have taken place. In this regard, *Veritatis splendor* has called to mind that on a social plane there are a number of negative norms which protect the inviolability of human dignity, which form the basis for social life and its development (Mat. 19:18, Thou shalt not kill).[60]

Concerning the objection that Catholic social doctrine before the Second Vatican Council was not sufficiently based on experience and thus a static social image was derived from natural law, we would like to call attention to the genesis of *Rerum novarum* and *Quadragesimo anno*.

The least that one can say is that this critique gives proof of insufficient historical knowledge. The encyclical *Rerum novarum* came into existence after long preliminary studies in various countries where one was well-informed of the statistics and the great surveys about what freely and generally began to be called "the social question." Many in and out of Catholic circles, led by their sense of justice and inventive love of one's neighbors, rejected the taboos of social Darwinism. Even *Quadragesimo anno*, in the context of which McCormick says the society should be equated with an organism, but in which an abstract model that was derived from traditional ethics is presented, was no deduction but the extrapolation of a historical model. A renewed vision of social affairs was established in the 19th century by Catholic sociologists, after they had perceived the pernicious effects of industrialization and of liberalism. The figure which was presented of business organization in the encyclicals was studied approximately in the same period, not just in Catholic circles, in England, Belgium, Holland, France, Germany, and other countries. It was a model derived from history, from which one thought, in a too idealistic way, that it would throw up a dam against the ruling economic power of the large business groups. Even the "New Deal" of President Roosevelt, after the great crisis of 1929-33, was a result of it. The Jesuit magazine *America* was, in 1933, full of praise for the attempt started by

Quadragesimo anno to show the way to the organization of business life and control by economic power-groups.[61] We can conclude that it is unjust to say that neither *Rerum novarum* nor *Quadragesimo anno* had any knowledge of empirical reality. These encyclicals, with a knowledge of situations, have pointed out injustices. That *Mater et magistra*, appearing thirty years after *Quadragesimo anno* and after a world war, comprehensively went into social, economic, and political changes, and that this *mutatis mutandis* is also the case with *Gaudium et spes*, does not mean that the highest teaching authority suddenly has more insight or is better informed about world affairs than before (we will omit the role played by the modern means of communication).

Surprisingly, in *Mater et magistra* is the now all-too-well-known expression about the importance of induction for Catholic social doctrine and its application. This induction would occur in three phases: the scouting out of the situation, the judgment of this situation in the light of principles, the establishment of what must and can be done, in short, seeing, judging, and doing (*Mater et magistra*, nr. 236). This methodology is even recommended in the *Guidelines* of 1989 (nr.7).

Father van Gestel, O.P., who at the time taught Catholic social doctrine in Leuven, pointed out first how this method was already recommended by Msgr. Cardijn in the Young Christian Workers Movement (J.O.C.), and second, how through this method the importantce of "pure positive sociology was acknowledged, that through an accurate perception leads to a sound scientific insight into reality and saves one from utopianism and false fantasies." One finds already with van Gestel, thirty years ago in his commentary on *Mater et magistra*, the cliché which now occurs in the texts of Charles Curran and others, "that the church developed its social doctrine following scholastic modes of thinking according to the deductive method, namely that it goes from the principles of natural law or of revelation in order to deduct conclusions or applications relevant to the treated subject."[62] Furthermore, van Gestel clarifies "that since the last century we knew of a development of many social sciences...," and names sociology which "applies the inductive method based on accurate perceptions and the facts in their underlying context."[63]

4.3 Thus, we come to the third question: the current interest in induction with relation to Catholic social doctrine. It is clear that not a single social encyclical was written in ignorance of social reality. The social sciences heralded after World War II, as a new humanism made quite an impression. New chairs were established in all European universities in this regard. We read in *Gaudium et spes* "that the practitioners of natural sciences and humanities, especially of biology, medicine, sociology, and psychology, can contribute considerably to the well-being of marriage and family and to peace of consciousness."[64] Since then people have spoken about the crisis in the social sciences. The importance of these sciences nevertheless may not be ignored. They have given us a treasure of information about the most diverse aspects of the social life, a conceptual apparatus, and a terminology which allows us to analyze and to point out the social reality.[65] Regardless of subsequent developments, Paul VI placed trust in these sciences but with an important restriction: "because humans are the objects of these sciences, they can produce a serious reduction which distorts humans, and as a result they are incompetent to understand humans in their totality." He was, nevertheless, unfavorable regarding certain models that some would like to impose upon humans as a scientific plan for their behavior. A few years later, one can read in the *Instruction About Certain Aspects of Liberation Theology* (1984) that everything which carries the label "scientific" is not yet, therefore, really scientific. Furthermore, the method used to approach reality "must be preceded by a critical epistemological investigation." In addition, it states that "the critical investigation of the methods of analysis derived from other disciplines is especially necessary for the theologian"; "the use by the theologian of the contribution of philosophy or the life sciences must constitute the object of a critical theological investigation"; and "it is in the light of the faith and what this teaches about humans and their destiny, that one must investigate the value of what other disciplines bring up, often by means of conjecture, namely in the form of hypotheses about humans, their history, and their destiny." People realized about twenty years after *Mater et magistra* (1963), even before liberation theology claimed Marxism was an acceptable method of social analysis, that "seeing" is not always the taking in of pure givens provided by a social science. The *Guidelines* for the study of the Catholic social doctrine rightly established on their part the importance of the social sciences. Because of this, one will learn to know the changing situations in social life and one will find in the everyday knowledge of this life a well-founded starting point for the dialogue with the world. After all, these social sciences speak about the context in which the social doctrine of the Church must be applied. "Still," the *Guidelines* add, "in the interest for, and the study of social (things), the danger must be avoided of being captured in the traps of the idealogists who manipulate the interpretation of data, or be gripped by the positivism that the empirical data overestimate to the disadvantage of an integral concept of the world and of humans."[66] Already, more than 40 years ago, people had come to the conclusion in a discussion about the methodology of the social sciences that it is not as easy as establishing "pure" facts. In 1946, J. Monnerot published with the pregnant title *Les faits sociaux ne sont pas des choses*, a phenomenological critique on the method of E. Durkheim.[67] In 1970, Peter Winch pointed out in his *Idea of a Social Science and its Relation to Philosophy*, how the "social facts" are carriers of a "sense" and how one only understands a so-called fact if one has grasped the human sense of it.[68] The German method dispute of the 1960's was completely about that problem. It is now generally accepted that the engagement of the social investigator colors not only the establishment of his research subject, but also the interpretation of the data on which conclusions will rest. Furthermore, even the establishment of the "indicators" which grasp the reality quantitatively is not free of value judgments.[69] The "seeing" or the inductive method must be handled with care to give to Catholic social doctrine good statistical data and sociographical studies, adequately interpreted to their needs so that these, in light of the faith, can be judged and used for practical applications.

The new conceptual apparatus and the terminology of the social sciences are often enlightening. Through these, categories are created through which new realities are able to be talked about. Still, a human is not only a "homo sociologicus" who only has roles to play and who may be socialized into whatever role. A human is not a mere product of an independent process, e.g., class conflict, and the "dynamic of history," which imposes its own order on the human.[70] Interesting in this relation is the use of the term "structure" in *Centesimus annus* by John Paul II, where he acknowledges that a human is "conditioned" by the social structures in which one lives. But the pope points out immediately that it is human decisions that "create sinful structures." Here, the pope clearly rejects the globalizing terminology in connection with structured compulsion and structural violence. With these words, the pope introduces a personalistic connotation, which places humans as the cause responsible for the structures.[71]

5. Finally, there is another attempt to explain the meaning of theology and social philosophy in the development of the Catholic social doctrine. In the *Guidelines* that we chose as starting-points of our

reflection, there is only a short discussion about the political order (the numbers 9, 13, and 63, and in the appendix 1, IV, 4). *Gaudium et spes* contains, nevertheless, an important chapter about the political establishment (Part II, ch. 4, 73-76). Let us trace how Catholic social doctrine developed in this matter.

With the encyclicals *Diuturnum* (1881), *Immortale Dei* (1885), and *Sapientiae Christianae* (1890), once called the Thomistic encyclicals, where all fundamental proclamations are still underlined by appeals to the Holy Scriptures, Leo XIII has bridged almost 1000 years of controversy.[72] In the conflict between pope and emperor, in which they, their theologians, canonists, legalists, and publicists intervened, arguments were systematically used to the advantage of one or the other party, supported by Holy Scriptures, sometimes symbolically and other times realistically interpreted. Emperors and kings mainly used texts from the Old Testament to prove the divine establishment of kingship (1 Samuel 9:17 and 10:22-25); the texts of Paul (Romans 13:1-17) and of Peter (1 Peter 2:13) to found the duty of subservience of the subjects and the story of the two swords to substantiate the assertion that one sword, the pastoral sword (the Church) must serve and obey the emperor, and the other sword, the imperial sword should force the people to listen to the *sacerdotium*. From the side of the Church, the two-sword story was nevertheless interpreted in this way: that the two swords belonged to the Church and that the royal sword must be handled *ad nutum ecclesiae*, whenever the Church deemed it necessary. In the papal camp, one mainly called upon the Gospel texts about the mission of the apostles (John 20:21-22 and Matthew 28:28, "To me all power is given") as well as upon the words "Feed my sheep," directed towards Peter (John 21:17). In the regime during a united Christendom, under which all Christians were subjected to the ecclesiastical authority, the Imperium was judged to fall within this Christendom and thus subjected to the same authority. This ecclesiastical authority let itself be valid inside the frame of feudalism and on the grounds of real or fancied property titles, and it played, in this manner, an important worldly role. There existed a remaining confusion between the different arguments to the advantage of the authority of one or the other party.

These are the so-called Thomistic encyclicals that have introduced distinction between the source of all authority as such, the institution of authority, and the bearer of authority. They have correctly formulated the distinction and the difference between Chruch and state with the description of both their competencies. With contemporary words and expressions, these theorems about the relation between Church and state were adopted and endorsed by *Gaudium et spes*. It is also thanks to these encyclicals that a great step was taken in the direction of democracy, even though the wording and the nuances were rather careful. We read in *Diuturnum* that Catholic doctrine does not oppose that the bearer of civil authority is chosen by the people. We must wait until the statements of Pius XII in 1941, and of John XXIII in *Pacem in terris* (1963), to read the principle of democratic elections are formulated in its full scope, together with a fundamental treatment of individual rights and duties of people.[73]

We can conclude from this important area of state organization that the philosophical reflection, which was prepared by the leaders of Spanish scholasticism (De Vitoria, Suarez and Bellarmine) and via the necessary intermediary stages took shape here and has come to us in order to give new possibilities to freedom in modern political life. We have trouble seeing how this could have happened from Old Testament models. There followed two centuries of absolutism and also the attempts to found politics on the Holy Scriptures. We think of the writings of Bousset. Finally, the French Revolution came. We agree with Nikolaus Monzel, when he proposes that revelation holds forth values and determines goals that start from far above natural social ethics. We intended to show that it also belongs to the signs of the time that interests and controversies about biblical texts can give contradictory interpretations. Concerning the three American theologians, we have the impression that their critique on the so-called static natural law and the conservative social image of the Church is really inspired by a critique through which they want to touch other areas of natural law, but their critique concerning Catholic social doctrine is neither intrinsically nor historically founded.[74]

3
The Human Person and Human Dignity as Basis of the Social Doctrine of the Church

Professor Dr. L. Roos

1. Contours of the Christian portrayal of mankind

All cultures which are known by available evidence, possess a reflection of what it means to be human. This is especially valid for European culture of the West, which has its roots in ancient Greece, and unfolds further in the Roman Empire, and finally is fused together as a whole through the union of concepts of the "human" in classical, Greek-Roman antiquity, Bible-Christian, Celtic-Germanic, as well as the Slavic cultures.

From the beginning, Christianity has sought a dialogue with non-Christian anthropologies and ethical systems, which is evident already in the "house-garden-and-kitchen-ethics" of the epistle literature—influenced by Stoic elements—of the New Testament, and which becomes even more visible with the early apologists. This entry of Christians into traditions of other cultures continually took place by taking this dialogue as a starting point or by protesting against it as a starting-point. This applies especially to the meeting of Christendom with the modern philosophies of the Enlightenment and the present time. Afterwards, one can no longer determine whether or not certain utterances in the Church's current social doctrine about the human person and human dignity were derived from "pure reason" or from "faith enlightened reason." To what extent do the current contours of the Christian portrait of mankind emanate from an already thousand year fruitful meeting of theology and philosophy? What are the essential coordinates of the Christian understanding of mankind?

1.1 Man as image and likeness of God

"Then God said, 'And now we will make human beings; they will be like us and resemble us.'...So God created human beings, making them to be like himself. He created them male and female." (Gen. 1, 26 and 27). From this passage one can call creation the theological foundation of the Bible-Christian anthropology. Nowadays, the fact that humans are made in God's image seems so evident and self-explanatory to Christians yet only a few still "understand the incomprehensible mystery even to realize what is expressed in this notion."[75] The question "Who is man?" is, according to the Bible "only to be answered from a comparison with God. Man is a being related to God, a being corresponding to God, God's conversation partner, his ally, addressable by God and addressing God."[76] This being God's likeness has bearing on all human dimensions, on soul, body, spirit and brings a relation into being with the creation with which humans are entrusted.

If a human is "the being related to God" then it follows in an analogous (more unequal than equal, but still real) manner that a human has a part of the characteristics of God. Everything that one can say of God, also has a meaning for humans and their concept of themselves. That a human is the image of God, comes fundamentally into the expression that humans shall "rule" (see Gen. 1, 28) over the earth entrusted to them and are indebted to God because of this responsibility. Therefore, an ecological ethics in Christian context must make use of anthropological categories. It knows no "rights" of plants and animals that one could formulate without referring to the rights and the duties of humans. These and other expressions of the Biblical creation story demand a human whose personality is characterized by very specific characteristics and which one can summarize in four points:

1.1.1 Reason and uniqueness

In experiencing of himself or herself, a human understands himself or herself as a person, which means an indivisible, independent someone, a unique individual. The basis and reason of this single individual uniqueness is a soul, a principle of life, created by God, which forms an intrinsic unity with the material, and in this manner brings the individuality of the individual human into existence. This means in the last instance that the proper responsibility of humans for themselves and their actions is understood biblically as responsibility to God. It is also the situation that humans can be "spoken to" personally by God and can be "called up" for a specific task. The person in his or her individuality can also never be merged completely into another person and wholly give oneself to another. This difference is the cause of desire. We desire a complete correspondence in love with (one) other person(s), even though we know that this desire, even with the deepest love, could never be satisfied completely. Augustine expressed this last cause of this experience with the famous words: "You have made us, God for Yourself, and our hearts are restless, until they rest in You."

1.1.2 Freedom and morality

That a human is the image of God, finds its deepest expression in the fact that God lets humans share in his freedom, in other words, the capability "that human self-determination, faced with different possibilities, can decide either this way or that—that a human can choose."[77] This freedom would be rather senseless, if it did not at the same time have the capability to recognize good and have the will to choose it. Freedom and morality belong intrinsically with each other.

In contrast to the divine, human freedom has limits placed upon it. As a finite being a human experiences the limits of corporality and spiritual capacity. Because a human is a social being, freedom depends in essence on the way in which others are prepared to work voluntarily with him or her. Finally, freedom is determined and limited by the historicity of the human, which means the historical circumstances of concrete existence. Of all the tensions between the intentional infinite and the categorial finite freedom of humans the one hardest to understand is the limits of human existence. In this regard, a human is a being that develops visions of another, better world, and wants to take no pleasure with the world as it is. Therein rests the danger that humans construct plans for a utopian society and "sacrifice" others for it. The experiencing of finiteness, the pressure of time, and the pressure of circumstances is saddening. Only a limited space of freedom is at the disposal of humans, and for this reason human freedom stands continually under the "pressure of time," as Jesus said to the faithful servant: " 'Well done, good and faithful servant!' said his master. 'You have been faithful in managing small amounts, so I will put you in charge of large amounts.'" (Mt. 25,21). With the non-use (compare the "lazy" servant) or the misuse of freedom a human can forget himself or herself and his or her responsibility. Life becomes purposeful, if one's free choices are directed towards good.

The organ which relates freedom and morality to each other is consciousness. Here a human becomes aware that he or she must make a choice for the sake of himself or herself, one's fellow human being, and in the last instance God. Here one stands directly before God and cannot let oneself be represented by anyone else.

At the same time one may not interpret conscience in the sense of an individualistically conceived autonomy: what a human is worth and worthy of, one cannot fathom in the short span of the individual's life. For that the historical-cultural connection is necessary in the sense of anthropologically binding experiences of a culture related to what is at the service of humans and what causes humans damage. In the moral tradition directed to Christians by God and life experiences of the community of believers, conscience gets its necessary orientation to the truth. This may and must be approached critically by the individual, because only in this manner can one consider and accept in freedom the truth about humans and the world extending from God. Freedom is oriented always to the truth and connected to the necessity of moral choice.

1.1.3 Dialogical personality

Further, it belongs to the being of a human that he or she possesses a dialogical personality. As it seems from the creation story, humans are the only conversation partners of God in the world. By creating humans and transferring creation to them to care for in a responsible manner (Gen. 1, 18), God makes humans his conversation partner, "the one who hears the word" (Karl Rahner). As long as humans listen to this task, which means appearing to be obedient, everything that God created is "very good" (Gen. 1, 31). Let humans rather be led astray to doubt God's wisdom and benevolence and to follow another voice, opposite to God, then destiny goes its own way (cf. Gen. 3 and 4). The fall, an alienation from God, and an alienation from fellow humans (fratricide) and nature, follows. The "city without God," the construction of the tower of Babel, ends in a general confusion of tongues (Gen. 11). Without obedience to the word and the task of God an end comes to the consensus of the people concerning fundamental truth. John Paul II put this into words in the encyclical *Centesimus annus* in this way: "If there is no transcendental truth which humans must obey to realize their full identity, there is not a single certain principle that brings the right relations between people into existence. The importance of their class, their group, and their nation bring them constantly irrevocably into conflict. If one does not acknowledge transcendental truth, the violence of power will triumph" (*Centesimus annus* 44, 2).

The obedience to God and the answer to it by humans given in freedom is rather not only essential for the success of human life, but also for the being present to one's fellow human. God created humans "male and female" (cf. Gen. 1, 27). Moreover the creation story's translucent division of labor (cf. the different jobs of Cain and Abel), God's covenant with Noah and his sons and in this context a national community (cf. Gen. 9 and 10) point to a collective cultural task of all people. Therefore, humans develop themselves in relationship to fellow humans. A human only becomes human in a social connection. One should not see this first negatively in the sense of pure utilitarianism: it does not work without the other; but positively: it works better with the other. Biological survival, the basis of being human, can only come into existence in a society of marriage and family. The individual can only reach a large part of his personal objectives with others. The more values the members acknowledge collectively apart from a society, the richer the society can unfold itself. The less this is the case, the poorer the society. A society which is still only "pluralistic" without coming to a consensus concerning fundamental values, falls apart or becomes totalitarian.

1.1.4 Subject of rights and duties

The dignity of a human, based on the acknowledgment that a human is equipped with reason and unicity, freedom and morality and being with one's fellow human is lastly assured by the originality and self-determination of the person. Rights and duties come to every human, in the first place, not based on the grounds of another social contract, but based on humans' origin. In this manner John XXIII says: "In each ordered and well-functioning society it must be valid as a fundamental principle that every person has an identity, which means endowed with reasoning and free will, and has therefore rights and duties that directly and simultaneously flow forth from one's nature. These rights and duties are therefore general, inviolable, and inalienable" (*Pacem in terris* 9). Such a conceived truth concerning humans and the rights and duties that can be derived from it for the individual, form the highest value in society. Therefore, the person should be at all times "source, subject, and goal" (principium, subjectum et finis) of all social activity. Regarding this, short and concisely: "A human is older than the state" (*Rerum novarum* 6), not in the temporal sense, but with the focus on human dignity and the task of the state that dignity serves. Humans and the communities, especially the family, which are formed by humans as a natural cause or from free will, do not exist because the state establishes them, but because they possess them—as Leo XIII says with the family in mind—"independent of the state, thereby having rights and duties inherently" (*Rerum novarum* 9).

1.2 Humans under the law of sin and alienation

The introduction to the pastoral constitution *Gaudium et spes* brings out the "division" of the human being, which the naive optimism of the anthropology of the Enlightenment had forgotten and which we experience again today (cf. *Gaudium et spes* 4-10). Behind the "disturbances of the balance" in the human society there are really no unknown causes, but "in reality the disturbances of the balance from which the modern world suffers are linked to the deeper lying disturbance of the balance that wrestles in the heart of man" (*Gaudium et spes* 10). The creation story illustrates this. If one does not accept this truth, one must postulate other explanations, for example a "metaphysical dualism of spirit and body, or spirit and matter," or, since Marx and Rousseau, a "dualism between the individual and the society."[78] Every anthropology that neglects the phenomenon of the sinfulness of humans remains inadequate, because it does not let the reality of the human possess any rights. Humans who honestly see their own sinfulness, see that they must protect themselves against themselves. This happens through a corresponding political order which one must treat anthropologically as the self-protection of the better me against the worse me that constantly threatens humans. In the biblical history of the prehistoric times this motif can be found in the new covenant with Noah. Strict laws are necessary to protect and preserve human life (cf. Gen. 9, 5-7).

1.3 Humans delivered from sin and death

There is a danger in holding the sinful in humans to be so "powerful" that God's trust in his creation, especially redemption, is not taken seriously enough. "With Jesus one man—in whom God subjected Himself to the circumstances of human existence and in whom God himself stepped up to counter the corruption which has crept into human nature by human uprising against God—has walked this earth."[79] In Jesus and his fundamental obedience the summoning of God to the people found the complete, adequate answer. Jesus, as the substitute of all, has done the will of God and lived the true life for us (cf. Rom. 5, 19) The hope, based on Jesus' obedience to the Father and to the incomprehensibility of his death on the cross, is that God is prepared to forgive all human guilt (cf. Heb. 5, 9). In Jesus' resurrection from the dead his salvation-giving power appears to be stronger than the doom-bringing power of the sin which leads to death. The resurrection of Jesus is the fundamental turning-point in the history of humanity. From this grows the power to resist sin and its alienating consequences in the certain hope that God's love is stronger than all human disobedience. This belief guards Christians from despair and frees them for love and the effort for more justice. On the basis of the life, death and resurrection of Jesus a human may see himself or herself in faith as that being whose hope is not in vain. Jesus, the Son of God, lived our life and opened for us the road to eternal life. By "obeying Him" (Heb. 5, 9) we are doing the will of the Father. We live from the gifts and the fruits of the Spirit, which the Father sent in Jesus' name, whose power "poured forth in our hearts."

2. Criteria for a Christian Humanism
2.1 Receiving and thanking

At the heart of Christian life stands the thanks to God for the gift of creation and salvation: "A 'Christian determined' human being is a being in receiving, a being in thanking."[80] Thanks to God is the first, fundamental life expression of the Christian. A Christian humanism means therefore in the first place that daily thanksgiving is given to God through prayer, especially in the celebration of the Eucharist on Sunday, for salvation and redemption deliverance from sin and death, and for the hope of eternal life. At the same time it follows from this that one should understand personal life in all its dimensions as a thanking answer to the received gift of life and to salvation. With this Christianity has freed us also from all 'moral overloading'. It is not the human who must create order in life or the world, but it is only God who can fulfill our life and the world and this is already fundamentally present in the Christ-event. We should, as Christians, live forth this truth about humans and we should bear witness to it.

2.2 Self-affirmation and "being there" for others

If God created all people, and Jesus Christ gave his life for me and for "many," then anyone who believes this must establish oneself and one's life as a summons from God and at the same time be there for all the others encompassed in God's holy will. If God has created humans in this manner and does all this with humans, then one can affirm oneself, but with weaknesses and limitations. It is precisely this absolute union with God which frees the human as believer from subordination to this world's claims to absoluteness and makes one free for an unselfish effort in the world. This applies both to the general calling of humans in their responsibility to God to shape the world and to collaborate with God's plan of salvation and the saving of all people, and to the personal calling of the individual, who receives it in his unique union with God and who follows it in his direct relationship with God and its accompanying peace.

2.3 Acceptance of, and giving form to the world

For the Christian the world has not been abandoned by God. One accepts the world as God's world and trusts that God grants "the people of good will" enough insight and willpower always to find and to go from "the path of less dignified to more dignified living conditions" (Paul VI, *Populorum progressio* 20). God said "yes" to this world in the word of creation and even more in the "The Word became a human being and, full of grace and truth, lived among us." (John 1, 14). Consequently people may and must likewise say "yes" to our life, no matter how threatened and in vain it may seem, to that which we call our work, to the continual fight which the hard-working economic person with tools that always are in need of improvement delivers in spite of the scarcity of goods, to the unending and tiresome efforts for a just division of opportunities and costs in society, even when this not always is honored, and to the nerve-racking effort of a politician in the context of conflicting interest and unavoidable polemics, who must wrestle with much ignorance, half-truths and anger to bring about something as a bit of order and justice that makes a life with dignity possible for people. The "proclamation of faith" and "instruction of its social doctrine" (*Gaudium et spes* 76, 5) are therefore both internally connected dimensions of the mission of the church.

2.4 The sense of suffering

Any image of a human that does not examine the problem of suffering would lack an essential element. Every humanism that deserves this name must address this problem. In this last case, Christ can give no answer that answers all questions. He can only refer to the answer that God Himself gives in the fate of the life and death of Jesus, and urge humans to follow him, even in suffering and dying. "Whoever does not take up his cross and follow in my steps is not fit to be my disciple. Whoever tries to gain his own life will lose it; but whoever loses his life for my sake will gain it." (Mt. 10, 38-39).

It is important, then, that the suffering is not simply something that one lets happen, but an essential subdivision of one's existence that a human in incomprehensibility finally leaves to God. Each suffering is not only in part a premonition of death, but also a preparation for it. For each human, having to suffer everything is an indication that he or she is on the road to God. Each spiritual being who is created to be directed to God, but has not yet found his or her fulfillment in Him, is necessarily a suffering being, because there is always a difference between what we wish and strive for, and what we can complete (Only God is *actus purus*). Only God can do what He is, which is to experience to the fullest. We can do that only partly and the "rest" is not *actio*, but *passio*. Suffering is a falling short in a possible fullness of being, and is finiteness to mortality. The "yes" of faith to suffering that we see in Jesus' life exists also as a comfort and guidance for us: "But even though He was God's Son, he learned through his sufferings to be obedient. When he was made perfect, he became the source of eternal salvation for all those who obey him" (Heb. 5, 8-9). The social doctrine of the church is also meant as the answer of faith to experiencing misery as well as justice in this world. The Church "feels that people are bound in their best aspirations and it is overcome by a great sadness, when their hope seems to be so often in vain. Therefore it desires to help them develop themselves completely and it therefore presents to them what is only its own: an all-encompassing vision of man and mankind" (*Populorum progressio* 13). It is convinced that in the middle of all the suffering of humankind "the way of the less dignified to more dignified living conditions" always can be found and offered. Its social doctrine is the expression of this conviction.

2.5 The vitality of the theological virtues

Christian life is fundamentally formed by the theological virtues—by the virtue of faith, which conceives existence as "receiving" and gives thanks for it; by the virtue of love that whoever is gifted with it is made capable of mercy, comfort and assistance; and by the virtue of the hope which is the conviction that all human striving for the betterment of social circumstances is not in vain, but that only God can make this happen completely (cf. *Gaudium et spes* 39). With a focus on the current, widespread despair that sometimes takes the form of a fear psychosis, no comprehensive proofs are necessary for the social relevance of a humanism that makes the theological virtues a goal. A similar humanism resists on the one hand any utopian optimism resulting in the movements on the one hand calling upon Adam Smith and on the other hand calling upon Karl Marx: the utopia of the liberalism believed that through the mechanism of the

"free competition in all markets" the egoism of the individual would
be transformed as if by a wave of a magic wand into a communal
well-being; the utopianism of Marxism believed "that by changing
institutions, e.g., by a changed sequence in production, the start of
the 'new human' immediately would happen."[81] The theological virtue of hope keeps Christians from falling prey to such utopias. On
the other hand Christian hope does not mean "do-nothingism." Precisely because it is not limited to earth-bound results, hope can more
impartially take the many, small, daily steps that are possible and
necessary to improve social situations. It avoids the anthropological
optimism of the "world-improvers" and utopians, as well as the pas-
sivism of those who despair and the catastrophe-theoreticians.

What the Christian view of humans means for the theory and the
practice of justice, John Paul II has formulated in his encyclical *Dives
misericordia*: it is the granting of the theological virtue of love with
the obstruction of an antagonistic pluralism of values in mind.
Nikolaus Monzel pointed out the reason for this with two arguments
unsurpassed until now: "In the first place: only love can bring the
economic rulers to move to abandon forever the prejudices and the
defense of an unjust economic and social order, and in the second
place: only love can widen the outlook of the political rulers, which
is limited through bondage to a social position, and make them see
the *suum cuique* of the different groupings."[82] This leads in no way to
a cheap harmony of values. It does imply, however, that the necessary
collision of values is conceived as a "normal effort" for a justified
good, not as "a fight against others" (*Laborem exercens* 20, 3). The
theological virtue of love assures that the Christian's point of departure is the God-given capability to conquer hate, and, with the good
will of all the concerned, to find ways to agree. What unites people is
always larger than what divides them, insofar as they trust their endowed powers.

2.6 Citizens of two worlds

The strength of the Christian image of the "human" exists finally
in the fact that he or she who lives from it is able to "endure" productively the tensions of human existence. Other images of the "human"
cannot do this in the same way. They tend to one-sidedness and lead,
for example, to individualistic or collectivist development of a society, to "a only having an eye for this world" or a flight from the
world. The Christian human image supplies insight and the Christian belief gives strength to "endure," to be called to transcendence
and to stand with both feet in this world; to become conscious of the

borders of immanence and not to rest with it; to experience that one is graced by God and not succumb to the daily pressure of inadequacy, even sinfulness (cf. Rom. 7, 19-25); and to take part in the community of believers and in this manner receive everything "from the church" and simultaneously personally be called by God to a mission that can be received only in the peace of the awareness of God. The Christian human image grants the capability to endure the tension between being orientated to the "goods of the hereafter" and the full effort in work and occupation, and the corresponding duties: to expect the "new city of God" and at the same time to take upon oneself the frequently ungrateful task of the politician (cf. *Gaudium et spes* 76); to subject oneself to the law of the "scarcity of goods" and still fall to neither greed and consumerism nor the avarice that grants no joy of life to oneself and others.

This means that one should not become satisfied with the hereafter, but take responsibility for the people in this world and in this time, with the knowledge granted by faith that eternal life by God is the goal of all. The Christian expects the completion of his or her own life and the history of humanity, and this fulfillment will take place not by human effort, but by God, who at the end shall create "the new heaven and the new earth." This expectation, the council says, may "not weaken care for forming this earth, but should rather stimulate it, since here the body of the new human family grows, and it is here that an adumbration already can be found of the new world" (*Gaudium et spes* 39, 2). Therefore, a more just and humane world is not unimportant for the Kingdom of God; one should rather proclaim a just, more humane world as a rough draft or silhouette of the new world and the new earth, which God will bring into existence. Faith in the fulfillment in the apocalypse promised by God should now already clarify the effort of the Christian for a more just world. This internal coherence between the salvation task of the church and the execution of it on the improvement of social relations corresponds exactly with the definition of the Church, according to which it is called "as it were, the sacrament of the instrument of the profound uniting with God and of the unity of the whole humanity" (*Lumen gentium* 1). Because those who believe in Christ avow and experience their belief, they form a connection between people and God, from which at the same time a new, more humane way of social society comes forth. In this respect the mission of the church appears to be "religious, and because of it very humane" (*Gaudium et spes* 11, 3). Our effort for love, peace, and justice does not bring a "paradise on earth" into being, but is possibly a premonition of the new heaven and the new earth. *Laborem exercens* speaks about a *lumen aliquod*, a "glimpse of the new heaven and the new earth."

As citizens of two worlds, the Christian strives not fanatically for an "earth paradise," but with resignation for "the way from circumstances less dignified to more dignified." Less dignified: these are the material needs of those who are lacking of the minimum for existence; this is the moral need of those who are consumed by egoism. Less dignified: these are the characteristics of violence that are based on misuse of property or power, on exploitation of workers, and on doing business in an unjust manner. More dignified: this is the climbing out from misery to possession of that which is necessary to live, the conquering of poor social circumstances, the expansion of knowledge, and the obtaining of education. More dignified: this is better knowledge concerning human dignity, defeat of the spirit of poverty, collaboration for the well-being of all, and the will for peace. More dignified: this is the acknowledgment by humans of ultimate values and the acknowledgment of God, their source and their goal. More dignified: this is finally "especially the faith, a gift of God, accepted by humans of good will, and the mutual unity in the love of Christ, who calls us to take part as children in the life of the living God, the Father of all people" (*Populorum progressio* 21).

Also, if this task, faced with a widely spread secularism and a disappearing piety, has become more difficult today, then the Church may "not abandon humans," but it must faithfully "make the way of the "human" to be its own" (*Centesimus annus* 62, 3). The Church owes the gift of "its social doctrine and activity" (*Mater et magistra* 6) to contemporary humans. After all, "the social doctrine of the Catholic Church" is and remains "unreleasably bound to its Christian doctrine about humans" (*ibid.* 222)

3. The culture-creating meaning and the current threatening of Christian humanism
3.1 Value, institutions, and virtues

Whoever wishes to understand the meaning of the Christian image of the "human" for our society must first obtain a clear insight concerning the structural laws of every culture. One can analyze and understand cultures by means of the mutual connection of values, institutions, and virtues. The philosopher Max Müller from Freiburg once established that world history is determined by shifts in sets of values. It is clear to everyone that these sets differ according to whether people believe or not and according to the image of God they support. If a society has reached an agreement about values, then it must provide its members with clear means or forms to best attain its goals. Solid social forms are also called social structures. If they are poured in a judicial form, then one speaks of institutions (e.g. marriage and family, property, right of inheritance). To hold on to a certain set of values and to maintain the social structures that are necessary for the fulfillment of these values, corresponding behavior and virtues are required by the members of the society.

How the mutual relation of values, institutions, and virtues receives a concrete form depends on the image of the "human" (and the image of God that is connected to it) of the people who form or have formed a structure with each other. He who believes in the God of the biblical-Christian revelation shall experience, judge, and give form to life and being involved in social processes and in political and economic conflicts in a different way than someone who shows no faith. The Christian is, for example, convinced that God gave humans a meaningful freedom, and therefore considers all deterministic philosophies concerning history and conducting social trade derived from it (like Marxism) to be faulty. The Christian is convinced that that which binds people internally is still larger than that which separates them, and therefore can protect neither the way of class hatred and class struggle nor that of a social-Darwinistic "survival of the fittest." From a similar fundamental position, the Christian tries to give social institutions a certain form. He or she discovers in the course of history those social structures which correspond more than others to the set of values and the personal stance from which he or she chooses as a Christian. In this manner, these institutions shall take on specific characteristics in which the essential choice for the faith also becomes institutionally and habitually tangible: the social institutions of family, state, education, social help, the "social giving form" to business, the condition of an enterprise, and the forms of value conflicts—this all takes on a certain form that they would not have, if the existential option of many or all people who live in the society for Christian faith would not have existed or would not exist.

3.2 The Christian cultural legacy of Europe

The first time in the West when there was reflection about the internal relationship of the image of the "human" and social order was with Socrates (Plato). He lays claim to knowing that in the final analysis morality cannot be determined only by existing laws. Therefore it is only logical, as he himself formulates it, that he must die as "offender of the law." A few hundred years later the Jewish Maccabees let themselves be sent to their deaths by the Syrian autocrat Antiochus IV Epiphanes rather than offend "God's law." In this exact sense Peter and John declare before the high council, the highest political committee of Israel, "We must obey God, not men." (Acts. 5, 29). The Christians obey indeed "for the sake of conscience" the authority legitimized by God (on the grounds of the natural law) (cf. Rom. 13, 1-7), but they resist until death against that apocalyptic animal (the state) that depicts the idolatry of the state as that which got form in the cultic honoring of the emperor at the time of Nero and the later Roman emperors (cf. Apoc. 13, 1-18). Also here it becomes clear how the image of God and image of the "human" are linked essentially with each other and how the corresponding convictions fundamentally put their stamp on the social order.

This applies then, as well as today. Also, in the 19th and 20th centuries, the Christian image of the "human" is for Christians the basis for giving form to a critique of society. The controversies with the great ideological trends, as those that came forth in the last 200 years and have developed socially, are controversies about spiritual causes which ultimately lie in ideas about "human" and the social theories and actions derived from them.

From all this a European culture came into existence that historically also helped form North America and, in a far-reaching manner, South America. Its foundation is the Christian image of the human, and in North and South America the historical encounter of Christian belief (of the church) and the culture of the indigenous peoples. From that, a certain form of culture came into existence that found its reflection in a set of values based on the Christian image of the "human" with its corresponding social institutions and behavioral models (virtues). Therein exists the true cultural accomplishment of Europe, a benefit not only to its member states, but also to the entire humanity. In the middle of this culture the human person stands with God given dignity, human rights, and the public-social institutionalizing of these. Because these human rights had to find a social acceptance in Europe where there was occasional ecclesiastical resistance, they then based themselves, anthropologically speaking, on the biblical-Christian understanding of the human person.[83]

Our cultural-historical long-term memory has become weak, and many can no longer recognize the internal connections between the social guarantee of human dignity, corresponding rights, and the Christian faith. The contribution of the Christian image of the "human" to a political, social, and economic order that rests on inalienable human rights preceding the state, can be sketched by means of the following elements:

• The founding of human dignity, unicity and freedom on faith to a personal God, who historically acts with humans, whose image and likeness humans are.

• The principles of solidarity, subsidiarity and communal well-being conceived and established in this personal relationship.

• The distinction between the transcendental salvation and the immanent well-being of humans. From that follows a certain function of politics and economics, which prevents both the absolutizing of these and the politicalizing and economizing of faith, as well as makes possible the ethical influence of religion on politics and economics.

• The family as life-long, based on one marriage of man and woman, a community, like a primitive cell of a social life which connects generations, and an existence that has found its fulfillment.

• The democratic, constitutional state that admits to inalienable human rights existing before the state.

• The right to personal property, including the means of production, and the link of this right to the provision of goods that are necessary in order for all people to live.

• An economic order that equally makes freedom and social justice the pillars of all economic activity and which as socially tied market economy avoids the deviation of both an individualism aligned only to market economics and a state-bureaucratic collectivism.

3.3 Universality and particularity

The Christian image of the "human" finds its center in the person of Jesus Christ. However, this Jesus did "not come to lift up, but to bring to fulfillment" (cf. Mt. 5, 17). If one cannot "understand" Christ without the Father, one cannot also fathom the Christian image of the "human" without relating the Christ-event and the creation-event. In this respect the Christian truth about humans must be accessible in principle to all people, insofar as it has a connection to the arrangement and shaping of life in this world.

St. Thomas Aquinas speaks of the divine gift of reason and the divine gift of faith. We as Christians are convinced that God as Creator of humans has given us the capability to at least recognize in principle, with the assistance of reason, the good and the ways to achieve it. In this aspect the social doctrine of the Church since John XXIII expressly and directly refers the contents to "all people of good will." Because of this the "fundamental principles" of the social doctrine of the Church "can be accepted by all" (*Mater et magistra* 220).

The Church knows that the Christian image of the "human" is anchored in the Gospels; however, it maintains that the God of creation gives all people the capability of reason, by which in principle they are able to acknowledge human dignity and the conditions to actualize it. We then speak of a "moral natural law." In spite of all this the fulfillment of that which constitutes the value and worth of humans is only to be completely fathomed in the light of the Gospels: "Christ, the new Adam, lets humans just now, in the revelation of the mystery of the Father and his love, see who he is, and reveals to them his highest calling" (II, *Gaudium et spes* 22, 1). The Christian image of the "human" sees humans therefore not only delivered by Christ, but also—as early as the creation—equipped with a responsibility to the world and with capabilities to make the most of it. The Church thinks therefore not only about its own believers, but also about all people who are created and called to salvation by God. The particularity of the Christian image of the "human" therefore does not exclude but implies its universal validity and the acknowledgment of its principles with the assistance of human reason.

3.4 The value-free and religionless society

The prevalent theme of modern society is consciousness and the active development of autonomous human subjectivity. This first of all comes into existence by a process in which the natural sciences and philosophy rightly make themselves free of misplaced theological intrusions.

However, the current separation of natural and social sciences and their original connection with ethics and theology led to the mechanical conception that in society one also could replace virtue with social "technology." The liberal variation of this conception believes that freedom is sufficient in all areas to reach the goal of a human economy. In such a sociotechnical conception personal virtues are superfluous: the sum of egoisms brings "by the invisible hand" economic well-being. The socialist opponent of liberalism functions in an entirely sociotechnical way: the class-conflict which takes place according to the laws of historical materialism, ultimately realizes the empire of social freedom. Personal, moral choices, and virtues are superfluous. Both ideological theories of a "sociotechnical" economy fall short. However, they have not yet lost their effectiveness in the minds of many.

One can also show this empirically. The sociologist Gerhard Schmidtchen sees in the last century an increasing "shift from the search of causes with the individual to the searching of these with society": the society as scapegoat! A sociologism ultimately hides behind it: the image of the sociotechnical design of personal happiness.[84]

3.5 New synthesis of faith, ethos, and culture

The illusion of a sociotechnical society which can forgo personal virtues continues in spite of contrary experiences for two reasons: on the one hand, because the Christian ethos up to today has drastically placed its stamp on our culture, on the other hand, because until now it had not been technically possible to destroy human culture through ethically incorrect choices. The facts—that the up to now determining Christian ethos threatens to lose its influence and at the same time the possibilities offered by science and technology for man bring forth not only usefulness and well-being, but also violence and possible death—summon in a strong way an understanding that one can no longer leave questions about value and sense out of consideration in treating life in connection to the state. Moreover, it becomes even clearer in larger circles: one can become less and less the manager of the great challenges of an ecologically and world-economically sound society without including values in this discussion. However, from where can the necessary ethical forces come? John Paul II sees the most firm basis for a society-obligating ethos in a "transcendental" motivating of human dignity. The core of this idea is based on a human being "a visible image of the invisible God" (*Centesimus annus* 44, 2). Seeing that human dignity is rooted in this "transcendental worth," a human is "subject to rights which no one may violate" (*Centesimus annus* 44, 2). Consequently "theology appears necessary for the interpretation of, as well as for the solution to the current problems of human society" (*Centesimus annus* 55, 2).

This does not mean that the conditions for a dignified society can be found only with assistance of faith. The task of the "social sciences" and "philosophy" is "to interpret the central place of humans in society and to enable them to understand themselves better as 'social beings'." Therefore it is the goal of the Church... "to stand by humans on the road to salvation by making use of the fruits of science and philosophy" (*Centesimus annus* 54, 1). The Church emphasizes the ethical and religious dimension of a real humanism without supporting a religious integralism. It pays attention rather to the "warranted autonomy" (cf. *Gaudium et spes* 36) of the culture.

It follows from this that a fundamental task of the Church is to point openly to the internal relationship between ethos, religion and society based on human dignity. It is not alone in this. In this manner, for example, the philosopher Leszek Kolakowski explained at the German philosophy convention in September, 1993, in Berlin, that a "popular relativism" in liberalism stands on the point of destroying the foundations of civilization "more consistently than communism." "The popular relativism" frees us of "the idea of responsibility and duty." Kolakowski warned of the consequences of such an ethical anarchy with the sentence: "At the end of each anarchy, tyranny stands waiting impatiently."[85] The new Europe can only serve people and peoples, when it does not let the necessary social-ethical connection between the social, political, and economic structures and the Christian image of the "human" out of sight.

Original translator's note: this text was initially translated from German by Drs. H.M.G. Kretzers; where the translation of the Biblical citations corresponds to the text of the Willibrord-translation and the cited passages from the different ecclesiastical documents have been translated directly from the original Latin text.

English translator's note: the English text is translated from Drs. H.M.G. Kretzers' Dutch text; the Biblical citations correspond to the text of The Good News Bible.

4
Institutions of Social Organization: Family, Private Property, State

Professor Dr. A. Rauscher

Human life is embedded in a mutliform world of social relations. These stretch from the first relations inside the family that are of great importance for humans and their personal development, through the experiences with brothers and sisters, friends and acquaintances, through the encounters in school and church, through contacts and relations that are built up in education, work, and employment, through a relationship that is directed to marriage and family, and through the many memberships of interest groups, cultural societies, sport organizations, and recreation clubs, to the relations that occur from belonging to a people, nation, and a political community. In social relations in all areas of life people experience various dependencies and also the possibilities to give shape to existence by being with each other and by being there for each other.

A human is not an individual who lives for himself or herself alone. The modern idea of the autonomous person misses the reality of that which is social. Certainly, the Christian conception about humans has always held fast that they possess an independence and a personal responsibility for all that they do. At the same time it has emphasized that a human is a social being; that a human, like Heinrich Pesch the founder of "Solidarisme" says, "lives and develops in the midst of the society."[86]

1. Social life needs structures

Social life exists in the solidarity and unity of people for the actualization of social values and goals. These values and goals can be of personal-social or economic, cultural, social, or political nature. Social life does not develop of its own doing. The solidarity and unity in values and goals need a judicial-organizational structure. This belongs, just as social life itself, to the fundamental experiences of people and peoples. The idea that a society could develop without judicial-structural organization, and in this manner seemingly emphasize a personal depth, leads to a faulty position. Just as social life does not come into existence without the communal values and goals upon which it is based, the collaboration between people and the actualization of these goals does not come into being without the organization of solidarity.[87] The reason for this lies in the fact that a human is a being that exists in body and soul and exists in space and time, and especially in the fact that individuals in general have different convictions about the manner in which communal values and goals can be actualized. The organization which comes into existence via rules of conduct, and even judicially binding rules and laws, to which compliance is required, serves to actualize values and goals.

In this respect it brings to mind the occasionally, but continually returning illusion of a "dominion-free interaction," a society that no longer needs any structures, order, or state authority, and that reduces the state to a pure ruling organ and uses it as "representative" of the society. It is indeed understandable in a time during which structures, laws, administrative rules, rulings in all areas of life have increased enormously, that people have the feeling that they are objects rather than subjects of social life, and an aversion to judicial-organizational "pressure" grows. What it comes down to in this situation is not a flight into illusions, but a reflection on that what structures must and can be brought into existence and their limitations in carrying out reforms where structures have had the upper hand and have choked the personal and unified life of humans.

Structures give durability and perseverance to humans who live together and work together. Binding rules of human conduct can also possess a permanence without being established in writing. This applies not only to less well developed societies and cultures: as is known, the constitution of Great Britain even today is not established in writing. As long as the communal values and the structures that guarantee them are respected and no inquiries are made about "how and why," a judicial form is not necessary. Experience also indicates that in developed societies which are liable to continual economic, social and political change, judicially established rules and in this sense binding structures considerably simplify the community and guarantee clarity and legal security. The judicial-organizational structure and government of a society is perhaps not needed primarily to hold outsiders, dissidents, or criminals in check; it does make possible an orientation of an individual—as condition for the actualization of communal values and goals—and orientation of the individual's rights and duties. The culture of a people is determined by law in service to fundamental values. Especially in a time of rapid change, judicial rulings need to continually test whether they fulfill their function and whether they should be replaced by other rulings if necessary.

2. What are institutions of social organization?

There are a number of communal values and goals in which people take interest and with which they associate themselves. Especially in modern society, which is markedly a "pluralistic society," the number of forms of association has increased considerably. They are the numerous free forms of association that place a stamp on the living-together of people. Importance should be attached to the organized interest groups on an economic level, in the first place to employers' federations and trade unions, which have a large responsibility for forming and organizing work and production, as well as for dividing economic profit.

Whenever there is talk of institutions of social organization, all these structures of the social life are not meant. Among the free, social forms of association and of interest groups with far-reaching governing tasks, those institutions of organization must be identified which are indispensable—and therefore were just as necessary in the pre-industrial society as in our highly developed industrial society based on the division of labor—and which are to be found in all cultures albeit in different forms. Therefore, there are three areas of human life that need particular judicial government, because from it the existence and the future of the society are naturally dependent. In the first place there is the area of marriage and family, because each society must see to it that life is passed on in a dignified manner and guarantee to the coming generation its connection in the succession of generations. Not less important is training and governing of humans in society with respect to the use of material goods, without which neither physical survival nor the development of the socio-cultural would be guaranteed. This entails the judicial organization of work and job life, in particular of private property and of property proportions. In the third place one must identify the political government of the society, which should anchor the state on the grounds of its responsibility for the general human well-being.

These three institutions of governing may not be considered individually; they must rather be seen in their mutual reciprocity. Marriage and family, private property, and state can guarantee only collectively the durability and the future of a society.

In the Christian-European tradition marriage and family, private property, and the political society were never seriously discussed.

However, in the Middle Ages there were utopian designs and critical reflections which did not threaten the existing order. It is different in modern society. The population growth that skyrocketed since the second half of the 18th century, the growth of the population density that took place in the 19th century, the transition from a decentralized and agrarian society based on self-sufficiency to an industrial society based on a division of labor and directed by market forces, the rise of natural sciences and technology, the upbuilding of the educational system and organization of education, the new traffic and communication systems, and especially the growing importance of the efforts on behalf of the state for the development of private life on a social level—all these have changed the landscape thoroughly. In contrast to being a static society, there is a mobility and dynamic particular to an evolving society which lead to continual changes within the society and accordingly ask for a continual application of structures and judicial rulings.

3. The social ideologies

It is not surprising that under these circumstances the stability of the institutions of social organization has come under pressure. The strongest attacks on marriage and family, private property, and state came from the social ideologies.

On one side there is liberalism. Its starting point was an individualistic human, who determined his or her own conception about society. A human was, in this view, an individual, sovereign in his thinking, deciding, and acting. Society had its origin not in the social being of humans and not in the communal values and goals which unite the individuals and require social cooperation, but purely in the decision of the individual to enter into a contract whose content, significance, and length would be dependent on the pleasure of the contracting individuals.

Marriage, which in the Christian vision is seen as founded by God and as an indissoluble contract between man and woman, degenerated to a marriage contract, that just like every other contract, was dissoluble. Even if marriage and family were considered for a long time as "civil institutions," then it comes as no surprise that as the traditional vision and motivation lost validity, the destructive powers of the individual thinking won ground. In the liberal perspective marriage and family were seen no longer as an institution of social organization, but rather as only private relationships.

In precisely the same manner, private property no longer qualifies as an organizing of social duties by which the owner has not only rights but also social duties, but it is still viewed as a private right. When the French Revolution and then the Napoleonic Code regarded the right to private property as a holy, inalienable right, which is only limited by the rights of a third party, then this stands in opposition to the Christian-European tradition. Liberalism has regarded work as a contractual relation, which is entered into and determined solely by employer and employee. Therefore, liberalism was by no means in a position to solve the social question and could do little more than offer symptomatic cures. Liberalism was not in a position to perceive the power problem that exists between employee and employer. On the other hand, the Christian-social starting-points for change—which precedes all contractual agreements and starts with human dignity of the worker and demands for a just wage—are integral parts of a work relation.

Furthermore, the representation by Rousseau of a social contract, through which the state would be founded, continues on in liberalism. While he has trouble with values and rights given beforehand, he is inclined to justify the democratically chosen majority's choosing the content of fundamental rights in circumstances of conflict. However, in the Christian tradition the state and the parliament are bound to values and legal norms established beforehand, and according to Rousseau, the state is not to be concerned about these pre-existing values and norms. The fixed anchor is missing from the liberal position.

Collectivist ideologies, like national-socialism and revolutionary socialism, have fought the institutions of social organization in many ways. Karl Marx started with private property, which he saw as the original sin of humans and the source of all social evil. His materialistic philosophy blocked him from understanding the human as a person, one to whom there is an inalienable value, and to whom there are fundamental rights and duties. He reduced society to the "collective," and especially to class warfare which takes place in history. For him, marriage and family were civil institutions, which gave priority to the individualizing of humans and impeded the rise of the individual into the collective. Indeed it is the family that is necessary for the development of the person and personal responsibility. In addition, the state appeared to Marx only as a class state, which would end at the end of the proletarian revolution, because there no longer would be any classes.

It was this concentrated attack of the great ideologies on the institutions of social organization that is the context for Heinrich Pesch's thinking about marriage and family, about private property and state, and about their meaning for the continued existence, the future, and realization of the modern society.[88] It was in no way a predilection for traditional models of organization, as later was claimed even by enlightened Catholics. It was rather a concern that individual trends emanating from the great ideologies could inflict damage on the institutions of social organization, social life, and solidarity amongst people. It was also the worry that revolutionary socialism, when/if it comes to power, could destroy the institutions of social organization and with this it could get a fertile medium for a collectivization of humans, their consciousness, and their actions.

Today, the spiritual-moral and social-institutional trash-heap that socialism left in all of the Eastern Bloc has become visible. What people want is freedom and understanding. It shall take a long time before they see that these goals could have been reached, if they were embedded in the institutions of social organization that are marriage and family, private property, just property proportions, and the state.

But in the societies directed to freedom we also run the risk of neglecting the institutions of social organization. This applies especially to marriage and family. A fundamental reflection is necessary here.

4. The social task of marriage and family

Indeed, if marriage and family only concerned purely personal private-matters, then it would not be understandable why these should stand actually under the particular protection of the state and would have a need for judicial rulings.[89] Now the choice of someone to enter into marriage and starting a family is certainly first of all an affair of those concerned. The state should not involve itself at this point. From an ethical standpoint these conditions come under individual morality. Social ethics only enters into play because marriage and family have meaning not only for the concerned people themselves, but also for the society and for the community that has judicial form in the state.

The social dimension of marriage and family is connected with the fact that these institutions in an eminent sense serve the transmission of life. This goal is—together with providing goods and services to the people and with guaranteeing the common good by the state—a task of the society which has priority. After all, it is only when the transmission of life to the next generation is guaranteed for a society, that essential cultural goals can be actualized. Only then do a people have a future. This is as a matter of fact not the direct task of the individual members of the society. It is a free decision of the individual whether he or she wants to enter into marriage, or if he or she wants to start a family. For the society, historic-cultural development and, with it, the future depends on whether or not the transmission of life at all takes place. Also childless citizens are dependent on the achievements and the services of the following generations in many ways.

Each society has the task of ensuring the transmission of life. Therefore the living together of the genders, as well as of parents with their children, is regulated in all cultures and societies and is not seen as a private matter. These regulations, which are determined by economic, social, cultural, and political circumstances and by often particular traditions, essentially lead to the institutions of marriage and family. Attempts to regulate the mutual relations of the genders and the number of children are only undertaken individually (Sparta) and remain utopian dreams against an ideological background. Otherwise, one must establish that an original connection between marriage and family community is given by focusing on the social-ethical dominating transmission of life. That is apparent from the fact that a marriage, if it has remained childless, is treated qualitatively differently in many cultures than a marriage from which children have come forth and a large family develops.

Against the notion of connecting the transmission of life with marriage and family one can raise the objection that in each society non-marriage relations are also a fact. Certainly, from such bindings children also come forth. But apart from the question of whether or not the continued existence of a society could be guaranteed in this way, one could claim that a grounding in stable social circumstances, as only the family can offer, is lacking for these children. This is also the reason that a considerable number of people in non-marriage situations, as soon as there is a child, welcome the commitment of marriage. Stability and security are only possible when living together is directed to durability.

Within Christian culture circles the organizing of the transmission of life was reached over a relatively long time period. On one hand, it is based on the personal dignity of the human, who was created as man and woman by God in His image, and on the other hand it is founded on marriage and family as on an individual life-community. The basis is monogamy and marriage fixed for one's entire life. The creation story in the Old Testament, and the statements of Jesus point to this. The sixth commandment demands: Thou shalt not covet another man's wife. Marriage between Christians is a sacrament.

However much marriage as a sacrament is binding in the end, nevertheless, it is the testimony of near-sightedness, if on a social level one would protect monogamous marriages, but not the indissolubility of marriage. Both forms truly came into existence on Christian grounds, but they can be demonstrated and made reasonable through the anthropology of the person. Personality implies a vision of humans in their totality. This means: all the areas of ones' life, including sexuality, are controlled by the spiritual principle which establishes a human, and these may not be separated from each other. With the personal structure of being "human," there is a desire and a will to enter into a complete union which would be permanent and would be carried through love, as well as through trust and reliability. Circumstances like the wavering of the human heart, especially when the commitment is missing or has diminished and situations in which the continued existence of the marriage community would be in danger do not change the fact that humans desire permanence in marriage.

From a social ethical aspect it is the anthropology of the person that seeks not only a permanent structure of marriage, but also an institution for the transmission of life. In the first place, there is the right of an individual to know his or her father and mother. Unfortunately, this fundamental right has up to now not found its way into the catalog of human rights. Indeed, the first legal actions which demanded this right point out that humans cannot be refused it. Father and mother are just not purely "permanent contact persons"— a sociological concept which is suitable to express certain qualities of a durable connection, but is misleading and falsifying when original relations are intended by it. The original relation of parents and their children is not to be undone; it remains existing for the whole of life.[90] Each child has the right to be educated by his or her parents. In this sense not only a right of parents exists, but also the development on the part of the child exists, which is directed not to society and also not to "permanent contact persons," but to parents. This fundamental right stretches out over the entire development of a human: the physical-psychological, the spiritual-cultural, the professional-social, the political, and last but not least the religious-ecclesiastical. In the family, the human experiences a security that makes it possible to trust in parents, brothers and sisters, relatives, friends, neighbors, acquaintances, and fellow human beings. Here one can develop one's capacities, acquire social virtues and responsibility, develop one's personality and ultimately take one's life in one's own hands and enter into marriage again and start a family.

5. Private property in service to the working person

The question concerning the institutions of social organization arises in the area of the use by humans of material goods. With this, we arrive at a discussion of the economy in which there is foremost the regulation of property allocation and the institution of private property. When we ask what is property according to the starting-point of Christian thought, we come to the conclusion that the goods of this world are intended for all people by God and for all of humanity by God, because each human is required to use these goods, if one does not want to starve and if one wants to develop one's life.[91] Nowadays people speak of the principle of the communal allocation of earthly goods for all people.

The question that arises here is: is this principle not guaranteed first by a social organization of communal property? How does Christian thought come to acknowledge not the communal property, but rather private property in spite of this principle? Would an organization of social property be better suited to resist egoism and the greed of humans, and even the practice of usury? With all criticisms that egoism, avarice, and usury met, private property was never fundamentally discussed in the Christian tradition. One condemned abuse, but not private property.

An explanation of the connection between the principle of the allocation of the worldly goods for all people and of private property was only given by the great theologians of the Middle Ages, particularly St. Thomas Aquinas. Decisive for him is the conviction that that which encompasses the earth, including "earthly goods," both quantitatively and qualitatively is not as people need it to be to satisfy their needs and to build a culture. If the worldly goods as the world contains them are sufficient for the people, then it would be a simple matter to divide the goods for all in an equal manner. The earth provides the goods, as people consume and use these but not without cost. The story of the land of plenty was and is a utopia. Today we know that clear water and clean air in the industrial society are no longer to be obtained without cost.

Certainly, without the goods of the earth (mineral resources)—in jargon identified with "sources"—no goods can come into being, as people need them (economic goods). The sources, which are divided very differently among the different countries, are intended for all humanity. How do economic goods come into being from the sources? That is the decisive question which is overlooked by all those who only concern themselves with a just division of worldly goods. The answer to this question is as follows: only through work do the economic goods which people need come into existence.

In such a discussion natural riches are always pointed out, as if the available natural resources are the reason for the wealth or the poverty of countries and peoples. Germany, Great Britain, the United States of America, and South-Africa are all rich with coal. The "black gold," as one calls oil, flows in the Arabian countries, Russia, the Ukraine, and in a few states of America. But do these natural resources motivate the wealth of a country, the well-being of the population? Must not much labor, and well-qualified labor, be invested in order to ensure that only oneself can have control over these natural resources?

Something similar applies as well for "capital," for means of production, and for machines. They are necessary, but only a condition for a good economy. Decisive is the work of the people who put these machines into motion. Labor may not then be simply regarded as a "factor of production" as Adam Smith believed, but rather as a result of the human person, who with his or her creativity, initiative, diligence, and responsibility performs work.

It is the human who through his or her work makes the worldly goods available, who discovers and extracts the natural resources, who also invents apparatuses and machines to make labor more fruitful, "more productive," and who in solidarity builds the economy in its branches and in its entirety. Through labor, which in all the phases of its development was and is of a physical-psychological nature, humans place their stamp on things. Work is the factor which forms culture.

When work is the main cause of economic actions and production, then profit, the quantity and quality of economic goods depends in the first place upon the circumstances in which work can be delivered as efficiently and as well as possible.

It is enlightening how St. Thomas Aquinas consults the question concerning the orientation of moral values in the area of the use of material goods. He establishes that people work more diligently and treat economic goods more carefully, when these goods, as well as the means of production, belong to themselves and are their personal property. This observation applies today precisely in the same manner. People are generally more careful and more economical with means of consumption and consumer goods, when these belong to them, than when these are property of the state or of a public institution.

Sustained responsibility linked to private property has been lacking in socialist countries to a great degree. The employees, like management, had only interest in the actualization of a previously established, planned assessment, but not in the manner in which sources and means of production were handled "productively" as economically as possible. From this there was an incredible amount of trash when compared to the factories with private ownership in free countries. When a machine no longer ran and no parts were on hand, it was simply discarded. Here was lacking personal interest by more, and especially qualified, labor and management, which through better machines and good maintenance could enlarge the economic profit and with that constantly could improve the provision of goods and services to the people. Also management was more intent on fidelity to the political line—the possibilities for promotion were not independent from such allegiance!—than to economic achievement and better methods of production.

The productive use of worldly goods by the working human is an absolutely necessary condition to reach the goal of the social intentions for worldly goods, namely to provide in the long run goods and services to all people. This is only possible if there is an organization of private property. Private property is the real condition for which humans devote their time, take initiative, search for improved possibilities of production, and proceed responsibly with sources and goods. Private property is not a goal in itself and not a means to enrich oneself, but it makes it possible for humans to work productively, to fulfill their personal and social duties, and to take part actively in the building of society and culture. Private property is at the service of the working human.

Private property is both: fruit of labor and at the same time the first cause of and the impulse to work, because only by this means can humans provide for their needs and build a culture. Fruit of labor: this was self-explanatory for most people in the pre-industrial society. Whoever worked diligently could also earn a corresponding profit on his or her farm or trade and guarantee favorable chances of development for his or her family. Work was and is the source of well-being for the enormous majority of the population. The connection between personal work and personal property of attained goods must be directly evident to members of a particular society. Therefore, in the society based on the division of labor, the just division of profit has such an important role.

Just as significant is that all who do not work (children and young people who still are being educated) and who no longer take part in the work process share in the profits. In the pre-industrial society the large family carried the responsibility for this. Today one needs a system of provisions for the elderly—and an effective family politics and sufficient laws for them—who for no matter what reason can no longer work, but are given help to live in a dignified manner.

This experience teaches that an institution of organization, like private property, is threatened when the property proportions are one-sided, when property and possession proportions are not "justly" divided, and when access to property is limited to certain groups. Here lies a challenge for the state.

6. The organizing task of the state.

The third institution of social organization that is essential for the development of social life of humans lies in a public and political domain. That which the Romans called *res publica*, public matters, is the state according to contemporary concepts. Its task exists in guaranteeing the common good. In the Christian-European tradition the common good encompasses two fundamental functions. First, the state should guarantee order and safety for its fellow citizens internally and externally. It carries the main responsibility for peace. It must guarantee legal order and its observance, heed good relations with neighboring countries, and work together with other states. The second fundamental function concerns the care for the well-being of its citizens. The state is in the service of justice; it must care for the balance between the strong and the weak, so that the mutual bond is guaranteed and the unity of the state is not jeopardized.

Three problem areas should be discussed briefly here. The form of government of democracy brings with it a temptation to put more emphasis on the representation of the different opinions and interests of the citizens than on the necessity of a government that is able to function properly. Certainly the convictions actually held by people and trends forming politics should emerge in parliament and also in governmental administration. This may not impinge upon the legal capacity and decisiveness of the government. The concept of the so-called basic democracy reaches its limits quickly when fragmentation of the political parties makes the decision making and the forming of a government difficult. Coalition governments that are not capable of solving pressing problems lead to political apathy. In a democracy a government of full legal capacity is absolutely necessary. However, no matter how desirable the representation of different opinions is in the political process, this must be in harmony with the responsibility for executive power.

Another problem concerns the multitudinous tensions and contrasts between the social (collective) interests and the common good. Within society there are associations and organizations that publicly represent the interests of their members. In itself the representation of values is also fully legitimate; a combining of values in order to implement values is also legitimate. Many developments in the economy, society, culture and politics would not come to existence without these initiatives and organization. However, special interests, especially collectively organized values, can also come into conflict with the general interest and with the common good, which is to be guaranteed by the state. It becomes especially difficult when the powerful interest groups succeed in allowing the interest advocated by them to pass as an element of the general interest, and initiate a broad publicity, especially in the media, for this purpose. Here there is a great danger that the real common good is neglected. Especially when the government is weak and yields to the interest of the unions to win support, damage can be caused by this "control by the unions." The modern society and the state in the long run will not be able to avoid special interest groups, their practices, and their lobbying governmental and administrative bodies. They must also scrutinize the media more and create general conditions in order to monitor and deter a division between special interest and the common good.

Another problem of the modern state should be mentioned. In contrast to the situation after the war, when the political parties and the social forces were interested in overcoming not only the material-economical but also the psychological-moral chaos that the totalitarian regimes had left behind, one now can perceive a distinct legal positivism. This development is all the more worrying, because it presents itself under the disguise of democratic legality and claims a legitimacy. The conflicts concerning an encompassing legal protection, which must commit the state to the life of every human, actually touch on the "inalienable" fundamental rights and values which are independent of democratic majority decisions, which always require a corresponding "interpretation." The questions concerning the inalienability of fundamental values and rights and with it the limitation of the democratic process to areas which properly are subjected to voting resurface again. Yes, we sit in the middle of this process. A state that no longer is in a position or no longer is willing to protect fundamental values and rights—which cannot be voted away and which resists attempts to be removed "democratically"—would no longer be the institution of social organization equipped with an independent task and with it a proper authority, but rather it is the accomplice of the majority at a certain moment. This concerns the process of stimulating contemplation and renewal.

5
Social Justice:
The Development of the Concept "iustitia" from St. Thomas Aquinas through the Social Encyclicals

Dr. B. Kettern

Forward

With entirely different concepts and ideas people try to clarify the rules and the laws of their society. The concept of justice takes up a central place in this connection. Ideas concerning justice have a long history. Classical Greek philosophy left its mark on this concept in a normative way. In contrast to this prominent tradition in the history of ideas we only encounter the concept "social justice" in the "century of the social question," as Joseph Höffner characterized in the 19th century.[92]

Now it should be obvious with the conjunction of the traditionally handed down concept "justice" and the adjective "social" to see one result, namely the change which "social" brought with it to the reconsidering of the original understanding of the concept of justice. For a long time one only saw being a companion and being bound with other people as the "social" aspect; but judicial relations and the orientation of society to the *bonum commune*, the welfare of all, which from time immemorial fell under this concept, remained far-reachingly out of consideration.[93] The great economic and social problems that came with the transition from an agrarian society to an industrial one recalled to mind the forgotten nuances of the "social" aspect, in order to characterize the deep disturbances in human society. The "social" aspect as characteristic of social needs and problems thus became a key concept in the 19th century.

Thus, one might ask: do we have with the term "social justice" only a concept adapted to the former use? Considering the discussions that took place about the introduction of this concept in the vocabulary of the ecclesiastical proclamations, it is difficult to answer this question with a simple "yes." Among theologians and Catholic ethicists the appearance and interpretation of the demand for social justice were controversial. *One can, according to the thesis presented here, notice a striking change in the starting-point of the ecclesiastical social proclamations when these invoke the concept social justice. Because successive popes took up the concept social justice, they took account of a change to the modern conception of personal and common good.*

The following explanations are grouped in three sections. First, a brief historical sketch should be given of the ideas of *iustitia* in St. Thomas Aquinas' teachings, because on the one hand this doctrine started from Aristotelian ideas and so definitively determined the current reflection on justice, and on the other hand this doctrine concerning social justice also became the basis of differences in interpretation in philosophy and theology. These controversies are indicated briefly here, because in these the above mentioned change of what is understood by personal and general welfare can be detected. The second part gives an overview of the development of the concept social justice in the statements of the doctrinal authority. With a concern for the processes of change in Eastern Europe, one final, short third part establishes the exact meaning which the demand for social justice has with the introduction of the governing structures of the market economy in Eastern Europe.

1. The doctrine of iustitia of St. Thomas Aquinas and the controversies about the concept of social justice
The use of Aristotle by Thomas

Aristotle describes humans in his *Politica94* as zoon politicon, as a being living in a community. The gift of language makes it possible for humans to speak of the useful and the harmful, and also the just or the unjust. Only humans, in contrast to other living creatures, are able to perceive what is good and bad, what is just and unjust. Home and the state, thus the private and public domain, are, for a person, instances that provide one with these linguistic forms of expression.

For Aristotle, the whole is more fundamental than the part; the state therefore is more fundamental than the domestic circle or the individual. Because humans cannot live and be economically self-sufficient, they are by nature destined for life in society. Law forms the organization of the state community and justice determines what is just. The *Nicomachean Ethics* explains that that which is just and complies with laws favors no one too much and is "a friend of justice."[95] The complying to laws is in a certain regard a criterion of justice for Aristotle. That which is legal is just, if it produces and preserves happiness and its components for the political society.[96] Justice so understood is characterized by Aristotle as complete virtue.[97] And for Aristotle, legal justice, δικαιον νομιον (*dikaion nomion*[98]) constitutes the totality of virtue.[99] This legal justice exists as a judicial and moral law, because it brings about virtue not only in the individual sphere, but also in the area of relationships with other people.[100] Aristotle divided justice into a general and particular.[101] General justice corresponds to legal justice. Particular justice is further distinguished into the distributing and apportioning of justice, διανεμετικον (*to dianemetikon*[102]) and rectificatory justice, διορθοτικον (*to diorthotikon*[103]). Aristotle distinguishes both from reciprocity, αντιπεπονθος δικαιον (*antipeponthos dikaion*[104]). Distributive justice characterizes itself by a geometric proportionality, αναλογια γεομετρικη (*analogia geometrikè*[105]), which means "in these it is possible for one man to have a share either unequal or equal to that of another."[106] Distributive justice is supported by the knowledge that neither business nor persons are always equal to each other and, consequently, justice is a proportionality of the middle.[107] "For in the case also in which the distribution is made from the common funds of a partnership it will be according to the same ratio which the funds put into the business by the partners bear to one another."[108]

Briefly formulated: public progress corresponds to the achievements previously provided by the citizen! Rectification justice on the other hand is characterized by an arithmetical proportionality, αναλογια αριθμετικε (analogia arithmetikè[109]). With it, both concerned members are mutually brought to equality and this comes about exclusively by focusing on the things to be compared. For example, contractual agreements rest on rectificatory justice. "The law looks only to the distinctive character of the injury, and treats the parties as equals, if one is in the wrong and the other is being wronged, and one inflicted injury and the other has received it. Therefore, this kind of injustice being an inequality, the judge tries to equalize it."[110]

Let us, focusing on the various interests, summarize social justice: already with Aristotle there are the essential elements of later attempts at interpretation. According to Aristotle, the citizen concerned with the community possesses general justice, which also can be summarized as legal justice. Not only are humans made perfect as human, but also they are made as citizens, because they feel obliged with regards to the whole. But particular justice is also of importance to the later development of social justice. Distributive justice regulates the allocation by the community to the individual members of the society; rectificatory justice on the other hand regulates the traffic between the members of the society, because it tries to rectify disadvantages.[111]

St. Thomas takes up the idea of legal justice. Its concern is the laws which govern the life of the community and the state towards the actualization of the common good. Legal justice (*iustitia legalis*) is, for St. Thomas, the justice of the common good. "The law pertains in the first instance and mainly to the common good."[112] Justice is the foundation of this being directed to the common good, because it arranges mutual human relations. It does this in a double manner. "In one way one approaches the other as an individual and in the other way one approaches the other in a community."[113] If it deals with the relationships between single people, then justice is individual justice. If it rather deals with the community, then it is justice of the common good. "And because virtue pertains to directing humans towards the common good... this justice... is called legal justice because of course through it humans are in accordance with the law which directs acts of all virtue to the common good."[114]

St. Thomas makes legal justice equal to general justice, because the whole moral human is under the influence of it.[115] It is at the same time higher in rank in relation to the other virtues, because it directs them all to the one goal, that of the common good.[116] Because with Thomas, in accordance with his time, legal justice still chiefly laid with the ruler,[117] one can agree with Utz in his commentary that in a modern democracy the individual citizen is responsible for the common good.[118]

Like Aristotle, Thomas divides individual justice into commutative justice (*iustitia commutativa*[119]) and distributive justice (*iustitia distributiva*[120]). Commutative justice seeks a complete balance between people. Distributive justice is concerned with allocations from the common good to the individual members of the society. The communal goods are supplied to each according to a certain proportion.[121] Also here the geometric proportionality [of Aristotle] is valid, because the goods of the common good are allocated to the individual according to his or her merits in relation to the common good.

Problems with Thomas's depiction of justice: social justice as a renewed emphasis on the justice of the common good

The Aristotelian legal justice cannot be equated with the justice of the common good. Law is for St. Thomas not the same thing as common good; it is an instrument to bring into existence the orientation of the state community to the common good.[122] The law is at the service of the common good because all members of the society are dedicated to the actualization of it as an ethical value. The basic fault of Aristotle exists in the assumption that human sociality, i.e., the tendency to the communal society, finds its fulfillment in concrete civilian life, that is in a concrete state. The effort to realize the common good was limited to the effort by the individual to realize this concrete state, a conviction that sufficiently brought Christian thought to this perspective: the personal fulfillment of humans has its place within an organized entity; individual and social fulfillment are possible only in connection with other people.[123]

Is there not a danger with this view of so emphasizing the general welfare that the individual is overlooked from the perspective of the whole, the *bonum commune*? Can it not result in a curtailing the legal claim of the individual? Does the scholastic urge of categorizing and systematizing make the human as person retreat in the background? Thomas accentuated the duty of the individual to adjust himself or herself to the society for the benefit of the common good. Here it would have been logical to draw attention not only to the duty, but also simultaneously to the right of each human to be able to take a place that belongs to him or her in the society. Here one can establish an internal tension between the otherwise very expressive, seemingly personalistic social theories of St. Thomas and the leanings of this society to justice concentrated on the common good; to the defense of Thomas one must add that in his time there was no reflection about the perspectives of the individual understood as subject of rights—this was the result of the transition to modern times.

The difficulties with the interpretation with respect to social justice arise from the trouble that St. Thomas had in his representation which connected the common good—the common good as an ethical value found in the state—to the Aristotelian justice system. This problem can be clarified as follows: Thomas sees in relation to distributive justice the contribution of the individual to the common good as a criterion for distribution. The goods of the society are allocated to the individual according to his or her merit with respect to the common good. Here lies an important difference with the current practice: in the modern social state the communal goods are allocated according to the need of support and the respective claim to it.

Moreover, St. Thomas did not postulate the identity of justice for the common good and distributive justice, which is defended by many today. Distributive justice must be part of the justice of the common good, if one wants to follow Thomas in the priority that he gives to the common good over each state authority.[124] Thomas overlooked the fact that this judicial proportion is two-sided: there exists not only a judicial proportion from the whole to the part with the duty of the contribution of the individual to the common good, but also the opposite—the right of the individual to a place belonging to him or her.[125]

What consequences did this vagueness have in the representation of legal justice for later philosophy and social ethics? Arthur F. Utz investigated and explained the development of legal justice according to certain points of view.[126] The subject of philosophical speculation was 1) the character of the legal justice as an individual virtue, 2) the demand for the judicial character of it, 3) for its rank and limits toward the other forms of justice, and so on. It appeared that the opinions about legal justice and its place in the framework of justice diverged. They freed the representation of justice from the representation of the common good, which was its foundation. The character of legal justice as justice of the common good threatened to pass into oblivion. The problem itself remained: how must the relations between the individual and the whole, between the individual and society be justly regulated? The rise of the concept social justice in the 19th century can be understood as an attempt to solve this problem in the conditions of the current time.

In 1840, with his *Saggio teoretico di Diritto naturale,* the Jesuit Luigi Taparelli presented the design for a natural law supported by experience, in which the old justice of the common good depicted social justice with a new concept.[127] The starting point for Taparelli was no longer the common good, but the individual human. Humans have received from God certain subjective rights and they should live together with other people in the concrete reality. "This view stands very close to real life, because it conceives the social actions in the first place not as a communal actualization of a difficult to define ideal value, but as a just agreement between concrete people, each of whom as free and unhindered as possible wants to pursue his or her goal."[128] Different individuals have the right that each one's individuality is respected. Proceeding justly for Taparelli entails the respecting of individual rights of the fellow human being.[129] However much these individual rights are recognized as the origin of the general welfare, there are degrees of importance of these individual rights, ranked according to their social meaning and acceptability. When compared to Thomas, the starting-point in this *thinking* has changed considerably: St. Thomas investigated the common good on an abstract level as standing above the individual, and as a value to be actualized socio-ethically and he chose going from the common good to the individuals. Taparelli, on the other hand, goes the opposite way: from the individual rights to the common good and investigates the conditions needed to actualize the common good.

In his *Progetto di costituzione secondo la giustizia sociale* (Milan 1848) Antonio Rosmini, who followed after Taparelli, made social justice the basis for a test of lawmaking. With Rosmini, it becomes clear why the traditional concept of legal justice was replaced in the 19th century by that of social justice. The concept of law had its roots in the state sphere; now one wanted to direct the state to the outgoing principle of the common good which is above it. From this point of view, the concept social justice hid in itself the danger of not sufficiently expressing the enclosed social dimension of the common good.

This new justice concept underwent for the time being a similar fate within the Church: a year after its appearance, the book of Rosmini was placed on the index: social justice as a concept did not fit in the traditional frame of justice. One saw its relevant demand a call to social revolt. The concept received every now and then—especially in France—the description "being a poisonous fruit of modernism."[130]

Gradually the concept received a firm place in Catholic moral theology, because it expressed the relation of the political order and the economic order of the common good, and once this happened the individual was understood as person and as a real subject of rights. Discussions took place concerning its systematic insertion into the division of justice. Sometimes social justice was identified with legal justice, sometimes it united legal and distributive justice, sometimes distributive and commutative justice were united, and sometimes it stood outside of the three-part division which had been passed down.[131] Apart from all differences between the individual authors, one can establish in a summary: Catholic social ethics understood social justice as being related to the common good which is to be actualized. It tested both political and social institutions against the background of common good and it pointed out their shortfalls with relation to justice. In contrast to the rather rigid division of legal, distributive, and commutative justice, one thought to have found in social justice a dynamic greatness and contribution which expressed in a fitting manner the duty to the common good and the right to make claim to it in different social emergencies. The papal social proclamations took up these considerations again and emphasized that the individual must be oriented to the common good in modern times, without curtailing the fundamental relation of the individual to the common good.

2. *Social justice in the papal social encyclicals and in subsequent ecclesiastical social proclamations*

One can perceive as central to the very specific papal statements concerning social justice the demands for a just establishment in the world of work, a correct sense of public responsibility, and a justice in international relations. This shall become clear in the following chronological summary.

The first social encyclical devoted to labor issues, *Rerum novarum* (1891), did not yet contain a reference to social justice. Leo XIII treats the *iustitia distributiva* and the *iustitia commutativa*, as he repeatedly reminds the state and employers to allow all citizens and workers to experience justice. To each one in society his or her own must be given. This includes among other things, the paying of a just wage, the guaranteeing of the dignity of the workers, the regulation of the working hours, and the possibility for workers to accumulate capital and property.

Social justice as given from a natural governing principle, which gives each human the place belonging to him or her, occurs for the first time in an ecclesiastical document of Pius X. In the encyclical *Jucunda sane* of March 14, 1904, he describes his predecessor Gregory the Great as "public defender of social justice."[132] The concept occurs afterwards in a composition of Cardinal Secretary of State Gasparri to General Castelnau (April 1, 1922), there is mention of a "peaceful solution in the spirit of social justice."[133]

After these somewhat incidental references to the principle of social justice, Pius XI finally anchored the concept in an ecclesiastical social proclamation. In a letter *Quando nel principio* on June 24, 1923, Pius XI cites social justice as a governing principle of the peoples of this earth that precedes and transcends the state. It is against the background of the occupation of the Ruhr district after World War I and the pressure of war reparations that the pope reminds the conquering forces that both social justice and social love, as well as the self-interest of the creditor states and of all nations, does not allow the restitution from the debtor of that which can be paid back only with the complete exhaustion of its powers and reserves.[134] We find another instance of a concrete social question in a statement of the conciliary congregation to the bishop of Lille, Msgr. Achille Liénart, concerning a matter in dispute between employers and employees in his region (June 5, 1929).[135] It explained that family bonuses in workers' salaries are in accord with social justice, a thought that we frequently encountered with Pius XI.

In *Quadragesimo anno* (May 15, 1931) much is said about social justice. This document fosters the social reform program of the Church, which is directed to preventing class-warfare type conflicts.[136] The pope invites the socialists to return to the Church and to cooperate with the renewal of society in social justice and social love.[137] After a renewed demand for just wages,[138] the pope sheds light in a more detailed manner on the state's responsibility for a just governing of society and economy. The narrow interweaving of the subsidiarity principle with justice must give free room for the state to act, as well as for smaller social units to actualize justice.[139] Social justice must strive for the actualization of the common good. From here onward it is warranted to understand justice characterized by Pius XI as *iustitia socialis*—as justice of the common good.[140] Social justice becomes the natural principle of the social governing "in which each possesses the freedom that belongs to him or her and also complies with his or her duties to the whole."[141] The pope also indicates the limits of striving for justice. Social justice may help eradicate social conflict from the world, but it definitely does not motivate—this social love brings this about.[142] Social justice finds its fulfillment in social love, which forms the actual foundation of social peace. It is bent on "bringing about the ideal social order, which strives for the common good, where the coordination of the different claims and achievements simply remains inadequate."[143]

Social justice finds its application for example, when it treats the conditions for the economic community. The pope makes mention of the limits of the free market driven only by competition. In contrast to the individualistically driven economic sciences he cannot allow or make significant within these limits freedom of competition as a regulating principle of the economy. Neither is the delegation of the economy in the sense of a centrally directed process a suitable principle of economic organization.[144] Here, one should uphold freedom and the orientation to the common good.

The intensifying worldwide conflicts of the thirties prompted Pius XI in his encyclical *Divini redemptoris* (March 19, 1937) to take a point of view concerning social justice.[145] Saving the world from the collapse toward which it was headed as a consequence of morally unrestrained liberalism was "not" to be found "in class conflict and terror," "much less still in the self-satisfied misuse of state power, but in the penetrating of the economic and social order by the spirit of social justice and Christian love." Again an urgent solution to the worker's question is called for:

> Indeed in addition to the so-called commutative justice there is also a social justice that imposes duties on its part from which neither the employers nor the employees can withdraw. It is the task of social justice for the individual to demand all that which is necessary for the common good. Just as not everything is taken care of in a living organism, if the individual parts and the individual members do not have everything that they need for exercising their functions, so also not everything is sufficiently taken care of in the social organism and in the well-being of the entire society, if one does not give to the individual parts, i.e., the individual members who are the people equipped with dignity, what they need for the fulfillment of their social function. If the demands for social justice are satisfied, then from it develops an increasing activity in the whole area of economic life.... [146]

As workers' demands for just wages and the social rights of the worker are enumerated, a plea is made to the employers to stand open to attempts to come to solutions.

Similar statements are found in a letter of the pope to the archbishops, bishops and priors of Mexico (*Firmissimam constantiam* of March 28, 1937)—this time formulated as an admonition to the ecclesiastical supreme pastors:

> If you truly love the workers—and you should love them in an exceptional manner, because they stand through their industrious life so close to the ceaselessly working divine Master—then you grant them also material and spiritual assistance, because you on one hand press for the guaranteeing of both commutative and social justice in order to relieve in every way the circumstances of life of the propertyless, and because you on the other hand supply them with the encouragement and consolation of religion, without which people are reduced to a humiliating cult of the material. [147]

The successor to the papacy, Pius XII, managed only incidentally to speak about social justice, although he formulated a number of positions and determinations to relevant social-ethical questions. He conceived justice as a just and legitimate sharing of all of the goods of a country. [148] The just division of goods is the central aspect of social and economic life. It is the expressing of social justice which becomes clear when the goal of an economy is realized. [149] The effort of

Christianity has led to a progressive actualization of social justice, through which the danger of class conflicts is banished.[150] The emphasis in all these papal and ecclesiastical determinations of the judicial aspect of social justice—social justice is a needed priority on behalf of the various layers of the population—was completed on September 29, 1955, in a papal letter of the substitute Secretary of State, A. Dell'Aqua, with a reminder of the binding character of the classic justice of the common good. At this time Canada held the then internationally popular social weeks with the theme "civil rights and duties." On behalf of the pope, Dell'Aqua recalled to mind that the rights and duties of citizens have roots in the common good, especially legal justice. In its orientation to the common good the well-understood civil and legal conviction guarantees the continued existence of the community.[151]

Rerum novarum and *Quadragesimo anno* had treated justice with priority in connection with labor issues; since John XXIII the formulation of the problem has been broadened. John XXIII makes the theme of *Mater et magistra* (May 15, 1961) the international dimension of social justice and the restoration of balance between the different nations and peoples, and he first demands as the fundamental area of social justice "that... social progress must correspond to scientific progress and must follow it, so that all layers of the population receive their corresponding part of the growing wealth of the nation,"[152] and then, in a separate chapter, he applies this thought to an international level. The economic trade between peoples of different levels of prosperity entails the duty of helping the poor and weak, fighting the destruction of resources, supplying scientific, technical and financial help, establishing no new colonialism, and taking care of a just distribution of goods and world government. The division of economic profit as well as the progress of the economy should be in accord with human nature.[153]

The Second Vatican Council explained in the pastoral constitution *De ecclesia in mundo huius temporis* (December 7, 1965) that all grave economic and social inequalities within a people as well as within humanity arouse indignation: "these go against social justice, equity, the human value of the person, and social and international peace."[154]

Paul VI in *Populorum progressio* (March 26, 1967) further developed this thought. He recalled the duty of the developed peoples to social justice, "which exists because people are bringing in order and improving the relations between the stronger and weaker peoples."[155] The pope supports the free market, but he takes into account the limits of free competition which make this just and social, "thus humane." The conditions and possibilities of free self-determination are unequal if one looks at differences in development. "Social justice demands that the international trade of goods, if it wants to be humane and moral, happens between partners that at least have a certain equality of opportunities. Indeed this is a remote goal. In order to realize this faster, a real equality in discussion and in price-making must exist."[156] Only through greater justice in trade relations can there be a lasting effect.

One year later, in the papal address on the occasion of the first anniversary of the encyclical *Populorum progressio* (March 27, 1968), the development problem moves:

> ...the famous social question from particular societies to the international level...to the whole humanity. If social justice, which changes the class structure of a society in the sense of a more just division of goods and culture so that no one suffers a lack of the means necessary for a humane life and no one enjoys goods in an exaggerated and selfish way while others have need of these, should be actualized now on the level of the relations of one nation to another, then one knows the magnitude and importance of the problems that are set up by modern progress...[157]

But once again the connection between social justice and legal justice is called to mind by the pope. Paul VI expressed himself in his speech on the 75th anniversary of the encyclical *Rerum novarum* (May 22, 1966). According to Utz:

> The [C]hurch has made the principle of the progress of social justice its own and this is the case not only in speculative teaching (this has been the case since the Gospel rang out, which blesses those who are thirsty and hungry for justice), but also in the practical teaching profession (cf. *Summa Theol* II-II 58, 5), which means that it has made as its own the principle that it is necessary to promote the actualization of the common good by a reform of the existing legal government, if this does not sufficiently consider a just division of benefits and costs of the social life.... In addition to the concept of static justice, which is sanctioned by positive law and which protects a certain legal government, there is another concept, dynamic justice, which is effective in the development of the human society and which can be traced back to the requirements of natural law: namely the concept of social justice.[158]

Here, Paul VI goes back first to St. Thomas, but recognizes the distinction of static and dynamic justice (see Gustav Gundlach[159]). Social justice is expressly placed in the realm of natural law.

After the pontificate of Paul VI, a new important aspect emerges in the next treatment of the meaning of social justice.[160] We encounter this in the apostolic letter *Octogesima adveniens* (May 14, 1981): time and time again the pope describes the particular mission of the church to penetrate the public domain with questions of social justice.[161] A few chapters further he maintains that with urbanization, which is especially noticeable in developing countries, the isolation of the individual must be resisted; humans must be offered a new home in the cities in which there is a "vital fraternity, and actual justice must bring the message of a new hope to the people congested in these cluttered and intolerable cities."[162] This can happen via the development of personal initiatives in order to bring social justice into action.

John Paul II treats justice mainly with a view to building a socially just economic order (*Laborem exercens* of September 14, 1981, and *Centesimus annus* of May 1, 1991). The latter social encyclical does not go back systematically to the concept of social justice, but it should be read as a plea for a socially structured market economy. That which the pope maintains there, concerning the fundamental ethical orientation of the economy and production process, is further treated by the new canon law (CIC/1983). Can. 222 par. 2 states: "The Christian faithful are also obliged to promote social justice and, mindful of the precept of the Lord, to assist the poor from their own resources." Here, the pursuit of social justice becomes a Christian duty and this is not only for individuals, but also for social structures. Therefore, the quick glance of the *New Catechism*, which has avoided using the term social justice, is not wholly satisfying. The numbers 1805 and 2411 are the only explanations about the traditional threefold division of justice, especially justice towards God as the virtue of divine worship. Likewise, one searches in vain for the term in the last published moral encyclical, *Veritatis splendor* (August 6, 1993). It is meant to be present in at least two places in the text, although the references are kept general. The pope, in the introductory section (5), maintains that the current moral crisis is dangerous, both for the community life in the church and for a just and social life. This danger culminates in a considerable lack of justice within many societies and nations (98). Human rights are trampled on and only a radical social renewal will improve prospects.

If one attempts to balance the papal points of view concerning social justice, then this concept would reflect the great concern for the common good, which runs as a thread through the doctrinal social proclamations. The popes know, according to their historical experience with totalitarian seizure and oppression in the name of the common good, of the possible risks for the individual. Their effort for social justice also essentially is directed to calling many social injustices by name, taking the side of the disadvantaged, and restating the duty to undo situations of injustice. They continually reject the incorrect effort of conceiving social justice as class conflict. For them, social justice is to be reached only by way of dialogue.

The most recent social encyclical *Centesimus annus* centrally places in its argument reflections on how a socially just economic government would appear. In a concluding third part this contribution takes up these reflections and asks the question of whether social justice is to be actualized against the background the changed situation of the Eastern European.

3. A concrete case: social justice as an essential forming element of the Eastern European reform process

The collapse of existing socialism left the democratic and market economy organized by the West as apparent winner in the field of history. As the introduction of competing market economy arrived everywhere in the East the hope surged that the ruinous economic situation would quickly be fixed. Already the complaints have piled up. The expected economic boom experiences delays and is still awaited. A critique of the market economy is growing. Already voices are being raised that plead for as radical as possible reversion away from these many unfulfilled promises. Instead of producing a functioning and just type of economy and production, the market only aggravated social injustice.

In the tradition of Aristotelian legal justice we recognize that social justice is always a relational term. Because social justice is a relational term, the relations naturally cannot be placed into the same category. First, with respect to the Eastern European complaints, it can be pointed out that the conditions for the introduction and building up of the market economy were different from country to country. One must thus always give a very different answer to the critique brought forth about the market economy, if one wants to run no danger of simplistic generalization.

Which form of market economy do we find today in Eastern Europe? The analysis of the different national economies gives the impression of a very complex, mixed situation: one finds remains of a centrally directed economy next to elements of a very free economic liberalism, in which each attempt to give some legislative framework on the part of the state strictly fails and a definite shadow economy profits from the weakness in the functioning of the not yet fully developed markets. One must thus, in many places, concede as a decisive shortcoming the absence of those social attainments, which constitute an economically and socially successful "social market economy." If people in Eastern Europe continue to have the option for an economy establishing itself via supply and demand, one shall be able to prove whether in the future there is a preference for a very liberally established market economy, or whether the model of a socially bound market economy can really be established.

Catholic social doctrine approached liberalism, or, more precisely stated, the different liberal, social, and economic philosophies, with great skepticism. Liberal starting-points lean to the theory of drafting individual freedom starting from a market paradigm.[163] The term social justice has not always been explicitly appreciated. Friedrich August von Hayek, one of the most important protagonists of a liberal economic government, finished off the concept with the statement: "The expression 'social justice' does not fall into the category of aberrations, but rather into that of nonsense, like the expression 'a moral support'."[164] One who sees market and competition as instruments for realizing social justice would underestimate reflective entry by government into the market. In such a government the individual must search for and find his or her own place.[165] Competition cares for the best possible coordination of this searching process. The plea for social justice distorts the spontaneous market organization to a system of norms; it regards regulation and organization to be identical. Hayek, as resolute opponent of a type of economy and production characterized by state regulations, rejects any conviction that is directed to place any earned income in the market under the ideal of distributive justice. Because justice would be a contentless category, there is consequently no standard. On the contrary, behind the demands of social justice there should stand values which are directed to protect the privileges or positions of certain groups and persons.[166]

It is not surprising that Catholic social doctrine diametrically opposes the liberal position sketched briefly here. As we have seen, it places the concept social justice in and connects it to basic ideas and important demands. Market and competing economies are here not the goal in itself, but are in service of the personalistically understood common good.

With respect to the situation of the upheaval in Eastern Europe, the demand for social justice presents itself with new urgency. The only prospect offering economically worthwile promise in the meantime is the introduction of the market economy. There is then talk of social justice, insofar as the chances to do business in a society are understood in such a way that all concerned parties receive an advantage from the social rulings and are not exploited by others. John Rawls correctly realized this in his *Theory of Justice*. The complete organization of the market economy must be structured so that there are socially just relations. The only alternative to a socially bound market economy is the relapse into the conquered structures of the centrally directed economy, containing all its limiting negative consequences.

Critics of the market economy, who by "social justice" exclusively understand distributive justice and drop the aspect of the contribution to the common good in favor of partial interest, must recognize that social justice cannot be brought into existence with a slide rule. In the democratically arranged state of today citizens and groups can then only live in freedom and peace, if this state makes an effort in the name of social justice and receives the necessary means from the citizens for that purpose. Then a peaceful organization of social conflicts becomes possible. The effort for social justice belongs to the democracy of the social state in the 20th century. In this sense social justice is "the other side of democracy" (Karl Homann).

Eastern Europe will be more successful if it takes into account the experiences learned in the West with the reformation process. One should fight two incorrect developments: first, the incorrect appeal to social justice, and second, a shortsighted view of this justice. In the discussions about wage levels, often demands are brought forth in the name of social justice and attempts are made to push these through by force. This loses sight of the aspect of social justice oriented on the common good. Social justice functions here as disguise for certain partial interests, which make an erroneous plea to social justice. For example, if during an economic recession the employers cut after tax wages, the employees answer with a strike because of this, and an outsider believes that both parties have not searched seriously for ways to settle the conflict in a peaceful manner, then this workers' conflict damages the common good by putting a third party at a disadvantage. As a result of the high degree of economic interconnections other perhaps not directly related enterprises are threatened in their economic success.

We now run the danger of viewing social justice shortsightedly, both with respect to the individual and in relation to the community. On one hand, we make the legal position of the individual absolutely opposite to the different social institutions. We accentuate the priority of the individual at the cost of that which is social. On the other hand, the community does not allow sufficient justice to befall the individual. If, for example, the relation between the whole and the individual is lastingly disturbed, as is sometimes alleged in the area of tax politics, then the judicial relation no longer functions between both: too high fiscal demands on the part of the state are met with a bad attitude toward paying taxes on the part of those taxable, which means that when the one side taxes too highly in order to provide contributions to the common good, the other side attempts to get out of paying it through tax evasion. Social justice is here a matter that must be practiced on both sides. If one neglects it, then the result will be negative consequences for the society.

6
Common Good as Goal and Governing Principle of Social Life: Interpretations and Meaning

Professor Dr. L. J. Elders

Little argument is necessary to convince people that in our western countries moral-social life has gotten into a precarious situation. The difficulties are known: the disappearance of social morality and of many virtues which in the past have promoted the development of Europe; the threatening of the family; the rejection of many values; a pluralism in fundamental questions; and a similar overexaggerated individual freedom that threatens to collapse the social structure that has existed to now. On the other hand, the anonymity and the bureaucratization of political life, the alienation that one experiences when one is constantly confronted with different convictions, cultures, and sometimes dangerous ideologies, and increasing lawlessness and uncertainty become reason to flee into smaller communities of like-minded people, into the exotic or even into nationalism.[167] Centrally the question arises, whether and to what degree humans are social beings and if they must direct their activities to the common good.

At the root of this question is the transition to individualism that took place at the end of the Middle Ages and during the first centuries of the modern era. Nominalism favors the decline of consciousness taking part in society: the society is seen as a sum of individuals and not one as demanded by nature. The word individualism was first used by J. P. Rouen around 1825,[168] but the spiritual attitude suggested by the term goes back to the end of the Middle Ages. Rouen had the thought of the 18th century in mind, since it shattered the relation of the individual and the society. According to Prof. A. Rauscher, the roots of individualism lie, from the viewpoint of spiritual history, in nominalism and Protestantism, and its economic roots in liberalism.[169] Deeper subsequent trends that were noticeable already before the Reformation and in Catholic countries played a background role.[170] Individualism maintains that humans are isolated beings and accentuates the rights of the individual against the other: mistrustful and calculating, the individualist searches his or her own advantage without worrying about others.[171] As Alexis de Toqueville writes in his book *Democracy in America*, democracy and the equality of all bring the danger with them that humans stand next to their fellow citizens, but do not see them, because they are there only for themselves... ; there exists a power that patronizes others, but others are only there to fulfill their wishes.

In the end of the Middle Ages and in the following centuries the European people began being concerned about themselves, society, and the world, and as a result they interpreted God differently. The organized world structure, in which humans had a fixed place, was replaced by a universe expanding to infinity, in which humans no longer felt safe and no longer had a governing principle. Through new economic and social developments, social institutions like gilds were pushed aside or discontinued. The feeling of belonging to a universal church also had been undermined by the Reformation and religious wars. The number of "free cities" increased: the citizens barely saw an all-encompassing society—to which they should belong— over them. In each instance the political society was experienced no longer as an extension of the family, and certainly not as a moral environment in which one lives, but only as a coincidental structure that one could change at will. The state is there only to help the individual obtain a well-being as great as possible and to protect from external threatening dangers. It is therefore not surprising that John Paul II speaks of a crisis in the democracies: they have, so he says, lost the capability to make decisions that are directed to the common good.[172] The pope adds to this that the decisions often "are made under the pressure of certain groups by elections by financial consid- erations," which in the course of time:

[by]…absences of political actions evoke mistrust and apathy, that when there is a return to participation in the political life, there is a decline in the sense of public responsibility. The consequence thereof would be that one is able no longer to fit private and group interest into the general vision of the common good. The pope adds to this that the common good is not purely the sum of individual interests, but rather an integrating of these interests on the basis of a harmonic hierarchy of values, and finally the common good demands a correct conception of the dignity and the rights of the person (cf. Gaudium et spes, 26).

The changes in social life, to which the above cited texts refer, are also to be seen in the development of justice. For St. Thomas, who refers to the old tradition and the sentiments of his contemporaries, justice means: first, the right affair (*res iusta*); second, the knowing or the knowledge through which one sees what is right; third, the place where right is spoken; and fourth, the right itself that is spoken. Justice is a compromise between two persons that corresponds to the norms of natural law, an objectively founded state of things. In modern thought justice is felt rather often as the moral power that humans possess over that which belongs to them.[173] As John Finnis has shown, we find an initiative to this new conviction with Suarez and with Grotius: the word justice means the decision-making power of people over themselves and personal property.[174] Thomas Hobbes goes still further and identifies justice with freedom.[175] Humans have the right to do that which is useful to them. The limitations of individual rights became motivated, as the 20th century *Universal Declaration of the Human Rights* (1980) maintains, by the argument that the rights of the other may not be infringed upon, so that peace reigns in society and well-being can be obtained. It shall be clear that much is extremely unclear here and a closer analysis is required concerning the relation of the individual to society and the common good. It is remarkable that Hobbes presented a model of human life *in statu naturae* that goes a long way back in every form of society. In fact, people live together because of their own needs; each society is there for profit and to obtain power.[176] John Locke carried out the separation of the individual from a life inside social structure: the profit of work, he writes, comes to those who accomplish it, a human can obtain wealth in an unrestricted manner and possess more than others ("man's labour is his property"). With this, the road for unlimited competition based on egotistical striving became wide open. The separation of individual and society was radicalized. The question is therefore: what is human nature in reality, and whether humans actually belong to society.

A closer specification of this theme is also of importance for morality. As is known, the liberation of the individual has also implications for morality: it is no longer fashionable to talk about morality, and the traditional morality is dismissed as an old fairy tale. In addition, the classical ethics of natural law is sharply attacked. One says that it is an empty shell of norms, that there is no uniform philosophy to ground it anymore. Because human thought is a product of its time, one cannot integrate any statements about the social life of humans in a doctrine that has a validity transcending time. Therefore, the whole social doctrine of the Church is outdated, or it would have to be that one only can make a series of theological statements without intrinsic coherence with respect to content and without methodological uniformity. To this other authors respond that the abandoning of natural law terminology in social doctrine and replacing it with a purely theological treatment has far-reaching consequences. It is superfluous to overemphasize how important these questions are. They are connected to the problem of the relation of the individual to society and the common good. In what follows I shall try to explain the traditional doctrine, especially that of St. Thomas Aquinas, about the common good and the relation of the individual to the common good, in order to indicate clearly the difficulties with an explanation of the *bonum commune* and the shifts in the interpretation of the modern era, and to accentuate their meaning for current society. Finally, a few thoughts are formulated with respect to the question: how can we, in the current situation, regain a commitment to the common good.

As is known, Thomas has used an Aristotelian range of ideas in his doctrine about the common good. Therefore it is useful to point out a few considerations of the Stagirite. The state's goal is to help human nature make itself complete[177] and it precedes family and household. The state is the condition for a complete, humane existence, because it makes the "good life" possible, not only as protection against threats and dangers, but also as a positive source of virtuous activity. The origin of the state, in addition to meeting the needs of the individual, is necessary for a virtuous life.[178] The "good life" (to eu ζην) of the citizens endures in work, spiritual activity, free time, and recreation. This goal of the individual and the whole is guaranteed by justice, and the "proportionally just" should be reached because it is to the advantage for the whole state and the common good (το κοινον).[179] The expression common good (το κοινον αγαθον) is in the second book of *Politica*.[180]

Let us now turn to St. Thomas of Aquinas. We encounter the term *bonum commune* approximately 370 times in his works, and most of the time the meaning is assumed to be self-evident. As Diego Ramírez first suggested,[181] this concept is used analogously by St. Thomas Aquinas. One can distinguish the following meanings:

• God is the common good of all creatures in an absolute sense, because He is the universal good to which all things are directed as their goal.[182] It is important that God has in mind the good of the whole, in which the goal of individual things is contained. This thought points the way to an interpretation of the relation of the individual goal of humans to the common good. "All particular forms of good that exist in the universe appear to be directed to the common good."[183] Consequently, the part, by its nature, holds the good of the whole more important than that of itself.[184] One should think that there is no contrast here: because someone searches for personal well-being, one directs oneself to the common good. One's deepest being is characterized by this being directed to the common good, which contains the personal well-being at the same time. To the extent which knowledge refers more to the general—as is the case with angels, love goes more in the direction of the common good.[185]

• On a spiritual level, Christ is the communal spiritual good of the whole church that is offered to us in the sacrament of the Eucharist.[186]

• Also, the whole world is a good that exists in the process of perfecting and ordering of creation. As such, as the basis of all forms of good that it contains, it has a greater perfection than humans.[187] Each has a place within the universe and is directed to the whole.[188] Also, humans have their natural place in the whole; and as people they are made such that they are directed to the universe.[189]

• The human community has its own direct goal, that is indicated directly by the term common good. Because of their social nature humans live communally. One cannot bring about a complete development of the person alone, but this must come into existence through the organized cooperation of several within the structure of the social life. Without community humans cannot reach the goal that God has set for them. Now there exists a multiplicity of communities: family, village or city, religion or population groups, and the state.

Except for those communities which are integrated within each other or help each other set up and complete each other, there exist sub-communities which within the previously mentioned social structures aim for a partial purpose (like culture, economy, sport). The state, in other words the community that is sufficiently complete to guarantee the well-being of all (and in which the other communities are contained), is named by Aristotle and St. Thomas as the perfect community.

With determining the relation of the individual to the common good, one must establish that the good of the individual never stands *against* the good of society.[190] Therefore, there is no contrast, since the good of the individual is only reached in the good of the whole, is contained in it, and is encouraged by it. Being thrown into each other's company is not a humiliation; letting oneself be helped be-

longs to magnanimity.[191] Humans desire to stand in a relation of
exchange with each other and to share their thoughts and possessions
with others. Even in a situation of paradise humans needed support
of friends.[192] Because of their nature, humans are concerned about
not only themselves, but also their fellow humans. According to St.
Thomas, a series of social duties results from this natural tendency,
as, for example, friendly contact, just treatment, provision of services, and honesty. Even friendship and love correspond to human
nature.[193] Therefore, it is incorrect to maintain that humans only
belong to the society as individuals, but transcend it as persons. First,
one can say that being persons and the being incorporated into a
society or the universe does not exclude each other: persons reach
their goal by being directed to the other, and their contemplation
and happiness need others; second, humans as persons are subjects
of social activity.

E. Welty shows that, according to St. Thomas, the common good
does not have a particular nature that is separated from the personal
well-being[194]: the common good is a unit of organization that exists
in its parts, in other words is rooted in the personal well-being of the
members; it consists of many components.[195] Well-being, understood
as the well-being of the people living in the community, is the encompassing goal of everyone's activities. As a goal it has not existed
first in its totality, but it is striven for and actualized only partially.
This comes forth clearly when one pays attention to the components
of the common good, like: a) life, health, and physical and spiritual
development of the members; b) the activities of the members with
the communal goal in mind—activity on the social-political level, in
other words the building up of an organized structure of the society,
belongs to the common good; it is clear that a community can only
exist when its members strive for and promote the goals of the community; and c) the structures, laws, institutions, proceedings, and
material goods that are necessary for or beneficial to communal life.

E. Welty has rightly emphasized that the common good, as well as
the good, is a goal and together with it the first cause, insofar as it as
beginning of all activity desires to be attained, albeit it may be actualized or reached only later. In this manner, the common good gives
to each community its meaning. St. Thomas even says that the part,
according to its nature, holds the good of the whole to be more important than that of itself.[196] One must understand this in such a way
that the original, natural order is meant here. In the situation of their
fallen nature humans strive more for their own personal well-being

than God, or if not they would have to have been healed by the grace of God.

The argument about the relation between the individual and the common good reflects the situation as it corresponds to human nature. In actuality there are tensions, a shortcoming in dedication to the communal goal, and even crimes against the community, and, on the other hand, oppression of individuals and absent or insufficient care for the poor and weak. Different people feel a contradiction between the personal well-being and the goal of the group. For some the necessity to comply with the general interest of the state is not clear; they do not see that the common good goes above self-interest. It would be useful to investigate the precise relation between the two.

With relation to the texts of Thomas, Welty[197] has described these relations as follows: (a) The common good is better, more divine than the particular good of the individual.[198] This expression, which goes back to Aristotle, is clarified as follows: the common good shows a greater correspondence with God. (b) Personal well-being is directed to the common good, as the imperfect to the perfect.[199] (c) Common good is more important than personal well-being; activity for the common good surpasses efforts for the personal good.

In order to properly understand St. Thomas one must think that in both *Summas,* and the commentary on the *Sententiae,* his interpretations are theological in nature; in other words, he understands social factuality as coming from God: from the perspective of God it is evident that the common good is the first and encompassing goal. Can one also say this from the perspective of humans? The answer is affirmative, if one thinks that the common good is the personal well-being of the members and essentially exists in their spiritual perfection. Now this is reached by the virtues, in which friendship, love, and social justice are primary. The part is indeed in accordance with the whole; therefore, each good of the part can be directed to the whole. Consequently, the good of every virtue, either that which humans arrange towards themselves or to other individuals, can therefore be connected in one way or another to the common good, to which justice is geared. "Consequently actions can belong to justice, insofar as they direct people to the common good."[200] "There is no virtue of which actions cannot be directly or indirectly directed to the common good."[201]

Thomas even says that personal well-being is directed to the general welfare, like the imperfect to the perfect.[202] The general welfare deserves the priority; activity for the good of the common good surpasses efforts for the personal well-being. Social justice comes first under the virtues of natural order. One would think that in a just society there would be no contrast between the two: through the common good which encourages the community, one contributes to the common good; and through the common good, one cares the best for personal, authentic interest. Humans cannot act for or against the common good without at the same time serving or damaging their personal goals. When one, on the other hand, cares for personal interests—within the framework of justice and laws, one contributes to the common good. Thomas writes therefore that the citizens contribute to the common good when they follow the orders of the government, in other words, the continued existence of the common good is guaranteed when citizens devote themselves to their own affairs and at the same time conform to the laws.[203] This is contingent on the government being capable and the laws being just. One can only reach the perfection of a virtuous life by conscientiously orienting the personal actions to the common good.[204]

There is a dimension of the "human" which starts from above the political community and is not subjected to it. By this, Thomas means one's personal relation with God and life in the universal community of the church.[205] Thomas expresses this, when he says that the common good is more important than personal well-being, when it concerns the same genus.[206] The supernatural forms of the good stand above goods belonging to the natural order.

Common good is a complicated concept, because it appears to contain something intangible, namely a goal surpassing everything, comprised of concrete components, while it is not concrete itself. One can approach the common good, on the one hand, with respect to its contents (*materialiter*), and in this respect it is identical to the well-being of the members. A second method of approach directs itself to that which is formal in the common good, in other words, the structure that results from the cooperation of the members of the community with safety, well-being, and the welfare of all in mind. The well-being of the individual is only reached when it is incorporated into the all-encompassing community.

With his definition of the common good Thomas starts from a conception of community that is based on the being of things and the demands that they entail. He sees the relation of the individual to the common good[207] as ethical rather than ontological. However, today, changes have taken place in the form of political community: the state has developed into a community which seems to possess great complexity of rules and laws; for the individual the state is not even a community in which one feels completely at home, insofar as the individual creates the conditions for his or her material existence. One resists against real or supposed interference by the state in the private domain. Many modern authors are of the opinion that the state should limit itself to supporting and protecting its citizens.

In this situation it is not surprising that different interpretations of the relation of the individual to the common good have arisen on the level of ecclesiastical social doctrine. To Antoine Pierre Verpaalen there is some value in working out the various interpretations of this relation held by Thomists.[208] The following is an overview of his summaries:

M. De Wulf has interpreted St. Thomas as an individualist; the community should serve humans.[209] One can find similar statements with authors such as V. Cathrein and H. Pesch.

E. Welty emphasizes, on the other hand, the meaning of the community and the common good as the ultimate moral goal of humans.[210] There is no conflict, since the common good actually consists of the perfection of the individual.

Th. Eschmann sees two different elements in Thomas' concept of common good: the Roman concept "society" as a judicial structure with different independent scopes and the Aristotelian theory, according to which the perfect *bonum humanum* would be a good political order. Eschmann believes that the first idea dominates: there would exist with Thomas no antimony between individual and state, because humans are always in a community. Thomas assesses the well-being of the community to be higher than the good of the individual; however, later he would allow the personal well-being to prevail.

Jacques Maritain is a clear-cut personalist: the human person as such can be no part of a whole, because humans are in themselves complete wholes, who can act freely and *sui iuris*. The person as moral excellence, so he writes, is the goal of all social life—the person appears as an autonomous subject, with personal rights preceding the state, who approaches the state. The state should protect the person. Verpaalen observes that with St. Thomas the state has a meaning other than that of a modern national state: it is the perfect society, in which and through which humans strive after personal moral perfection.[211]

Ch. de Koninck restates the personalism of Maritain and emphasizes the concept of participation: the individual shares in the perfection of the whole; the common good is the communal goal of all. A new dimension comes into existence in humans through being directed to the whole: the more perfect humans are, the more they are directed to the order of the whole. The common good stands above personal well-being because it reveals a grandeur which humans share: it exists in all.[212]

The French author S. Michel goes back to Thomas himself: the common good is the harmony, the coordination of the individual forms of good within a larger unit; it simply cannot be in conflict with the personal well-being.[213]

L. Janssens observes that the distinction used by different authors between person and individual cannot explain the relation between personal well-being and common good. Since humans must find their way through the community to personal perfection, Janssens believes that the community is a means in this respect. On the other hand, communal benefit is also a goal, since it is comprised of the perfection of the members.[214]

F. A. Weve regards the general welfare both as a good which one sets as one's goal (all human actions are determined in their structure) and as a good which governs. The good which governs exists in the just order, in peace, and in an efficient and easy functioning of the community. In this regard, the community is a means because the order is in service to welfare and perfection. As a good which one makes one's goal, the common good can be examined concerning content. In this sense it does not differ from the goal of the individual. Concerning the formal meaning, the common good can be distinguished from the personal well-being of the individual.[215]

As we have mentioned before, **Diego Ramírez** is credited for first indicating that the concept of common good is used analogously by St. Thomas. Further, he has used the concept *totum potentiale* to clarify the nature of the common good: while God as *analogatum principale* is the perfection and goal of all creatures, those who actually share in personal well-being exist only in the well-being of the members of the different communities and their being directed to a group and society, through which the personal perfection is promoted and constituted.

The widely popular personalism maintains conversely that we must start from the individual and not from the whole. According to **H. Pesch**, the individual precedes the state historically and logically.[216]

O. von Nell-Breuning distinguishes: as the community of people morally bound to each other the community stands above the individual members as the whole above the part; as organization of people amongst themselves, the society has a servicing value and is subordinate to the individual members.[217]

G. **Gundlach** is of the opinion that the Thomistic conception of Welty attributes too much meaning and power to the common good: one cannot say that humans as individuals are completely subordinate to society. On the other hand, there is no contrast between a correctly conceived common good and a correctly conceived personal well-being. Both have the same root, namely the human person. Since the common good inevitably is the principle of the organization of society, one can never derive measures from it which entail an interfering with the existence of the person. The public authority has a character of service and should protect the inviolable rights of the human person. In this manner, Gundlach, because of his personalism, believes that one can never justify the death penalty by making reference to the common good of the community, which denies the killing of criminals as something desirable. Gundlach does not deny the tension between individualism and collectivism, but he tries to solve it with his solidarism.[218]

A certain type of personalism was endorsed by the ecclesiastical doctrinal authority: **Pius XII** accentuates repeatedly that the state must serve humans and not the other way around. It is clear that the concept "state" that is being used here is different than Thomas'.

In a commentary on the treatise of St. Thomas, **A. F. Utz** first treated the development concerning the virtue of justice in the history of thought of the idea of common good.[219] Utz emphasized that, according to Thomas, the political community does not come into existence, as many modern authors claim, via the free choice of the participants, but is demanded by the social nature of humans. What is dependent upon the free will of humans can only be an accidental structure. Utz points out that currently personalism has gotten another meaning in society: one no longer starts from the *persona humana* in its ontological condition, but one overemphasizes the free initiative of the individual. Utz explains that the life in community serves the perfection of the virtues and thus "the just and good life": the good life can only be reached when the citizens possess the necessary spiritual qualities; and material goods are a preparation for it. As St. Thomas explains, moral virtues are the natural supplement to the capacities that help them—humans—to act according to their deepest being and to direct them to their goal. In this manner, Thomas can write that a virtuous life is the goal of the legislator: the perfection of the virtue exists mainly in an abstaining from unjust pleasures, which are attractive to people.[220] Although this objective appears to be very distant from what politicians and citizens generally assume about the objectives of the state, a deeper approach teaches that this vision is correct. Utz points out again that there really is no contrast between personal and common good: seen from the point of view of *causa materialis*, the common good is comprised of the forms of personal good, while the *formal* starts from above it. There are forms of personal good (of the supernatural order, as for example the virginal life for the sake of the Kingdom of God) that stand higher than the common good of the completely natural community.[221] I would like to emphasize that this exception does not hold true for the *natural* forms of the good of the human people, who are part of the community with their rights, capacities and achievements.

Utz mentions a text in which St. Thomas writes that personal well-being cannot be reached, if at the same time the well-being of family, city, and mother country are neither sought nor guaranteed. Utz means that Thomas, possibly under pressure of the Aristotelian tradition and of his own time, did not completely acknowledge the personal, because schematization of the different types of virtues that Aristotle presented were forced upon him. "Exactly the acutely accurate distinction between justice of the common good and distributive justice has caused confusion."[222] According to Utz, Thomas would not have succeeded to recognize the identity between justice of the common good and distributive justice.

Now one must realize that the relation between individual and community is not purely symmetrical. The justice of the common good is naturally justice because it offers the framework in which human existence and the virtuous life develops.[223] As St. Thomas himself says, the part is to correspond with the whole; therefore, everything containing the well-being of the whole can also be directed to the whole (*est ordinabile*). Humans have this orientation even when they are not conscious of it. Since the essential content of the common good and the well-being of the individual are formally separated, social justice cannot be the same virtue as distributive justice.[224]

For Thomas, people are not subject of rights that precede the state; he thinks of humans starting from their moral fulfilment and sees them therefore wholly in the framework of the community. One must add here that Thomas' vision is a theological one: he sees humans, as God thinks of them, as members of the community, citizens of the world, and as summoned to belong to God's chosen people. Since in the West religion and the moral feeling of dignity have partially or even entirely lost their uniformity, the individual lives in the same state, and the tendency is to limit the tasks of the political society to care for security and material well-being. The social structure is approached from the individual and not from the social nature of humans. Utz can write therefore: "It is a senseless undertaking starting from our current society to discuss whether Thomas emphasized the person more than the community."[225] For the modern person the society is only a structure that depends on a free choice of citizens. With that, it only has a purely organizational value. When favorable circumstances for the life of the individual citizen are reached it has fulfilled its task. Thomas looks conversely to the fundamental social nature of humans to come to the conclusion that the community as a whole is more important and is prior to its parts. Instead of being a requirement for the well-being of the individual, the common good is the perfection of the members living together. The norms that concern the society as a whole are not the product of a free will of the members, but come forth from the social nature of humans.

Utz also emphasizes that "the general intrinsic value which we indicate by the term common good, is not at all definable, but must be continually found again and again, corresponding to the situation and especially corresponding to the consequences.... Therefore there is a continual, dynamic testing of the reality necessary to grasp the real 'public interest'."[226]

It would also be interesting here to hear the voice of a representative of the Christian social doctrine from the United States. **Michael Novak** maintains that the nature of the common good exists really to protect the advantages of voluntary working together in the social life. Earlier a rigorous application of fixed rules was needed; in a modern society the common good must be open to changes and new inventions. In homogenous and collective societies it was possible to hold a communal goal in front of the individual, but in pluralistic states the situation has become completely different. Because of this Novak is of the opinion that a conception about the common good that sees its meaning in communal fundamental ideas and communal objectives must be replaced by a working together of free persons.[227] Novak points out that in modern times the common good was felt as something that must be realized through the communal efforts of all. The free market economy is a means to that, although it cannot attain everything. The modern conception about the common good has the following characteristics: it is an institutionalized framework, a concrete attainment, and an ideal to be sought. In earlier ecclesiastical documents the term was used with a number of meanings, but the social dimension of human existence was always accentuated. The Second Vatican Council sees in the communal well-being the sum of the circumstances of the social life that guarantees the road of perfection to the social groupings and their members.

Novak cites a text of Cardinal Höffner,[228] which likewise seems to reduce the common good to a means. The above discussion is partially theoretical. The representatives of personalism, solidarism, and the Thomistic doctrine should, practically speaking, not have to differ so much. All see the fulfilment and the well-being of the individual in a life not only in which one strives for what is good for oneself, but also in which one is there for others, shares in the constructing of the society, and directs oneself to what is good for the whole world. Also, all emphasize the meaning of the moral good as a goal of the personal life. On the other hand, one must admit that the description of the common good is often determined normatively through the impressions that one has formed from the state, as well also through personal experiences and ideals. As Utz explains, the concept state as perfect community has become strange to us. The question forces itself upon us for many reasons: should we not think differently here? In the pastoral constitution *Gaudium et spes*, with the subtitle "The Church in the Modern World," the Second Vatican Council stressed the necessity that humans transcend the conceptual universe of purely individualistic ethics, and called for another style of living.

Through goal-oriented education and with the help of the media consciousness should awaken to the fact that we live in larger communities and personal, individualistic values must not be imposed at the cost of the other. We must learn to live in the all-encompassing European community and exchange with other countries, including those of the third or fourth world. It is a fortunate development that the insight is growing among many that we are responsible for others, we must share with them, and we have the obligation to help the hungry and to promote peace in the world. In the area of Catholic ethics one can really ascertain a shift: one distances oneself from micro-ethics and accentuates more macro-ethics (obligation with respect to the other, the community, and nature). The extremely individualistic conception of an unlimited right to private property has been rejected already in many countries; the social dimension of property, as St. Thomas Aquinas knew it, could have found a far-reaching acceptance.

It seems that the common good is already functioning in a certain respect and has become a principle of acting in the thinking of more layers of the population. This applies almost exclusively to the material aspects of the common good. One cannot say the same for moral fulfillment. It is difficult in everyday life to keep the common good in mind and only in a limited way to strive for personal advantage without risk to higher ideals. It is a long way from understanding that the main goal is not the possession of material goods, but rather reaching the organization of purposes through the exercising of virtue.[229]

It is clear that life in the spiritual community of the church encompassing all peoples can be an important help to broaden the perception of the common good of the political society. The weak spot of the current society lies in this: the religious dimension, the perception of God, and the transcendental common good have died off greatly, and therefore now that which is not only the ultimate purpose of the world and human societies, but also the best support of social humans life, is lacking and takes shape in freedoms corresponding to the demands of nature.

A last observation is related to the functioning of the communal well-being in reality: one cannot deductively derive the rules and laws of the communal life beforehand from the communal well-being. In order to fulfill it one should: find the spiritual and material conditions that make possible the development and perfection of the members; protect the rights of all, especially of the poor and weak; and help the members of the community to obtain their own property and with that to provide the awareness of the dignity of free people. The fundamental agreement and harmony of personal well-being and common good should be continually emphasized. Besides that, care must be taken to protect political morality and religion.

7
Common Good: Practical Orientations

Professor Emeritus Dr. E. De Jonghe

1. Terminology

The term "common good" is used often, even by non-believers. There is also the term "general benefit." Also much is written about general interest (*intérêt général*). J. J. Rousseau spoke about the "intérêt commun," which he opposed to the "intérêt particulier." The general interest, according to him, is served by and cannot stray from the general will ("*volonté générale*"). It must be the result of the majority decision. The general interest became, in this perspective, a sum of the particular expressions of will. We find in his contract theory the beginning of an individualistic, purely utilitarian and quantitative expression of the common good.[230]

In the modern social doctrine of the Church one encounters the use of the term "common good" in the first so-called political encyclical of Leo XIII, namely *Diuturnum* (June 29, 1881), which deals with the origin of civil authority. The civil authority is called a guarantee for the public well-being (*salus publica*). The authority shall direct the striving of the citizens in a lawful and orderly manner to the communal well-being (*bonum commune*). There one finds also the term *communes utilitates civium*, which eventually is translated the "general benefit of the citizens."[231] The terminology does not appear to be fixed yet. In *Immortale Dei* (November 1, 1885) Leo XIII establishes that the state authority is not necessarily bound to one or the other form of political organization, but that it must be at the service of the general benefit and the common good: it was established not with the individual interest in mind, but rather for the well-being of all (*cum ad commune omnium bonum constituta sit*). The laws shall have the common good as its goal (*leges spectant commune bonum*), also *salus civitatis*, called the spiritual welfare of the commonwealth. When the citizens are urged to take part in political life, the expression communal benefit (*communis utilitas*) is used.[232] After Leo XIII discussed the origin and the task of authority, the relation between church and state, and freedom as a moral concept in *Diuturnum, Immortale Dei*, and *Libertas praestantissimum* (1888), he spoke in *Sapientiae Christianae* (January 10, 1890) about the task of Catholics in the political order. This is almost a forgotten encyclical, which must be read together with *Gaudium et spes* in order to judge the true scope of the term. This encyclical is strongly under the influence of Vatican I and the fight against philosophical and political liberalism that in most countries was not favorably disposed to the Church. *Sapientiae Christianae* states that for humans, the families and the state, God is the highest goal. A state that would not acknowledge this would not act according to the goals appointed to it by nature. The believer is member of a large and holy community under its invisible head, Jesus Christ, and the pope as visible substitute of Christ, who runs the Church by virtue of the task commanded by Christ. On the other hand, natural law lays the obligation on the believers to love and to protect the civil society in which they were born and raised. Christians should accept the same position towards the Church. In this respect, the unity of the Church demands a complete subjection to its doctrinal and administrative authority. No law worthy of that name can be brought into existence in the civil order, if it does not comply with the needs of the common good. The encyclical remarks that the highest common good demands that the legislators take into account moral law, with the duties that religion imposes and with the interests of Christianity. There is a difference between *prudentia politica*, that the politician must exhibit, and the practical wisdom which the citizens exercise in daily life. One is the caution of the architect, the other that of the craftspeople who execute the architect's plans.[233] In *Rerum novarum*, the fundamental encyclical of the social doctrine of the Church, a central place is granted to the common good. A number of tasks that the state henceforth shall have to take upon itself are integrated in a broad vision of the common good. In the encyclicals about the political order and authority, the institutional framework and the legislative activity in the modern state are the main concerns. This penetrates through to the social-economic level. The "solution to the social question" shall become an important element in the realization of the common good.[234] When the common good entails the restoration of the social order forty years later in *Quadragesimo anno* (1931), after the great crisis of the 1930's, the professional organizations and the so-called intermediary bodies were clearly set to the task of serving the common good. It is to be both a goal of as well as a limit to their activities.[235]

In the encyclical *Divini redemptoris* (March 19, 1937), directed against communism and the evolutionistic materialism of K. Marx, one finds a résumé of the ecclesiastical social doctrine, as it had developed until then. Pius XI repeats here that the organization of business, perceived by him as a new organization of the society, must form a harmonic unity in the function of the common good. Social justice, a concept introduced by *Quadragesimo anno*, is to inspire politics, so that everything is provided to the members of the community that demands the actualization of the common good.[236] *Mit brennender Sorge* (March 14, 1937), directed against national-socialism, expresses the resentment of Pius XI and his protest against the manner in which the church in Germany became the victim of opposition and imputations which could be seen in the opposition to Catholic schools, in the attempts to undermine Christianity, and to exterminate the belief in the God of Bible and Gospel, the starting of a German national church apart from Rome, the spreading of a non-Christian morality, and the resistance to Catholic youth movements. All this is considered irreconcilable with the common good, as it was described by the Church in other documents. All these negative elements make the actualization of the common good impossible. This same thought guided *Non abbiamo bisogno* (June 21, 1931), in which Pius XI protected the freedom of religion, the Christian family, Christian education, the church, and Catholic organizations from politics executed by the fascist state. We see here once more the contrast between the ecclesiastical conviction about the common good and that of a totalitarian state. Once the contents of later encyclicals are examined, it shall be evident that the first encompassing formulations of human rights were brought forth from the opposition against the totalitarian state convictions.[237]

Pius XII in *Summi pontificatus* (October 20, 1939) with *Immortale Dei* of Leo XIII (1885) adds in the statement that the sovereign authority of the civil government, provided it observes a number of universal principles, is willed by the Creator to organize the social life, so that one can reach one's complete development and actualize one's supernatural goal. It is the noble task of the state to govern the activities of the citizens and of the public bodies such that the common good can be brought into existence. This common good cannot grow from the will of individuals and cannot be found in exclusively material welfare, but can be found in the natural and harmonious growth of humans. This is the goal that the Creator gave to the community. Maintaining that the state is a goal to which everything is subordinate can only damage the permanent actualization of the common good.[238] According to Pius XII, the human capacity to reason brings him to the conclusion that all state activity must be directed to the permanent actualization of the common good. One finds in this text a first synthetic approach to the contents of the common good, as it shall be adopted and further developed in later documents. According to this document:

> These external conditions, which are to the advantage of the whole are necessary for the development of human talents, functions, material well-being, and intellectual and religious life. This is even more so because the possibilities of the individual persons and families which have a natural priority are limited and they are not capable of reaching their goal alone. The church has, on the other hand, its own mission and has its own means for salvation.[239]

The obligation of the state to promote the common good does not also give it the right to curtail or to hinder the individual activities of citizens in its development, to decide for itself about the beginning and end of life, to prescribe the life of humans, to mandate how they should behave on the spiritual, moral, and religious level. This is completely in conflict with the duties and rights of humans. Similarly, one cannot ignore the natural right of humans for material goods. This all would eventually lead to maintaining that the only goal of humans on earth is the society, that it has itself as the highest goal and one has no other goal than the earthly existence in the prevailing society.[240] Pius XII shall repeat with emphasis in *Con sempre* (1942) that the service of the state to the community demands the absolute respect of the human person in serving one's supernatural goal.[241] The pope has more comprehensively and more principally expressed what his predecessor Pius XI has brought forth in his encyclicals in a critical manner against the totalitarian regimes. It is also in Pius XII's texts which concern war, that we find a first establishment of human rights as they were present in the judicial tradition of the West, and treated here from a Christian perspective. With relation to the statements of Pius XI about the common good, J. Y. Calvez has noted that the pope places two limitations with respect to this interpretation, namely the subsidiarity principle and the rights of the human person. The state must honor these limits.[242]

From *Mater et magistra* (1961), *Pacem in terris* (1963), and *Gaudium et spes* (1965), the term common good (*bonum commune*) is continually used in the papal documents in diverse contexts. Those who are involved with the socialization process that takes place in modern society must work together with the common good in mind (*Mater et magistra*, nr. 65). *Pacem in terris* (nr. 53) urges that it is everyone's duty to contribute to the common good. *Gaudium et spes* (nrs. 26, 74, 83) emphasizes particularly that the mutual dependence of humans on the world level brings with it a duty to strive for the common good on the world level. Clearly now it is specified more and more that it is everyone's moral duty to contribute to the common good. All parts of society, individual persons, families, and diverse groups that because of their inadequacy have called the state to life, must contribute to the common good. The same duty rests on the public authority and the public institutions. Within the limits of the morally permissible, what the public authority imposes in the name of the common good which must be recognized as a dynamic reality, may not be refused by the citizens who are obliged in conscience to obedience.[243] John Paul II, like his predecessors, has pointed to the meaning of the common good where it was needed. When in *Laborem exercens* he discusses the role of the unions, he emphasizes that the defense of the rights of the workers must fit in the framework of the common good (nr. 20). In *Sollicitudo rei socialis*, published on the occasion of the twentieth anniversary of *Populorum progressio* (1967-1987), he introduced the concept "sinful structures." These have, according to him, their roots in personal sin and always are connected to concrete actions of persons who introduced them and consolidated them, so that they can be removed only with difficulty (nr. 36). In the exhortation *Reconciliatio et poenitentia* (December 2, 1984, nr. 16), he had already spoken about social sins, the results, the piling up, the concentration of many personal sins concerning justice, and pointed to the responsibility of people in situations where injustice exists. It is in this context that the statement of John Paul II should be understood, namely those who are responsible for the life of their fellow humans must reform according to the common good, and that they must recognize that the common good demands a constant united effort for the well-being of each and everyone (*ibid.* nr. 38). In *Christifideles laici* (December 30, 1988), John Paul II emphasizes the willingness of Christian laypersons to help society. Proceeding from the establishment of the dignity of the human person, he explains that this is completely irreducible to all that would like to crush and destroy it in the anonymity of the collective, the structure or the system (nr. 37). This assumes the acknowledgment and observance of all human rights and on the political level the acceptance of the criterion of the common good, which is described in this text and in *Gaudium et spes* (nr. 42). Very important is the emphasis that the pope in *Christifideles laici* places on justice and solidarity, and with the need to actualize a new style of living by these. In *Centesimus annus* (1991) the meaning of transcendental truth of humans is again contrasted to every form of totalitarianism. It demands that democracy and the *trias politica* originate in an adequate conception of the common good which is above the mere sum of particular interests (nrs. 44, 46, 47).

Finally, one must point out that the *Catechism of the Catholic Church* (published in 1992) comprehensively treats the common good. The pastors of the Catholic Church will have to watch that all charismatics contribute in their diversity and complementarity to the common good (with reference to *Lumen gentium*, nrs. 801 and 951). The *Catechism* teaches that moral virtue, which starts with respecting others and acknowledging their rights, is justice. This virtue will have to introduce harmony and fairness in human relations and thus help to actualize the common good (nr. 1807). Recaptured is the statement from *Gaudium et spes* (nr. 24, 3) that in each society respect is due to the authorities, because the care of the common good is entrusted to them. Still, the importance of the subsidiarity principle is indicated (nr. 1883). The text of the *Catechism* about the common good and its concrete meaning is the most comprehensive synthesis of the doctrine of the Church about this matter since it was developed from Leo XIII. It is, with respect to content, the most encompassing document.[244]

2. The content of the common good

Whoever traces the term common good in the modern encyclicals can conclude that in the so-called political encyclicals of Leo XIII the role of the common good is primarily accentuated with respect to the role of the state authority and the responsibility of the legislator for actualizing a harmonious society. In the so-called social encyclicals after *Rerum novarum,* the particular task of the government improving working conditions is identified as the solution of the social question. In this context, the concept social justice was introduced in *Quadragesimo anno* and the necessary restructuring of the society was called for. In the encyclicals directed against the totalitarian regimes, the issue of human rights is the central focus. In each the common good is put forward as a standard. The first time one finds a short summarizing definition that appears later in many papal writings is only in *Mater et magistra* (1961). "The common good is a complex of many social conditions that enables people to actualize their personal perfection more completely and more communally" (*Mater et magistra* n. 65, *Pacem in terris* n. 58). In the same sense we read in *Gaudium et spes:* "The common good is the totality of the social conditions under which both groups and individuals more completely and quickly can reach their own perfection" (n. 26, 1); or again: "The common good encompasses the totality of the social conditions of life through which people, families, and unions can reach more completely and more easily their perfection" (*Gaudium et spes*, n. 74, with reference to *Mater et magistra*).

The content of these social conditions of life was specified more and more, between 1961 and 1965, according to a clear pattern. In the first political encyclicals from the end of the nineteenth century the emphasis is placed on the formal element of common good, order, peace, and security, that must be guaranteed by the authorities relative to the state. *Divini Redemptoris* (1937, n. 51) expressly started from the dignity of the human person, which demands that all humans have everything at their disposal to shape their lives. Both the government and individuals must take into account what people need for their completion, both on the material and the spiritual level, and respect an objective hierarchy of values (*Pacem in terris*, nr. 56 and 59). The material well-being contains all that is necessary for the self-preservation of humans. Those mentioned are employment, food, clothing, housing, etc., with great emphasis on the fulfillment of the needs of the family. On the spiritual level, the common good encompasses in the first place the freedom of conscience and religion. Slowly, especially during and after the war, more emphasis was placed in more or less systematic depictions of the entire range of human rights. These social conditions of life must be actualized formally, materially, and spiritually—not just in the developed countries, but around the world even for the less endowed on the world level. Even though the social encyclicals have always recognized that there exist forms of natural inequality among humans that are the sources of differences in intelligence, talent, dexterity, health, strength, and chance (*Rerum novarum*, nr. 14), they have always demanded that the legislator intervene in a particular way to protect the weak (the workers in *Rerum novarum*, nr. 27), concerning both their bodily and spiritual needs (*Quadragesimo anno*, n. 126, *Pacem in terris*, n. 56-59). In the document *Justitia in mundo* of November 30, 1971, about the promotion of justice in the world, the second general bishop synod connects the realization of the general universal well-being to the right of development in the underdeveloped countries. The striving after justice on the world level, including among other things the promotion of the developing of these countries, categorizes this new right under the concept common good: the right to development. In 1971, the world economy found itself in an emerging trend. There was a great uneasiness, because the "takeoff" of the developing countries anticipated by the United Nations in the 1960's did not take place. The new decade did not offer much hope. The above mentioned synod document continued building on *Populorum progressio* of 1967. On May 14, 1971, *Octogesimo anno* of Paul VI had opened the way in the eyes for what one then called "progressive front-forming," but the synod document kept this out of consideration. It pointed mainly to the crisis in international solidarity and the already clear failure of the development policies of the rich countries. It proclaims the right of the Church to make the demands of justice clear on both the international as well as the national level and to bring charges against injustice. This document, which was only advisory, was published accompanied by a papal confirmation.[245]

The last summarizing definition in an ecclesiastical document of what is understood under common good is in the *Catechism of the Catholic Church* (1992). This important text begins with a personalistic declaration: "In agreement with the social nature of humans there exists a relation between the well-being of everyone and the common good, The latter can only be determined by its commitment to the human person" (nr. 1905).[246]

Immediately after follows the definition that we already know from *Gaudium et spes* (nr. 26, 1). The common good demands that all bearers of authority put practical wisdom or the virtue of prudence into practice (nr. 1906). With regards to content one can distinguish three essential elements:

• The common good, in the first place, assumes a *respect for the person* as such. It imposes the task on public authoritative bodies to respect the fundamental and inalienable rights of the human person. This means that the common good demands that everyone can exercise the natural liberties which are required for the fulfillment of their calling (nr. 1907, nr 1925. nr. 1926 with reference to *Gaudium et spes* nr. 26, 2).

• Secondly, the common good requires the *social well-being* and the *development* of the group itself. The authoritative bodies must make it possible that everyone gets access to everything that they need to lead a humane existence: food, clothes, health, work, education and culture, sufficient information, the right and the possibility to start a family, etc. This shall fundamentally promote the real flowering of the group (nr. 1908).

• Thirdly, the common good implies peace, in other words, the security and permanence of a just order. This assumes that the government uses fair means for the preservation of its own security and that of the citizens. This aspect of the common good founds the personal and collective right of legal self-defense (nr. 1909).

In the first place, the duty rests upon the state, the unique political society of the community, to insure the common good of the civil society, of the citizens, and of the intermediary bodies (nr. 1910). Still, the unity of humanity which assumes an equal natural dignity of all implies a universal common good (nr. 1911). Also here, the goal must be the universal development of the people. The order of things shall have to be subordinate to the order of the people (nr. 1912). The *Catechism* comes back to the intrinsic determinations of the common good, when it treats social justice (nrs. 1928-1930), the right of freedom of religion (nr. 2109), the rights of the family (nr. 2203), and the duties of the political bearers of authority (nrs. 2235-2255). Finally, this document establishes the right of the church in its social doctrine to express a moral and religious point of view whenever the fundamental rights and the welfare of souls demands it. When the Church strongly directs its attention to the material content of the common good, then it is because the adequate use of material goods enables humans to reach their ultimate goal, the highest good. On the level of the social-ethical events the Church shall then first and foremost emphasize the demands of justice in relation to property and the use of material goods (nr. 2420, with reference to *Gaudium et spes*, nr. 76, 5).

3. The discussion about the common good

In the 1930's, a number of totalitarian theories claimed to give an answer to the individualism that was held responsible for the great crisis of 1929-1933 and its social consequences. Some countries promoted racial politics accompanied with so-called eugenic measures that were unacceptable for Catholics. In communism, fascism, and national-socialism the person was subordinate to the dominating state ideology. This was at times the expression of the liberating proletarian revolution, and, at times, the epitomization of the spirit of the nation or of the soul of the people. In these three instances every religious perspective containing a monotheistic conception about humans and society was expelled and it was maintained that human happiness must be sought in an order exclusively of this world.[247] Then questions were asked concerning the relation of the person to the community and the state, and the relation between personal and common good. Between 1930 and 1960, an extensive discussion in Catholic circles was held about the meaning of common good in the texts of St. Thomas Aquinas. A *de facto* end came to this discussion with the definitions of the common good which were repeated in *Mater et magistra* (1961) and which were, in some cases, completed in subsequent relevant ecclesiastical documents.

Dom Odon Lottin more specifically has brought forth a brief, but nonetheless important, synthesis of a number of texts of St. Thomas Aquinas.[248] It cannot be denied, writes Lottin, that a rather large number of statements of Thomas Aquinas are to be found in which he expresses the subordination of the individual person to the community in terms of the subordination of the part to the whole and in which the whole is often called "*divinius*" or "more divine" than the part.[249] However, it seems that the thinking of St. Thomas shows an explicit unity that by no means subjugates people to the community. With this it must also be mentioned that St. Thomas never gave a systematic exposé about this matter and in some of his texts it is the influence of the writings of Aristotle that gives the impression that for him the social whole or the political commonwealth starts from radically above the individual. One must thus, according to Lottin, carefully investigate in their context similar passages influenced by Aristotle.[250] One must understand that the Greek city-state formed a political, moral, and religious unit, and the civil and moral education was entrusted by Aristotle to the state.[251] With Aristotle it even goes so far that the state must not only bring the citizens by means of the law to a virtuous life, but also monitor their physical suitability for marriage and prescribe the death of undesired children.[252] According to Lottin, one cannot always discern from the commentaries of St. Thomas on the ethical and political writings of Aristotle what his own vision adds to the ideas of Aristotle. Other texts of Thomas are then more clear. The context of these is important. The law about which Thomas writes in his commentaries is the law of the civil society issued with general benefit in mind. This law wants to promote justice in the commonwealth and aims at a goal higher than the personal exercise of virtue. This legal justice is led by the "*prudentia politica*," which draws up the laws for the entire society and has a broader goal than justice seen from a familial or personal point of view. In this Aristotelian perspective the whole of ethics is arranged under politics and Thomas endorses the necessity of bringing into existence legislation that would lead citizens from their youth to forming virtuous habits.[253] The eventual goal toward which the legislator must strive, according to Aristotle, is happiness in life. It is a happiness bound with a virtuous and contemplative life. In the Greek city-state this was an ideal meant only for an elite. Slaves fell outside of the consideration of this vision. St. Thomas shall open a broader perspective for the meaning of human happiness, as well as the ultimate goal of each person. In this he shall not be immediately followed, but he pointed to a new direction. Also, in the *Summa theologiae*, an Aristotelian terminology concerning this material is present and exposés are also present which appear to be very Aristotelian when placed out of their context. Thus we read that the goal of each legislator who is worthy of that name is the common good, conceived as the happiness of the commonwealth.[254] Aristotle and St. Thomas speak about legal justice (*justitia legalis*). The virtue of justice goes together with this and directs humans to the common good and is called piety by Cicero.[255] The civil task of the legislator, which according to Aristotle exists to bring humans to moral excellence, shall be defined more closely by Thomas. He adds to this that the civil legislator is subject to the divine law, which specifies the ultimate goal of humans.[256] The meaning of the eternal law, natural law, and the decalogue is connected to positive law, according to the *Summa theologiae*.[257] Concerning the many places where St. Thomas, in following Aristotle, makes use of the image of the part-whole relation, Lottin remarks that, according to St. Thomas, the unity of the society is a "*unitas ordinis,*" an order-unity, endorsed by reason and willed by humans, where the common good must take into account the goals of the individual persons who are concerned with it. A commonwealth cannot bloom if the citizens and they who have leadership do not exercise the virtues of political wisdom and justice. According to St. Thomas, people are not subject to all of the civil society, but they must in all what they are, own and can do, be directed to God.[258] Incidentally, it can be pointed out that a few often-cited texts of St. Thomas, where each time the part-whole image is used, are in the context of the deaths of murderers and criminals, even mutilations (Medieval criminal law), and that in this context they are called sinners. They should, like sick limbs, be removed from the body. The metaphor is applied in a concrete situation that does not easily prove the total subordination of the individual person to the society.

A totalitarian or racist eugenism would search erroneously here for a point of departure. This would then ignore the ecclesiastical doctrine of human dignity.[259] O. von Nell-Breuning remarked in his commentary on *Quadragesimo anno* with relation to the subsidiarity principle, that speaking as if the whole has priority to the parts is a dangerous use of a logical connection of words in the form of a metaphor that can have different meanings. He meant, more specifically, that when it is about a whole that is an order-unity, a whole of which free people gifted with reasoning are a part, these people in their own goals must be respected as such. These are not wholes as a pile of rocks or an antpile.[260] In the same sense J. Maritain wrote that in society the people themselves must be regarded as whole units with personal goals and well-being.[261] The texts quoted by Lottin teach us that people must be regarded as independent beings and that the nature and the social forms of organization are made instrumental in their personal perfection.[262] Furthermore, we read in *Summa contra gentiles* that being gifted with reason is not just a species for God, but that Providence wants this personal fulfillment.[263] Therefore, God gave laws to the people which have as their goal this personal perfection.[264] These laws help humans on the way to God's love. They have a personal individual range: leading humans to their ultimate goal, the personal purpose that constitutes their dignity.[265] When St. Thomas uses the expression in the *Summa contra gentiles* that the well-being of the community is "more divine" than that of the individual, it appears from the context that he means that God represents the highest value as *summum bonum* and the highest common good for all; the well-being of the community is a more extensive approach to this highest goal, and in no way the well-being of the person should be subject to everything of the community.[266] From a theological perspective, God is the ultimate goal of creation and all the beings that it contains.[267] In the first part of the *Summa theologiae*, where Thomas is discussing God and creation, one encounters a number of statements that show a similarity to the analogous passages in the first three books of the *Summa contra gentiles*: God wishes to give expression to his perfection and his goodness through creation.[268] From the perspective of finding a hierarchy of perfections in the different parts of the creation, from the highest perfection of the angels to humans, living beings, and physical nature, St. Thomas shall also write that the well-being of the species (whole) surpasses that of the parts.[269] In his global vision, the ultimate personal goal of humans surpasses all forms of collective perfection. St. Thomas shall always say that the happiness of the saints at the end of time is the most perfect personal well-being.[270] The conclusion can be short, from a practical perspective. Normally, there shall be no contrast between particular and common good. By fulfilling their tasks where Providence has placed them in the community, people shall work together to a bringing into existence the common good. The "*prudentia politica*" shall lead the public bearer of authority to create the conditions so that all people would be able to reach their fulfillment on the three levels that are stated in the ecclesiastical documents: a harmoniously organized society where peace and order rule, a necessary material welfare, and a cultural development that gives a central place to the true ultimate goal of humans. General and particular well-being can unfortunately get into conflict and conflict is present everywhere in the world. In the three mentioned areas, people can be oppressed or the common good can be endangered. A well-organized society has at its disposal the necessary procedures to cushion conflicts and to resolve them. The emphasis here must be on the common good, the meaning of the virtue of justice, and the necessary education for a just life. Obtaining knowledge of everything that belongs to the common good and confronting everyone with the demands of the common good are indeed necessary. For everyone it is a moral duty to dedicate oneself to the common good. The discussions about the demands of the common good and the acknowledgment of human people and their rights, however abstract these sometimes seem, are significant and always actual. Ethnic violence, racial hatred, a lack of civility, unrestrained striving for profit, exclusion denial of personal rights and the rights of children, and hardship and inhumane poverty are, for the entire world, still daily realities.[271]

8
Solidarity and Subsidiarity

Professor Dr. J. Verstraeten

In the instruction of the Sacred Congregation of Faith, *Libertatis Conscientia* (1986), solidarity and subsidiarity, which are directly based on the dignity of the human person, are mentioned together as the fundamental principles of the social doctrine of the Church: "People are the active and responsible subjects of social life. Profoundly connected to this basis of human dignity are the principles of solidarity and subsidiarity" (LC, 73). The first principle refers to the social responsibility of humans and implies a rejection of individualism; the second refers to the responsibility of people and intermediary communities, and implies a rejection of collectivism.

At first glance the meaning of solidarity and subsidiarity is clear. However, a study of the evolution of the meaning of both concepts brings to light a number of problems.

Both concepts were introduced late in Christian tradition. There is no mention in the Bible of solidarity *sensu stricto*, although the most important aspects of the meaning are present in the biblical vision of love and justice. Moreover, the meaning of the terms solidarity and subsidiarity in the history of the social doctrine of the Church has evolved. This doctrine is more than a collection of detailed and concrete non-historical norms. It is the confirmation of a history of experiences in a doctrinal system considered in the light of the Gospels and century-old social tradition. It is, to use in the words of O. von Nell-Breuning, a "permanent process of learning," in which the continuity of the fundamental principles are always paired with new insights (McCormick, 1986, 228).

1. The period before John XXIII

Originally solidarity was not an ecclesiastic concept, but a concept that since the second half of the eighteenth century turns up in secular discourse. Among others, Adam Ferguson demonstrates in his *Essay on the History of Civil Society* how through the division of labor a belonging together or a solidarity comes into existence between people who are concerned with different skills or functions in the work-process (Walgraeve, 1960, 110). One of the most well-known definitions of the concept comes from E. Durkheim. In his work *De la division du travail* (1893), he makes a distinction between the "solidarité mécanique," which is characterized by a unity based on equality characteristic of primitive communities and the "solidarité organique," which is characterized by a unity in diversity and which is the case in modern society characterized by the division of labor. The solidarity concept also received an ethical content by extension, namely an obligation of belonging together. One finds this as early as 1840 in the work of Pierre Leroux *De l'Humanité*, who wrote about the duty of mutual help, which is founded on the idea that the community of which one is a member forms one whole (Walgraeve, 1960, 110).

Inspired by the French sociological school, the solidarists have developed and systematized the thinking about solidarity. According to the "social ontology" of solidarism, of which Heinrich Pesch and Gustav Gundlach were the most important representatives, humans are "intrinsically social beings" directed ontologically by their concrete nature to the community, as also the whole community by nature is directed to humans. Because of the ontological mutual relation between humans and society, according to the solidarists, also an ethical communality of person and community comes into existence (Klüber, 1980, 2576), as the duty to solidarity. Further, solidiarity is for them also a legal principle that forms the basis of a specific solidarity social model, of which the harmonious working together between the different work positions is one of the most important characteristics.

Heinrich Pesch did not hesitate to define the church in its whole as "solidaristic." Such a conception is susceptible to critique. Solidarity is not always the only fundamental principle. Furthermore, Pesch's point of view can lead to a far-reaching identification of the social doctrine of the Church with a social model which during the interbellum period willingly showed affinities with a number of variations of the corporatist "new order" (von Nell-Breuning, 1986, 60-68).

It is, in any case, remarkable that even the encyclical *Quadragesimo anno* (1931), often described as "solidaristic," maintains a critical aloofness.

1.1 This encyclical, which nevertheless was influenced by the ideas of Pesch and Gundlach, does not take "solidarity" as a starting-point, but rather "social justice" and the "common good" (QA, 56-58). Social justice refers not only to a redistribution of the goods according to the demands of the common good (distributive justice), but also, and according to Calvez, primarily to the duty of each one to contribute to the common good (the so-called "general" or "legal" justice that was reinterpreted later in 1986 by the American bishops as "contributive justice") (Calvez, Perrin, 1961, 145-153).

On the other hand, there is a clear preference for a harmonious mutual cooperation within the work force (QA, 81) and Italian corporatism is discussed in covert, careful, and positive terms, which is nevertheless an extension of Pius XI (von Nell-Breuning, 1986, 63).

1.2 *Quadragesimo anno* made history primarily by making the subsidiarity principle explicit. According to Utz, this principle has a twofold meaning. First and foremost it refers, in a negative sense, to the restriction of intervention by the state. It is thus a principle of non-interference of the state in the rights of the individual or of the higher or more encompassing communities in the activities in the smaller communities, namely where the individual or the small community is capable to fulfill its tasks itself.

In the second instance, the subsidiarity principle refers, according to Utz, also to the help which the individual of the small community may expect from the larger community, but only when it is no longer capable of fulfilling its tasks itself. The conditional expression "only when" is not incidental. The state may only intervene when it is really necessary (Utz, 279-280).

O. von Nell-Breuning clearly places a different emphasis: first, subsidiarity is no principle, but a *subsidiarium officium*, a duty of the community to be helpful to its members in the fullest sense of the word, namely to give them the possibility to develop themselves to the fullest as people (1979, 177-178). In other words, the community (which means "all *in solidum*") has the duty to extend and develop itself so that it becomes an effective establishment of help to meet their individual needs and as best as possible fulfill their tasks as humans. However, with the developing of the community, the relations of the groups to their members and of the higher and broader groups to the lower and more limited must be conceived in a such way that these two supplementarily help to accomplish their tasks (the positive aspect of the subsidiarity principle). This must be conceived in such a way that they are helped to be able to develop themselves through free self-activity within the broader scope and only are subjected to coercion when and insofar as they would counter the general good of the higher community (the negative aspect of the subsidiarity principle) (Walgraeve, 1960, 117).

The history of the social doctrine of the Church teaches us that the accent lies sometimes on the negative, other times on the positive aspect of the subsidiarity principle. In *Quadragesimo anno* there is a tendency to emphasize primarily the negative approach, as it appears in the classical formulation in nr. 79 and 80, which says that, "what individuals can actualize on their own initiative and through their own power" ... "cannot be taken from them and assigned to the community." What is "done by smaller and subordinate communities and brought into existence" cannot be taken by a "greater and larger community." "After all, each social activity must by virtue of its nature bring help (*subsidium*) to the members of the social body, but never destroy and absorb them" (*QA*, 79). This implies that the state authority (must) leave to subordinate groups the executing of less important tasks and worries through which it otherwise would be deeply engaged, in order to execute "more freely," "more power-fully" and with greater "effectiveness" that which "belongs to its exclusive competence" (*QA*, 80). The state authority must not assume the free initiative that can be developed on a lower social level.

Later, John XXIII shall in spite of his general theoretical confirmation of the point of view of *Quadragesimo anno*, put more emphasis on the positive "intervention of the state," that "supports, awakens, organizes, supplements, and complements" and is "based on the subsidiarity principle" (*MM*, 53). He pleads for a state intervention in different concrete areas, like the obtaining of state property, the receiving of taxes, the granting of credit facilities, the supporting of social security, price regulation, etc. According to him, the state must see to it that a gradual, simultaneous, and balanced development takes place in the three sectors of production: agriculture, industry, and public services. The private initiative which is necessary for this must be supported (*MM*, 151). With this as the background, the thought is always present that the Western social market economy model is valid for developing countries (Dorr, 1992, 138-142).

Later, John Paul II shall again put the emphasis on the negative aspect of the subsidiarity principle in the framework of a sharp critique of the welfare state. We will come back to this later.

2. The period from John XXIII to John Paul II
Going back to solidarity, we can establish that, particularly since the pontificate of John XXIII, its meaning has shifted in more that one respect.

2.1 There is a remarkable shift in emphasis from an ontological to a personalistic vision. Already Pius XII, but especially John XXIII, emphasized that the central starting-point comes to be expressed not so much as an "immutable order" in an ontologically interpreted natural law, but rather as the dignity of the human person. Human people are, according to John XXIII: "the foundation, reason for existence, and end of all social institutions, because due to their nature they are social and elevated to an order that transcends and overcomes nature" (*MM*, 219). In *Pacem in terris* (9) he expresses it in the following manner: "This principle must lie at the basis of each well-organized and fruitful human society: that every human being is a person. This means that they are gifted with the power of reasoning and free will. Therefore, they obviously have rights and duties that directly and simultaneously result from their own nature. They are therefore universal, inviolable, absolute, and inalienable."

In the distinction between an ontological and personalistic approach to solidarity lies, according to J. H. Walgraeve, the great difference within solidarism. Personalism does not base the community on an ontological solidarity as a fundamental principle (although the actual situation of already being in the society is important), but to the being of humans as humans, i.e., as people who are for themselves an ethical assignment, a calling to actualize themselves as people in a life for others.

2.2 Secondly, there is also a shift from an ontological to a sociological foundation of the communality of humans. This deals, among other things, with the transition from a purely deductive, natural law method, to a more analytical approach to the social reality according to the principle of "observe, judge, act" (*MM*, 236). Through that, the social sciences received more attention, and, among other things, this resulted in the introduction of the concept "socialization." In certain groups this was met with so much resistance that in the Latin and the English translation of the Italian text the concept "socialization" was omitted out of fear for a possible identification with socialistic thought and it was replaced by a more vague wording (*socialium relationum incremental increase in social relationships*). Nevertheless, there was not a single reason for this, because the sociological concept "socialization" (which was used by Pierre Bigo, among others) refers to the fact of the "growing mutual dependence of the citizens," that "[is] both cause and effect of a continually increasing interference by the state" and is also the result and the expression of "scarcely resistible inclination of humans, an inclination namely to unite with each other to the reaching of goals which each one desires, but which exceed the capacity of single individuals" (*MM*, 60). In spite of the fact that he is aware of the negative consequences of socialization, the optimistic John XXIII especially points to positive possibilities. According to him, the socializing process allows "the satisfaction and the pleasure of numerous personal rights, especially of those which have relation to the economic and social life." With this he remains at a distance from the liberal tradition which is oriented solely to freedom rights. Socialization contributes after all to the actualization of "the right to those means indispensable for a real dignified existence, the right to health services, the right to the expansion and deepening of elementary education, the right to more appropriate occupational training, to housing, to labor, to suitable leisure free time, and appropriate recreation" (*MM*, 61). In short, socialization can contribute "to a repairing of the human society."

The Second Vatican Council associated itself, especially in *Gaudium et spes*, with the vision of John XXIII. Again the concept socialization was referred to. Although the possible dangers are indicated, the emphasis is placed mainly on the advantages that the socialization process brings with it "for the strengthening and the expansion of the qualities of human people and for the protection of their rights" (*GS*, 25). The ethical norm which this socialization must satisfy is the common good, justice, love, and respect for the human person (*GS*, 26-27).

2.3 A third aspect of change is the shift from a perspective of a "national-economic" vision of solidarity to "world solidarity." For John XXIII, the development problem is, henceforth, the "most pressing question of our time" (*MM*, 157). He brings up this problem expressly in terms of solidarity: "now the solidarity, which unites all people to one family, compels as it should all nations that are saturated with an overflow of goods, not to stand indifferently towards the countries in which the inhabitants find themselves in such difficult situations that they nearly die of want and hunger and cannot even enjoy the most elementary human rights" (*MM*, 157). This world solidarity is not only described as a duty of love (*MM*, 158 and 159;

PT, 129), but primarily as a "challenge of justice and humanity" (*MM,* 161). It is "necessary and just" to divide the riches "in fairness" (*MM,* 168). The ultimate norm of this international justice is unmistakably human dignity: "This economic development and social progress must be actualized in a way that corresponds to human dignity..." (*MM,* 192). This is established expressly in *Pacem in terris:* "The relations between the political communities must be regulated according to truth and justice" (*PT,* 91, 98). And it is added immediately: "But they must also be inspired by an effective solidarity" (*PT,* 98).

With this, different forms of solidarity are identified: on the economic, social, and political level, in the cultural sphere and health care, and in sports. John XXIII refers especially to what he described earlier as fundamental human rights. In other words, solidarity cannot be understood without the universal actualization of human rights (both freedom rights and social rights).

In spite of the more "liberal agenda" in *Gaudium et spes,* this international perspective is also clearly present. In this manner the international peace is described implicitly in terms of solidarity: "Peace cannot be obtained on this earth, if personal values are not safeguarded and the people in mutual trust do not let each other share spontaneously in the riches of their inner spirit and talents. The solid will to respect other people, peoples, and their dignity, and the studied practice of brotherhood are absolutely necessary in order to reach peace" (*GS,* 78).

In general, it should be established that *Gaudium et spes* especially expresses the meaning of "solidarity" with the two concepts "justice and love," as for example in nr. 30, where there is talk of the duty of justice and love which "[finds] more and more its fulfillment in this that everyone... promotes and helps according to their personal capacities and with the needs of others contributing their own to the common good and the institutions in mind..., which have as their duty to improve the living conditions of people...."

The problem of international solidarity was especially expressed in the authoritative encyclical *Populorum progressio* of Paul VI. In the consciousness of the "world-encompassing dimension" of the social question the necessity is indicated as early as in the introduction to "this deciding turning point of history... to act in a solidarity manner" (*PP,* 43). With the description of the obligation to share the resources with others, Paul VI makes a distinction between three elements: "first, the duty of human solidarity, which entails the assistance of richer nations to developing countries; then the duty to so-

cial justice, which demands that the inadequate trade relations between the wealthier and the weaker peoples are improved; and finally
the duty to universal love of one's neighbors..." (*PP*, 44). Here solidarity gets a specific meaning, in spite of its connection with other
elements. This is described in the numbers 44 up to and including
55 as: the fight against hunger, the building of a world in which
everybody, without distinction of race, religion, or nationality, can
lead a true human life; an increase of production in order to be able
to contribute in such a way to a united development of human nature; the sharing of that which remains; the building of aid programs;
the establishment of world funds for assistance to underprivileged
peoples; bilateral and multilateral agreements; and a dialog that leads
to the solution of the debt burden.

3. The theologizing of the social doctrine with John Paul II
3.1 Solidarity

With John Paul II, solidarity is unmistakably a concept with a high
priority. It is so important for him that he even changed the definition of peace from *opus iustitiae*, used by Pius XII, to *opus solidarietatis*.

However, his vision cannot be understood without a general insight into what could be called the theologizing of the social doctrine.

From the beginning of his pontificate, he gave remarkable and great
attention to the in-depth study of the doctrinal foundations of the
social doctrine of the Church. By this he emphasizes two things: on
one hand, a personalistic element, insofar as the centrality he gives to
the human person, on the other side a theological element, insofar as
he bases the meaning of human dignity on the mystery of salvation
through Christ (Dorr, 1992, 270-273). One could also speak in this
regard of a Christologization of the social doctrine (Soria, 1982, 133).
According to John Paul II, the ultimate foundation of this is the
confession of faith (in the fullest sense of the word) in Jesus Christ.
Believing in Christ implies the task to love his world-transforming
process in history. The opening words of the encyclical *Redemptor
hominis* can be interpreted in this respect as an announcement of the
platform: "The Savior of the people, Jesus Christ, is the central point
of the cosmos and history" (*RH*, 1). For John Paul II, Jesus Christ is
the "immovable principle and the permanent central point of the
mission that God Himself has consigned to the people." All believers
must, according to him, work together and concentrate with all energy on this mission, "because it is necessary more than ever for hu-

man nature of today." Referring to *Gaudium et spes* he says: "in reality the mystery of humans shines only in the mystery of the Word that has become human" and he continues, "through the revelation of the mystery of the Father and his love, the new Adam makes humans clear to themselves and gives them insight to their high calling" (*RH*, 8).

The emphasis shifts clearly from a natural law and/or a sociological understanding to a theological conception, which was also present earlier, but now is placed completely in the center: "The church receives the meaning for humans from the divine revelation" (*CA*, 55). By this the contribution of the social sciences is not denied, but rather put into perspective: "The social sciences and philosophy help to affirm the central place of humans in society and to enable them to understand themselves better as social beings." But only faith reveals to them completely their full identity and the social doctrine of the Church uses exactly this as its starting-point. While it uses all contributions of science and philosophy, it plans to promote people on the road to salvation (*CA*, 54). He calls Christian anthropology "a chapter of theology" and according to him the social doctrine belongs "to the area of theology and especially moral theology" (*CA*, 55) for the same reasons.

Now this preference for theology is not purely a theoretical matter, because for John Paul II this also has practical implications. Moreover, his "doctrine" is characterized by a widening of the perspective from theory to engaged practice, from a moralizing language to the testifying language game of the Gospel itself without fading into a naive evangelism without the mediation of ethical reason (Nothelle-Wildfeuer, 1991, 782).

In this respect the political theologian Peter Eicher regards the encyclical *Dives in misericordia* primarily as a turning-point (Eicher, 1982, 84). According to him, in this the church becomes visible by presenting itself first as a reformed community which gives evidence of Christ's Gospel in the world. Without agreeing with the radical conclusions of Eicher, one can establish indeed that John Paul II openly pleads in *Dives in misericordia* for a "complete and inner transformation (of the church) in the spirit of love of one's neighbors" (*DM*, 14). From this practice of love, which is founded in a radical conversion to Jesus Christ, the church must "draw deeper spiritual forces, which determine the order of justice themselves" (*DM*, 12). For the church community this means that its social ethics may not be an informal preaching design. In his speech *Salvador de Bahia*

(Brazil, July 6, 1980), John Paul II explained that the experience of love demands that the believers "continually convert themselves, revise personal positions... in order to expose fruitless prejudices and to discover the personal mistakes in order to open oneself to the orders of a formed consciousness... ." Converting oneself means "opening one's heart and spirit so that justice, love, and the respect for human dignity and destiny penetrate through into thinking and inspire actions."

This unmistakable plea for a radical conversion to a "lived faith," to an "experienced faith," and for an integral humanistic engagement on account of the church community is also strongly present in the encyclical *Centesimus annus*, where John Paul II unmistakably insinuates that the social message of the Gospels must not be regarded as a theory, "but above all else as a foundation and motive for action" (*CA*, 57) and he adds immediately to this: "The church is conscious more than ever that its social message shall be more credible from the witness of actions than through the connection and the internal logic of it" (*CA*, 57).

This emphasis on the "testimony" of the members of the church community is also one of the points of attention in the encyclical *Veritatis splendor*, where repeatedly the importance of "martyrdom" is pointed to, a concept that refers to the testimony of the truth about humans and to the preparedness to give one's life for one's dignity. For John Paul II, this is a task for all believers: "Even though martyrdom represents the high point of the testimony to moral truth, to which relatively few can be called, there exists nevertheless a consistent witness which all Christians daily must be prepared even at the cost of suffering and heavy sacrifices" (*VS*, 93).

Solidarity gets a new meaning in the framework of this radicalizing and theologizing of the social doctrine. Its meaning is described in detail, especially in *Sollicitudo rei socialis.*

In the first place, solidarity is considered as the moral answer to the actual global interdependence, as it was described in *Populorum progressio.* The actual "interdependence," namely the mutual dependence, understood as a system that determines the relations in the current world in its economic, cultural, political, and religious elements, calls on the necessity of a solidarity that takes interdependence seriously, "transforms [this] into consciousness," and gives it in this way a moral character (*SRS*, 38). "The mutual dependence must be transformed into solidarity based on the principle that all goods are destined for all" (*SRS*, 39). Solidarity is an ethical task, which demands the "fixed and tenacious decision" in order to direct actions on all levels to the common good, which necessarily implies a redistribution of the goods of the world (*CA*, 39), and thus also of labor and property (*CA*, 43). The object of solidarity can be a person, a people, or a nation. Subsequently, this ethical vision of solidarity is radicalized theologically. As "Christian virtue" solidarity prompts a human to "transcend oneself and to accept the specific Christian dimensions of complete unselfishness, forgiving, and reconciliation." According to John Paul II, the fellow human being should not be seen solely as a human being with equal rights, but also as "the living image of God the Father whose freedom is purchased by the blood of Jesus Christ and is placed under the lasting influence of the Holy Spirit." This particular solidarity with one's fellow human being as image of the Trinitarian God is immediately connected with the already mentioned demands of self-sacrifice: One must "be prepared for sacrifice, even the highest sacrifice, *giving one's life for one's brothers*" (*SRS*, 40 and 38).

In addition, the interpretation of solidarity as the virtue that founds the unity amongst people and the model of the divine Trinity is important from a theological point of view: "This highest model of unity, which is a reflection of the internal life of God who is one in three persons, is the model that we, Christians, refer to with the word *communio*." In the light of this, solidarity becomes a task of the church as "sacrament" of salvation.

John Paul II also greatly emphasizes the meaning of solidarity as a faithful answer to the "sinful structures" (*CA*, 38 and 39): "The 'evil mechanisms' and 'structures of sin'... can be overcome only through the exercise of the human and Christian solidarity to which the Church calls us and which she tirelessly promotes" (*SRS*, 40).

Immediately it appears that the theological foundation does not lead to a spiritualizing of the social doctrine, because John Paul II does not delay in connecting it also with the "choice or love preference for the poor" (*SRS*, 48, 42, 39) rediscovered in the liberation theology. This is for him an "option or special form of priority in exercising Christian love, to which the whole tradition of the Church bears witness..." and this is "also applicable to our social responsibility and therefore to our lives, and to the decisions and the use of the goods, which must be made in a logical way" (*SRS*, 42). For John Paul II this option for the poor is so important that he does not delay in commiting the whole church community to it.

In *Sollicitudo rei socialis* he explains: "By virtue of her own evangelical obligation, the Church feels summoned to stay on the side of the masses of the poor, to discern the justice of what they demand, and to contribute to meeting this demand, without losing sight of the well-being of the groups in the framework of the common good (*SRS*, 39). In *Centesimus annus* he adds to this: "To those who now search a new and authentic praxis and theory of liberation, the Church offers not only her social doctrine and in general her instruction about the human person who is redeemed by Christ, but also her concrete commitment and help for fighting marginalization and suffering" (*CA*, 26). With that he warns not to regard this solidarity with the poor exclusively as a deed of love. The love for people, in the first place for poor humans, should after all receive form "by the promotion of justice."

An important detail which needs to be added here is that John Paul II speaks not only of a solidarity to the poor, but also of a solidarity of the poor amongst themselves.

This point of view is already present in *Laborem exercens*, where he defends the solidarity of the workers and the right to labor unions:

> Movements of solidarity in the sphere of work—a solidarity that must never mean being closed to dialogue and collaboration with others— can be necessary also with reference to the condition of social groups that were not previously included in such movements, but which in changing social systems and conditions of living are undergoing what is in effect 'proletarianization' or which actually already find themselves in a 'proletariat' situation, one which, even if not yet given that name, in fact deserves it (*LE*, 8).

The right to rise up in solidarity for just demands is recognized even more expressly in *Centesimus annus* where John Paul II, in spite of his dismissal of class-conflict and precisely in this context, indicates that "the positive role of conflict" must be acknowledged, "if it has the form of fighting for social justice" (*CA*, 14). Poor people or workers may resist an economic system "in the sense of a method which insures the absolute supremacy of capital, of the possession of the means of production, and of land, over the free subjectivity of people's work." In this respect he pleads for the creation of a "society of free work, of enterprise, and of employee participation" (*CA*, 35).

In conclusion, John Paul II actualized solidarity by connecting it to "ecological care" (*SRS*, 26). In his message on the celebration of the World Peace Day of January 1990, he explained that he drew attention to "the urgent moral necessity of a new solidarity"... and in imitation of Francis he pleads for "an authentic and total respect for the wholeness of the creation." According to him, "the respect for life and for human dignity" contains "also the respect and the care for creation, which is summoned together with humans to glorify God." The new solidarity implies that "states must show themselves to be constantly more united and complimentary in order to stimulate the development of a naturally and a socially peaceful and wholesome environment." However, according to him, one cannot bring about a good ecological balance, if one "does not directly join battle against structural forms of poverty in the world." He regards poverty as one of the most important reasons for ecological disasters in the third world. Ecological care and social justice may not be played against each other.

3.2 Subsidiarity

Together with the great attention he spends on solidarity, John Paul II also develops a critical vision on the intervention of the state. In this manner, the previously mentioned negative aspect of the subsidiarity principle comes to the foreground.

With his experience of the "real socialism" in the back of his mind, he warns that the underestimation of the subsidiarity principle and of the right to economic initiative leads to serious social problems (*SRS*, 15): there exists a slavish dependence on the (state) bureaucracy that is as faulty as the traditional dependence of the workers-proletarians on the nineteenth-century capitalism.

He applies this not only to the communistic regimes. Especially in *Centesimus annus*, he works this out further in relation to the welfare state after the fall of the Berlin wall: "Malfunctions and defects in the social assistance state come forth from an inadequate conception about the tasks of the state. Here again the principle of subsidiarity must be respected..." (*CA*, 48). In spite of the fact that he does not ignore the positive aspects of a system of social security, he imposes a negative accent: "By directly interfering with and taking away responsibility from the society, the social assistance state brings about the loss of human energy and the exaggerated increase of governmental apparatus, which are ruled more by bureaucratic ways of thinking than by the concern to serve their clients, with an enormous growth of expenditures" (*CA*, 48).

As an alternative, he places a restoration of the subjectivity of the society with volunteer work, efforts for solidarity and love, and the bringing into existence of "specific networks of solidarity" by means of "other intermediary communities" (*CA*, 49). Without ignoring its value—more appreciation is necessary for the dynamics of the middle ground between individual and state—one can ask oneself if this reversion to spontaneous "love and solidarity" will be capable of actualizing in a satisfactory manner in a complex industrial society the demands of "social justice" (Schokkaert, 1992, 75). Perhaps a critical rereading of *Quadragesimo anno* can be of some help.

Consulted literature

Baum, Gregory, Ellsberg, Rober, *The Logic of Solidarity. Commentaries on Pope John Paul II's Encyclical "On Social Concern"*: New York, 1989.

Calvez, Jean Yves, Perrin, Jacques, *The Church and Social Justice: The Social Teaching of the Popes from Leo XIII to Pius XII*, 1878-1958, Chicago, 1961.

Dorr, Donald, *Option for the Poor. A Hundred Years of Vatican Social Teaching.* Revised Edition, Dublin, 1992.

Eicher, Peter, "Er ist unser Friede. Von der Sicherheitsmoral zum Friedenszeugnis," in *Das Evangelium des Friedens. Christen und Aufrüstung*, red. Eicher, Peter, München, 1982, pp. 42-104.

Kluber, F., "Solidarismus," in *Katholisches Soziallexikon*, red. A. Klose, W. Mantl, V. Zsifkovits, Innsbruck, Graz, 1980, pp. 2574-2578.

Kondziela, J., "Solidaritätsprinzip," in *Katholisches Soziallexikon*, red. A. Klose, W. Mantl, V. Zsifkovits, Innsbruck, Graz, 1980, pp. 2578-2585.

McCormick, Richard A., "*Laborem Exercens* and Social Morality," in C. Curran, R. A. McCormick, *Official Catholic Social Teaching* (Readings in Moral Theology, 5), New York, 1986, pp. 219-232.

Nothelle-Wildfeuer, Ursula, *Duplex ordo cognitionis. Zur systematischen Grundlegung einer Katholischen Soziallehre im Anspruch von Philosophie und Theologie*, Paderborn, 1991.

Schokkaert, Eric, "*Centesimus annus* en de verzorgingsstaat," in: L. Van Liederkerke, J. Verstraeten, *Naar een samenleving met een menselijk gelaat. Kritische beschouwingen over de encycliek "Centesimus annus"*: Leuven, Amersfoort, 1992, pp. 61-75.

Soria, Carlos, "Elementos para una comprension de la doctrina social: problemas epistemologicos y theologicos," in: *Rerum novarum, Laborem Exercens 2000*, Rome, 1982, pp. 115-136.

Utz, Arthur-Fridolin, *Sozialethik. Mit internationaler Bibliographie. 1 Teil: Die Prinzipien der Gesellschaftslehre* (Sammlung Politeia, X), Heidelburg, Leuven, 1958.

Von Nell-Breuning, Oswald, "The Drafting of *Quadragesimo Anno*," in: C. E. Curran, R. A. McCormick, *Official Catholic Social Teaching* (Readings in Moral Theology, 5), New York, 1986, pp. 60-68.

Id., *Soziale Sicherheit? Zu Grundfragen der Sozialordnung aus christlicher Verantwortung*, Freiburg, Basel, Wien, 1979.

Verstraeten, Johan, *Sollicitudo rei socialis. Een niewe stap in de ontwikkeling van de sociale leer van de Kerk*, Leuven, 1988.

Id., "De sociale leer van de Katholieke Kerk en de "Derde Weg," in *Metafysiek en engagement. Een personalistische visie op gemeenschap en economie*, red. L. Bouckaert and G. Bouckaert , Leuven, Amersfoort, 1992, pp. 51-63.

Walgraeve, Jan Hendrik, "Sociaalethische beginselen," in *Welvaart, welzijn en geluk. Een katholiek uitzicht op de Nederlandse samenleving*, Hilversum, 1960, pp. 107-128.

Zsifkovits, Valentin, "Subsidiaritätsprinzip," in *Katholisches Soziallexikon*, red. A. Klose, W. Mantl, V. Zsifkovits, Innsbruck, Graz, 1980, pp. 2994-3000.

List of the used abbreviations:

QA Quadragesimo anno
MM Mater et magistra
PT Pacem in terris
PP Populorum progressio
RH Redemptor hominis
LE Laborem exercens
SRS Sollicitudo rei socialis
CA Centesimus Annus
VS Veritatis splendor
LC Libertatis conscientia

9
Participation in Historical Perspective

Professor Emeritus Dr. E. De Jonghe

1. The concept *participation* with *common good, solidarity,* and *subsidiarity* forms one of the central concepts of Catholic social doctrine as they are presented in the *Guidelines of the Congregation for the Catholic Education.*

In the document mentioned above, the term participation is used to indicate that one of the ways to do justice to someone entails involving the person with communal tasks with which he or she can assume responsibility. This is definitely the case, according to the *Guidelines,* if capital and labor work together in various enterprises and if between the state and the individual intermediary bodies emerge, in which employers and employees can take part in communal decision-making processes.[272]

We read further that the demand for social justice is met through participation. The just, fitting, and responsible participation by all parts of the society in the development of social, political, economic, and cultural life is the most certain way to come to a new society. The church will therefore not refrain from restating this principle, because it is so beneficial to the quality of the life of people and community. Participation, the text says, is also a deep desire of humans to express their freedom and skill in the world of science and technology, and of work and political decision-making.[273]

2. One can only situate these statements of the *Guidelines* in the context of Catholic social doctrine when one verifies via the document's footnotes, those documents of the tradition to which an appeal is made. With further investigation these footnotes appear to be about texts especially over the past thirty years, approximately from 1960, which have shed light on the term participation.

Then the transition from political to social and economic democracy appeared as an apparent and gradual process which was naturally accepted. People spoke of a ubiquitous democratization process. Democratization became a battle-cry which was used without much reflection "in and out of season." It was the student revolt of the late 1960's that lead to further discussions. In some groups, participation was then contrasted with a situation of subordination, manipulation, tutelage, and systematism. There lingers a type of emancipatory concept of freedom that searches an expression in new social forms characterized by participation. Since then, forms of participation in schools, universities, parishes and dioceses, families, and a number of groups have developed, with a great diversity in dialogical structures in the execution of responsibilities, although the existing forms of participation and involvement in business developed in their own ways.

Octogesima adveniens (May 14, 1971) of Paul VI reflects the discussions of its day. We read that the demand for the acknowledgment of freedom and human dignity will manifest itself in the coming years in primarily two ways: more equality among the people and the right to employee participation. According to Paul VI, this shall lead to a fundamental democratization of society. This shall happen on a much broader level than in the area of the purely political democracy. Along with these texts of Paul VI, a discussion about the eventual interecclesiastical democracy developed. In this regard, passages were cited from *Lumen Gentium,* the decree about the lay apostolate *Apostolicam Actuositatem,* and the document *Justitia in mundo* of the Italian bishop conference (1971). However, later papal and other ecclesiastical documents are concerned primarily about employee participation on political and economic levels. In the terms of the *Guidelines* "just, fitting, and reliable forms of participation and participating decision-making" are proposed.[274] "Laborers and farmers seek not only to provide for the necessities of life but to develop the gifts of their personality by their labors, and indeed to take part in regulating economic, social, political, and cultural life," according to *Gaudium et spes,* n. 9. The *Guidelines* can also say that participation "holds a very prominent place in the recent development of the Catholic social doctrine" (n. 40).

3. We will first investigate what is said in the recent texts about political particiation. Here we shall not go into particulars, because these will not sound very new for someone who lives in a democratic form of government. In recent ecclesiastical documents, one finds established—by the highest ecclesiastical authority—a number of principles which, for an important part of the world population, are still greatly problematic or new.

3.1 In *Pacem in terris* (1963), John XXIII recalls that, according to ecclesiastical doctrine, the foundation of all authority is not the decision of the majority, but rather the will of God. From the consciousness of their dignity, people wish to take part in the processes of political decision making. This assumes that the various ways of participating are secured in a constitution which acknowledges the right of the citizens to vote and which points out the way in which the people are represented. Furthermore, the separation of powers determines and acknowledges fundamental human rights which must be respected by the legislative, executive, and judicial powers.[275]

3.2 Paul VI, who calls the desire for equality and participation a fundamental aspiration of civilized and informed humans and an expression of their freedom and dignity, sees a better formulation of human rights as a guarantee for their acknowledgment. This can best happen in a democratic society that can be built up with the contribution of the diverse ideological and pragmatic trends according to different models. *Octogesima adveniens* (1971) not only invites Christians, but even says that it is their duty to work together for a realization of a democratic political order.[276] These statements of the Church about democracy are important. Nonetheless, it is in the footnotes of the *Guidelines* that this becomes apparent in the documents of the Congregation for Catholic Education. By summarizing a number of central words in that document one can find all the important themes of the ecclesiastical state doctrine, because they are mentioned together with the problems of the relation between church and state in different encyclicals.[277] We recall the encyclical *Immortale Dei* of 1885, in which Leo XIII described the sovereignty and the personal goal of church and state; and in *Quadragesimo anno* (1931) in which the Church established its duty and its right to proclaim its doctrine on all questions that touched the moral law, particularly as this is related to social and economic life (n. 41 and n. 42). It must certainly be stated that it was Pius XII who connected the future of democracy to the acknowledgment of human rights in his important Christmas addresses of 1942 and 1944. These documents occupy a classical place in Catholic social doctrine and were subsequently endorsed and instituted by John XXIII in 1963 in *Pacem in terris*. John Paul II has finally connected the development of poor countries and other countries with the bringing into existence of a democratic state governments.[278]

4. The meaning of participation on the social and economic level occupies an important place in the sources, as these are mentioned in the footnotes of the *Guidelines.* Here the present concern is only about texts published between 1961 and 1986. *Centesimus annus* (1991) is not taken into account, because this encyclical appeared in August 1989 in the English version of *Osservatore Romano* and thus only after these *Guidelines* of December 1988. Important texts from before 1960 were not mentioned.

4.1 The first text that belongs to the specified period of the *Guidelines* is *Mater et magistra* of 1961. This stands closest to the discussions that were held in 1949-55 in Germany *in economicis.* We shall devote the necessary attention to this, because during this period both the foundations of employee participation were investigated and important participation attempts were made in Western Europe.

We read in *Mater et magistra* that John XXIII and his predecessors are convinced that the striving of workers to participate in the life of enterprises where they are employed is a just striving. Furthermore, the pope says that the nature and the scope of this participation is difficult to establish in rules and laws, because this depends on the condition of each individual enterprise; well then this condition is not ubiquitously equal, and it changes, sometimes suddenly and radically even within the same enterprise. Still, the pope means "that employees should have an active part in the affairs of the enterprise for which they work." Not unimportant are the concluding observations that in each case one must strive "to give to the enterprise its character of a true human fellowship, which penetrates with its spirit the mutual relations and the different functions and services." The encyclical clarifies that "that mutual relations supposes respect, appreciation, benevolence, loyal, active, and unified working together between all those who fulfill a function in the enterprise." This supposes then again, according to John XXIII, that the workers make their wishes known, and that their cooperation must be asked for where it involves the well-functioning and the expansion of the enterprise. However, this may not prevent a powerful central leadership from continuing even if it lowers the workers to executors of orders who are incapable of self-government, who cannot express their own wishes and experiences, and who must passively undergo the decisions of others with respect to their labor. John XXIII cites Pius XII, who explained in 1956 that humans in their economic and social functions should not be completely dependent on the will of

others. John XXIII is finally of the opinion that within any enterprise greater responsibility should be granted to the modern workers,
who are better schooled and educated than their predecessors.[279]

In no single more recent text of the highest doctrinal authority is
the theme of economic participation treated as comprehensively. We
shall attempt to explain it.

4.2 A few years after *Mater et magistra* (1961), *Gaudium et spes*
also spoke about the participation "of free and autonomous people
in businesses." People must, in a subsequently to be determined and
efficient manner, be able to take part in policy decisions, but with
the restriction that they must necessarily be in harmony with management. *Gaudium et spes* is of the opinion that a form of participation similar to that mentioned in *Quadragesimo anno*, texts of Pius
XII, and *Mater et magistra*, "should be encouraged." *Gaudium et spes*
adds to this the consideration that decisions about the business politics, which can have often far reaching consequences for the workers
and their families and are not always limited to the business where
the workers work, are made, but that it is desirable that the workers
participate in the decision making on a higher level, be it personally,
or be it via their representatives. In addition to this, it is noted that
workers can found free labor unions which represent them in order
to come in this manner to a just government of economic life. Through
such a participation, workers will in due time become even more
conscious of their own responsibility.[280]

4.3 John Paul II writes in *Laborem exercens* (1987) only briefly about
participation. According to him, there must be in the light "of what
the experts say of Catholic social doctrine, an important meaning
attached to the proposals concerning the joint ownership of the means
of production, the shares of the workers in the profit or participation
of the management of the business." He remarks that "no matter
what one decides about this, the acknowledgment of the right position of the worker in the production process demands adjustments
regarding the right to ownership of the means of production." Here
another reference is made to *Gaudium et spes* and even to *Quadragesimo
anno*.[281]

4.4 It is in a non-papal document that started from the Congregation for the Doctrine of the Faith, namely the *Instruction about Christian freedom and liberation* (1986), that one finds the strongest expression from this period concerning participation. In addition to

maintaining that wages are the basis for all forms of material, social, and cultural development of workers and their families and that work is an expression of personality, this document argues that human dignity is the criterion to judge the situation of the employees. *Libertatis conscientia* concludes "that participation is a necessity which beyond just sharing in the fruits of work must accept a true communal dimension on the level of projects, businesses, and responsibilities."[282]

4.5 The idea of participation is also present in the letter of the American bishops *Economic Justice for All* (November 18, 1986). Chapter 4 bears the title *A New American Experiment: Partnership for the Public Good.* After recognizing the fatal consequences of competition for family life and the situation of economic weaknesses, the letter urges and calls for participatory structures—even if first in an experimental manner—to bring into existence a better cooperation in economic life. The letter states that all groups, in the language of the American "business ethics," are called "shareholders" and "stakeholders" and that all have an interest in the business and must work together to bring a flowering business life into existence. What this new "partnership" must contain is clarified by a summary of a whole series of possible initiatives and measures. We state: the better organization of the workplace (safety and hygiene), sharing of profits, worker shareholdings, participation in the administration of the enterprise (a reference is made to *Mater et magistra*), acknowledgement of the role of labor unions, consultation of the workers with important decisions for the business (closings, mergers, lay-offs) and the re-evaluation of the role of the shareholders relative to managers.[283]

4.6 Finally, there is *Centesimus annus* (1991), a text in which the elements of what has been called the social market economy are treated rather positively. The alternative for capitalism, the pope says, is not socialism but rather "a society of free work, business, and employee participation."[284] A little further on, John Paul II points out that the Church has no models to offer, but rather that it in its social doctrine holds forth a number of desired orientations. Clearly it establishes that the rightfulness of workers' efforts to come to justice in their dignity as humans, through more room for participation in the life of the business among other things, so that, while they work together with others and under the direction of others, they can work for themselves in a certain sense through the efforts of their intelligence and freedom.[285]

5. It is remarkable that the legitimization of employee participation is so brief in the documents of the last thirty years and it is sometimes very simply stated that an aspiration to employee participation exists. The striving of the workers to participate in the life or the administration of the business is called, in *Mater et magistra*, a rightful striving. In *Gaudium et spes*, it is said that participation "must be encouraged." In *Laborem exercens*, we read "that a particular meaning" must be attached to the participation of workers in the administration. The *Instruction Concerning Christian Liberation and Freedom* (1986) acknowledges as well participation to be "a necessity." *Centesimus annus* endorses and acknowledges the efforts of workers to "receive a larger participation in the life of the business." The letter of the American bishops points in the direction of "experimentation" in this area.

6. What are the causes of this brief treatment and limited legitimization in the documents of the last thirty years? It appears to me that the remarkable reserve and the nuancing with which participation is treated can be attributed to three factors: 1) the discussion concerning the basis in justice of the claims to participation after the explanation of the conference in Bochum, Germany, and what followed it; 2) the fact that in all of Western Europe different forms of participation are actualized on the socio-economic level; and 3) the fact that participation on the socio-economic level in large parts of the world, where the political and social participation had not yet been actualized, is not a priority.

We shall not discuss the last factor, because it is a rather plausible hypothesis. However, we must discuss the "Bochum" question and the subsequent attempts to legitimize the economic participation in Catholic circles. Finally, we will treat a few actual concrete models.

6.1 First, something about the most important phases of the Bochum matter must be stated. Pius XI described the employment contract in *Quadragesimo anno* as a legitimate means to regulate the relations between employer and employee and dismissed the theorem of those who were of the opinion that it must be replaced by a social contract. He also thought that the labor contract could be moderated by elements derived from this last type of agreement.[286] Otherwise, more attention was directed in this encyclical to the reconstruction of the social-economic order by the rise of the business organizations, in which, as one assumed, the workers would be involved.[287] In September 1944, Pius XII held a radio address in which he treated the future new social order and in which he explained, among other things, that "where large businesses would appear to be more productive, they must offer the possibility to moderate labor contracts by elements of the social contract." A few lines before the pope had spoken with sympathy about small enterprises.[288] In May 1949, the pope held an address for the *Union internationale des associations des patrons catholiques,* in which he fought the idea that every business must be regarded as a "community" from which one would then derive that because of distributive justice each would have a right to a part of the business' property and profits.[289] On September 4, 1949, the same year, a motion was approved by the *Deutsche Katholikentag* in Bochum which stated "that Catholic employers and employees agreed to acknowledge the participation (Mitbestimmung) by all coworkers of an enterprise with relation to social, economic, and personnel affairs, was a natural law in correspondence to the order willed by God, with, as a corollary, that all therein would carry their responsibility." It was asked whether this right would be acknowledged in legislation.[290]

Regarding the character of this participation concerning natural law, this statement was incorrect and not in correspondence with the doctrine of *Quadragesimo anno.* A few weeks later, it was corrected by an explanation of Cardinal Frings who noted that one only wanted to say with the use of the word "natural law" in connection with the "Mitbestimmung" that it was about a matter that was so self-explanatory that one could no longer resist it in the current state of affairs. According to him, one must make the distinction between the social, economic, and personal areas and one must not give to the "Mitbestimmung" the same meaning in these three areas. The Cardinal concluded that now the way had been indicated, but it would still be a long journey. Doubts were ended by a letter of Cardinal Montini on September 21, 1952, to the Social Week of Italy, in which he explained that fundamentally one cannot speak about a natural law with relation to co-administration. This does not prevent the entrepreneur, the Cardinal writes, from letting the workers participate in one way or another in the administration of the enterprise, and this does not prevent the state from giving to the employees via a specific legislation the possibility to participate in the diverse affairs that belong to the sphere of administration of the enterprise... especially in the enterprises where anonymous capital left to itself can cause a disadvantage to the community.

Msgr. Montini based his statement on the speech of Pius XII of September 1, 1944, which we already have mentioned, held on the occasion of the fifth anniversary of the beginning of the war, in which he then stated, in imitation of *Quadragesimo anno,* that large enterprises must offer the possibility to modify the labor contract with elements of the social contract. Msgr. Montini also mentioned the large enterprises whose business administration can be harmful for the common good. In this regard, he does not mean the enterprises that have kept a human dimension among, for example, those like traditional business, the production cooperative, and the family farm.[291]

6.2 We can establish that in practice, since around 1950, and primarily in Western Europe, already a whole road was laid out in the direction of the legal obligation for the introduction of employee participation in businesses. In Catholic circles, the so-called natural law argument was no longer used in favor of co-administration. Instead, there came a personalistic vision of which we find an example in the texts of Fr. O. von Nell-Breuning, S. J., which he published when the debate was still raging in Germany. He established two noticeable justifications in order to support the claim of the workers to employee participation. O. von Nell-Breuning first rejects utility as the foundation of the demand for employee participation. He nevertheless accepts that it is possible that participation would also improve the material position of the worker in an enterprise. According to him, the first and foremost argument is that the workers who can participate in forms of co-administration no longer will be used as a pure means of production like raw materials, half-spent products, machines, and fossil fuels. It is important that they as humans will have the opportunity to develop their personalities better. From this follows the being and the size of "the naturally undeniable right to co-administration." Working people have the right not to be treated as a pure receiver of orders, a pure executor who can be replaced with a machine as soon as it is cheaper to do so. If it is inevitable that people must perform spiritually draining work then this should be regarded as the cost of work. However, demanding this from them when avoidable is unjust. Reducing humans to such work, concluded von Nell-Breuning, is a crime. From this comes the demand to acknowledge workers in the business as people gifted with understanding and a sense of responsibility.[292]

A second series of considerations of von Nell-Breuning starts from establishing "that workers in their business do not want to be living machines, but they as humans are valued in their human dignity." This opinion implies, according to von Nell-Breuning, that not only do they want to be treated in a dignified manner, but also they want to play a full-fledged role in the enterprise according to their capacity and competence. They do not want to be a simple subject, but want to face the employer as sensible and responsible humans and be treated as such, not as immature children. In short, they want to be taken "au sérieux." If they want to develop to the fullest in the enterprise according to their professional and intellectual gifts, then responsibility must be given to them in the organization of their work in a way that is reconciliable with the demands of a businesslike and good business administration. The employees want to speak person to person with the administration and not be patronized with the help of psychotechnical methods or used as a lab rat for work and time studies; one must search for fitting forms of employee participation.[293]

This predominantly anthropological and socio-ethical argumentation can naturally be integrated in the theological vision of John Paul II who has characterized work in the first place as a cooperation in God's creation plan—a very large and broad task, because working people can offer not only a physical, but also an intellectual contribution.

Opposite and parallel to this argument in favor of co-administration, a more negative judicial argumentation was developed. This actually had a starting point in *Rerum novarum* and *Quadragesimo anno* themselves, where first and foremost the right—be it of physical people, be it of ficticious people—of the personal owner to ascribe to the shareholders of a corporation or their authorized agents the exercising or disposition of the rights of administration, and this in an exclusive manner. It is the private owner of the enterprise who is qualified to make decisions that comprise the business politics of the enterprise. That person alone can decide whether or not he or she shall permit forms of employee participation and if these are reconcilable with the objectives of the business. Whether the labor contract will be modified by elements of the social contract (*Quadragesimo anno*), depends on him or her alone. The ecclesiastical doctrine has always preached that the wage structure, if it includes an adequate compensation for work and takes into account familial duties of the employee, is not unjust. This all, the jurists say, can be found clearly in *Rerum novarum* and *Quadragesimo anno*.

The Deutsche Gewerkschaftsbund (German Federation of Labor) has answered this type of argument with an extensive judicial note in which it is carefully determined how in a publicly limited company (Inc.)—which it assumes manages a large business—the problem of property rights is highlighted. In this document, the distinction is made between ownership rights (property rights) and the right to management as it is exercised by the different parties. According to this note, the following are included as property rights (property in the strictest sense): a) the ownership of the shares; b) the right to dividends; c) the right, upon liquidation, to a part of the social property; d) the eventual "right to claim," the claim that with the distribution of new shares a right of priority is given to the holders of the original shares. To the right of administration belong: a) the right to participation in the general meeting of shareholders; b) voting rights in the general meeting; c) the right to certain business economic information; d) the right to approve or disapprove the balance sheet and to discharge the board of directors. Subsequently, the difference in the way in which the shareholders own property rights, on the one hand, and the administration rights on the other, are pointed out.

The above-mentioned property rights especially belong to the shareholders. Administration rights fall individually to each shareholder, but this only receives meaning through an arithmetic sum, in other words, by means of a counting in the general meeting. It is the general meeting of the shareholders, an electoral college, that possesses all rights in principle. It decides about the statutes, it is the mandator against the administrators and governors and it makes a number of important decisions with respect to business politics of the enterprise, capital increases or decreases, mergers, discharging of administrators, approving of the balance sheet, and the calculation of profits and losses. The note of the Deutsche Gewerkschaftsbund is of the opinion that it is of the greatest importance to point out that the individual, isolated shareholder exercises only a right of co-administration, which has only a small importance in many instances. Only the combining of a large pack of shares in one hand gives a real power in the general meeting. One notices the consequences of this immediately, when one sees that the banks, institutional investors (e. g. insurance companies), or holding-companies are those that control the power in many public limited companies.

The note acknowledges that by introducing the right of co-administration by the workers, the rights of administration of the general meeting become rather limited. It must also choose a number of administrators from the workers. However, the rights of the individual shareholders are only slightly touched by this. The individual shareholder possesses only a limited right to co-administration. The influence of the "power groups" comes to stand under a new supervision.

The goal of the note of the Deutsche Gewerkschaftsbund is to prove that the co-administration of workers in the community gives a better control over the anonymous economic powers. Otherwise, it starts from the fact that the presence of delegates from the workers in the administration of the enterprise does not now naturally mean that more economically unfavorable business decisions shall be made.

A few years before, the well-known French jurist Georges Ripert, in his *Aspects juridiques du capitalisme moderne*, pointed to the confusion that had been caused by legislation concerning share-corporations where the public limited company was made an equal corporate body with natural bodies. The liberal legislation of the nineteenth century intended to strengthen capitalism through this equalization by making possible a reference to natural law, and to provide the protection of the rights of the corporate body with the same basis as those of the natural body. In the evolution of capitalism this corporate body has become the real "*homo economicus*," striving after profit and economic power.[294]

Some, building on *Quadragesimo anno* where there is talk of the "repairing of the social order" and of social politics in the framework of a business organization, where the employees would exercise co-administration on the level of the business branch and of the national economy, were of the opinion that all this material was situated on the level of social justice. This implied then that the problems of co-administration must be treated on the level of national administration and it was a development belonging to the realm of politics. This led to different initiatives, only in reference to Europe, and to publications about co-administration that can fill a small law library.

Prior to giving a short summary of the actual judicial situation, mention should be made of yet another form of argument in favor of co-administration that, along with others, emerged in Holland and in France at a certain time. This argument was developed in Holland by Professor J.J.M. Van der Ven (Tilburg), who began with the nature, goal, and function of business. According to him, an enterprise is to be regarded as a:

> …whole of people, who, regardless of judicial situation, are summoned to set themselves to a communal human activity, i.e., work, and through that have an environment and an objective goal, which in effect, both sociologically and social psychologically binds them to a community (irrespective of the many mutually combatant and occasionally tension-giving forces). The well-being of that community demands then

the effort and the understanding of the responsibility of everyone, no matter how small the contribution of some might be. In a western society, someone who plays a role in a community may at least get advice concerning the reasons for actions and behaviors that the community expects from him or her.

On this basis, one can establish, according to Van der Ven, a right to co-administration.[295] J.Y. Calvez also concluded that such a type of reasoning was applicable in France, and is sufficient to lead to the conclusion that an enterprise would have to come into existence in the form of a social or association contract. Pius XII sometimes nevertheless discussed an enterprise as a "communauté de travail," where the employers have still obligations to the employees other than those which merely flow forth from a labor contract.[296] O. von Nell-Breuning has investigated this possibility under the title *Über das Lohnarbeitsverhältnis hinaus* in 1982. Starting from the expression "Au delà du salaire," which one often encounters in the literature of French social Catholicism and which expresses the idea that a labor contract should be replaced by another relation, namely a type of association, he has come to the conclusion that this contract—complete with all the many possibilities that this participation can develop—gives the employee a safer position than when he or she, logically speaking, would have to accept some of the risk involved with the enterprise. Also, according to him, on the basis of and around the labor contract a business community can be built.[297]

7. When one limits oneself to specific cases promoting employee participation in German, Dutch, and Belgian legislation, then one must first recognize that the treatment of this theme is to be found in the discussions of the nineteenth century, and that after the war of 1914-1918, important legislative initiatives were taken. This happened under the influence of the role of the "soviets" or workers' councils from the Russian revolution. but the meaning, which this term theoretically had, was accepted only for a short time. Between the two world wars, the problem of business organization and of unemployment work politics dominated, as a result of the great crisis of 1929-32, in many countries. It is after World War II that the discussion about employee participation came to the foreground. From this came the organizing legislation during the last 30 years.

Undoubtedly, one of the most progressive countries in the area of participation was Germany. In the framework of the judicial statute of an enterprise (Unternehmensverfassung), a real business economic consultation (Mitbestimmung) developed. This happened through the introduction of worker delegates and even people who were named by the unions in the Administrative Council of the corporations (Aufsichtsrat) and named in the daily administration. This presence of workers in the Administrative Councils (Supervisory Boards) comprises one third of the members in businesses with less than 2000 workers and one half in businesses with more than 2000. In addition, there was the special regulation through which workers took part in the business economic management of coal, iron, and national companies, where the employers and employees had an equal number of members in the Administrative Council and this was chaired by an added and extra member. In the daily administration, the workers had their own labor director. Finally, in Germany what was called "the evolution from the monocratic structure to the democratic structure of business" took place. Economic freedom of property was colored by the "Sozialstaatsgedanke" and on the basis of this the right to regular information and the raising of issues was granted. This happened via works of councils in all enterprises where at least five employees were entitled to vote and three were eligible for election. We seem to have here minimum and maximum ideals in comparison to the organization of employee participation in different European countries.[298]

Concerning the competence of a work council and the scope of employee participation there where the presence of the employees is absent from business economic administrative bodies, one can find the following in the countries in the European community in enterprises with three to more than two thousand employees (in Belgium at least fifty, in Holland at least one hundred): there exists an obligation to form a work council; work councils consist of an equal number of representatives of employees and employers, and are chaired by the head of a company or his or her representative; and these councils meet at established times and the members are appointed according to democratic procedures. The extensive right to social and business economic information, which is periodically exercised, is indeed remarkable: it concerns the flow of business in the undertaking, productivity, the balance, the profit and loss calculation, the annual reports, etc. All financial documents must be verified by certified public accountants. In addition, there exists an extensive advisory right: about terms of employment and work output, the received business economic information, workplace regulations, job qualifications, and vacation regulations. Finally, works councils have advisory powers or complete administrative powers over the social provisions created by the business for its personnel. Here one must add that in different countries the unions—via collective agreements, committees having equal representation, and participation in the processes of business organization and of the administration of the institutes that run the social security (the social funds)—exercise an important participatory function in bringing into existence social and economic politics on the national level. Last, but not least, in most countries of Western Europe, there exist in businesses so-called union delegations which enjoy a particularly protected charter in the business, through which it can enter into discussions with the business administration and directly be to the advantage of the workers.[299]

This development in Western Europe helps one to understand why the documents of Catholic social doctrine of the last thirty years speak in rather general terms about participation, especially on the socioeconomic level. So much was already actualized via legal roads that the current task is to make the existing maximum come to justice from the perspective of a true cooperation between employers and employees. Now, there even exists a legal model for the European Union, developed by the European communities, which provides different modalities of participation. It is not possible that the documents of the highest doctrinal authority would have gone futher than the establishment of principles; no models are given. Some models already are in use in different countries. Other countries can still develop their own systems on the basis of these principles. This is handed over to those who bear political responsibility in different countries.[300]

10
Catholic Social Teaching and American Society

Professor Fred Crosson

Forward

The title is not intended to suggest differences in the way that the principles of a century of papal teaching are understood, but rather in the way in which that teaching comes into view or is appropriated because of different social and economic conditions. Not only is the Church's vision of the meaning and supernatural destiny of human beings the same for every land, but its understanding of human life and of human society is rooted in the very nature of persons and communities as that nature can be discerned by reason. Catholic social doctrine is not based only on revelation, but also makes use of the insights accumulated over the long tradition of philosophical reflection.[301]

The language of that tradition is appropriated by the social encyclicals to articulate the moral teachings that they address to Catholics—and to the world—concerning issues of justice, freedom, and the common good of political society, just as theology has always appropriated philosophical language to assist its reflections. So we will begin by reviewing the language and conceptual framework in which the social doctrine of the Church has been formulated over the last century.

Before turning to that, it is worth noting that Catholic social teaching—which is generally agreed to have begun to be promulgated in its modern form with *Rerum novarum* (1891)—did not have a prominent role in the life of the American church until the Great Depression in the late 1920's and 1930's.[302] And since Catholics have always been a minority in America, when that teaching was taken up and proposed to the country at large as a guide to the goals of social justice that America should pursue, it was not surprising that the principles of that teaching should be presented not only as Catholic but as convergent with both American Constitutional traditions and the nature of justice (natural law).[303]

Moreover, the then strongly Catholic system of higher education, especially colleges and universities, incorporated the social teaching of the Church into curricula, even devoting whole courses to the subject in departments of economics, business, political science, philosophy and religion. So for a generation or so, the social doctrine of the Church was familiar to many Catholics and to a part, at least, of the wider public.

1. According to the first chapter of Genesis, we human beings were created as complementary creatures, as parts of a community, as male and female, because (as the second chapter adds) our good lies in not being alone, not being merely individuals. Human persons are meant to love and be loved, to share and to increase, and so to be images of God. Indeed a sign of that is that all of us are from birth members of a community, the community of a family.

And families themselves are members of a larger community of families, who also share in the tasks and the goods that are made possible by living together. (It takes a village to raise a child, as the saying has it.) It is not good for families to be alone: not only do we need the good of friendship that living together provides, but the sharing of different and complementary skills for providing other goods such as means of subsistence, tools (appliances), mutual defense, rituals and ceremonies, singing and dancing, and most important of all, a decision-making authority for deciding the patterns of our life together.

However that authority is constituted, its responsibility will be to direct the actions of everyone toward the shared good life that is common to all of the members of the group (whether it be a family or a community of familes), leaving to the individual (family member or family) to pursue those goods that are private, i.e. peculiar to the individual member or family. Of course the good that is common or communal is also a good for each of the parts of the community: it isn't as if the good life we achieve in common, together, were not the good of each individual member. It is called the common good (or communal good) because it cannot be adequately achieved by individuals, not because it isn't a good for individuals as well as for the group.

Three of the essential components of the human good we seek in common are, first, to facilitate the acquiring of the "necessities of life," of some standard of living; second, to be *with* one another, to live together; and third, to become better human beings, to learn—

by rules in the family and by laws in the social group—e.g., to treat others fairly, justly, to be honest, etc.

Because the common good[304] is the good of everybody in the group, and not just my personal good, it takes priority over my private good: it's wrong, selfish, for anyone (or any group) to put their own private good ahead of the good of everyone else in the community of which they are part. So even in the family, where there is a natural inequality between the roles and responsibilities of parents and children, it's wrong, unfair, unjust for either parent or child to put their own gratification ahead of what's good for everyone.

Any member of such a group,[305] by the very nature of being a part of a whole, has moral obligations toward the whole, toward the community. These obligations prescribe or restrict those actions of the individual that concern the good of the whole, and the traditional name for those obligations is justice. More precisely, we can say with St. Thomas Aquinas (who follows Aristotle here) that there is a species of justice that regulates what we owe to the communal or common good: call it "communal justice" or, since it is generally the laws that specify what the good member of the community (the good citizen) owes to the political community, call it "legal justice." [306] It prescribes what, as citizens, we owe to the community and it proscribes what is wrong to do to the community and its members. For example, it prescribes taxes and proscribes treason.

Conversely, the community owes something to its members, for example, protection from attack, the means necessary to participate in our common life, and formation in the practices and skills required for that participation. There is a species of justice that concerns what the community owes to its members, that regulates the distribution of, the various ways of sharing in, the component parts of our communal good. This second species of justice has been called "distributive justice," because it guides the actions of the community—normally the actions of the government , i.e., the decision-making authority for the community—in determining who shall receive what and how much. What is due to different members of the community may differ: for example, in a democracy children are not in justice due the right to vote, although they are in justice due the preparation that will enable them one day to exercise responsibly that right. Distributive justice discriminates between different individuals, it takes into account the different roles and kinds of persons—although unfair discrimination is opposed to distributive justice. So, not only are children under eighteen years of age not entitled to vote in the United States, neither are those convicted of a felony, or resident aliens even though they may have lived here all of their lives. And finally, there is a species of justice that guides what is due to the parts (individuals, families, groups, etc.) from other parts: fairness in exchange between buyer and seller, for example, or what restitution is required when a contract has been broken. This species of justice has been called "commutative justice," and unlike distributive justice it is no respecter of persons: whether the person is rich or poor, old or young, makes no difference to the requirement that exchange should be fair. Whether the purchaser is rich or poor, for example, deliberate overcharging is unjust.

Justice is thus the most encompassing of the components of the common good of a political society, and it is a central goal of the government, whatever form the organization of political authority may take. As James Madison wrote in *Federalist Papers* (No. 42), "Justice is the end of government. It is the end of civil society. It has ever been and ever will be pursued until it be obtained, or until liberty be lost in the pursuit."

2.I propose to review and comment on, in an American context, four principles of Catholic social teaching: the responsibility of civil society, and in particular of the the state (the government): first, to pursue the common good of justice by intervening in the economic sphere; second, to respect and foster the principle of subsidiarity; third, to acknowledge the right to religious liberty; fourth, to recognize and implement what is entailed in the solidarity of all human beings.

The first of these takes priority not only historically—it is the major focus of *Rerum novarum* (1891)—but also in terms of the harm for individuals and families that follows from the state's allowing a laissez-faire economy to go its own way. As economic production became more and more industrialized, more and more a production based on machines, less and less were workers capable of owning the means of production. Rather capital provided the machines and the labor of the workers was individually contracted for. But as individuals they had little bargaining power, and so the exchange of labor for wages tended not to be a just exchange, tended to diminish, as Karl Marx said, to a bare subsistence level.

Marx's solution to this problem was for the state to take over and become the owner of the means of production. But laissez-faire capitalists responded that it was beyond the legitimate power of the state to deprive citizens of their private property by nationalization or by requiring them to pay higher wages than was necessary.

Leo XIII defended the right to private property against communism, but he asserted the right and indeed the duty of the state to intervene in the economic sphere in order to secure justice:

> We have insisted... that, since the end of society is to make men better, the chief good that society can possess is virtue. Nevertheless, it is the business of a well-constituted body politic to see to the provision of those material and external helps, "the use of which is necessary to virtuous action".... Justice, therefore, demands that the interests of the working classes should be carefully watched over....[307]

> Let the working man and the employer make free agreements, and in particular let them agree freely as to the wages; nevertheless, there underlies a dictate of natural justice more imperious and ancient than any bargain between man and man, namely that wages ought not to be insufficient to support a frugal and well-behaved wage-earner. If through necessity or fear of a worse evil the workman accepts harder conditions, because an employer or contractor will afford him no better, he is made the victim of force and injustice.[308]

> Whenever the general interest of any particular class suffers, or is threatened with harm, which can in no other way be met or prevented, the public authority must step in to deal with it.[309]

A central teaching of *Rerum novarum* was that the government of a political community had both the authority and the responsibility to promote the common good, the good of the community. That meant that the government had the right and the duty to intervene in the economic sphere in order to foster justice between capital and labor.

It may be that the Church's teaching about the state's responsibility to intervene in the economic sphere would have been less influential in the United States were it not for the concurrence of three eventualities: the powerful restatement of that teaching by Pius XI in the 1931 encyclical *Quadragesimo Anno*, the Great Depression of the 1930's, and the Democratic New Deal beginning in 1932. Many spokesmen for the American Catholic Church forcefully promoted the Church's teaching on such things as miminum wages and labor unions. Father (later Bishop) Francis J. Haas spoke and wrote on the situation of American labor.[310] Msgr. John A. Ryan was a prolific writer on the social teaching and its relevance to the American scene.[311]

And indeed, it came to pass that socially and juridically Americans came to recognize the need for the government to intervene for the sake of justice in the economic dimension of society.

It should be noted that the papal concern was not only with justice as a general good—a principle of right order—in the society as a whole. The law, in requiring a just balance in the relations between labor and capital, for example, simultaneously requires the individuals involved to act justly. That requisite action, however much it may be simply mandated by law in the beginning, aims, according to traditional Catholic teaching, at ultimately forming the character of the individual citizens, at making them better human beings. Similarly, the law, in forbidding unjust discrimination by one citizen against another (for example, on racial or religious grounds), aims at forming the virtue of justice in the individual citizen, and thereby making him a better person.

3. Pius XI, in *Quadragesimo anno*, not only joined his voice to that of Leo XIII to insist on the responsibility and the right of the state to intervene in the economic sphere on grounds of social justice, he also enunciated clearly in that encyclical a complementary principle. Just as the responsibility of the government to intervene legislatively in the non-political area of economic markets was made clear, Pius XI articulated in the same document (for the first time explicitly) the principle of subsidiarity, which limits such intervention.

The principle of subsidiarity has two aspects. Since political society is a community of communities, the government—the administration, or set of offices constituting the supreme decision-making authority—does not have sole jurisdiction over everything that needs to be done in the society. The family has the right and competence to pursue its common good, for example, to arrange its internal affairs (e.g., what to do with its leisure time), to monitor the education of its children (e.g., what kind of religious education they receive), etc. Similarly, the groups intermediate between family and state—provincial or regional governments, municipal governments, voluntary associations of various kinds—have goods that they are themselves capable of pursuing and achieving. The responsibility of the state here is *not* to intervene: it should allow and indeed help those subsidiary bodies to accomplish their own proper ends, and not usurp their perogative. Whatever individuals and groups can do for themselves in pursuit of their proper goals should not be done by the state.[312]

The principle underlying subsidiarity thus stated is that a society is more just and more functional if the work that *can* be done by the parts *is* done by the parts, rather than being taken over by the whole. The responsibility of the state in this sphere is to assist the subsidiary groups in achieving their proper ends, and to implement those ends itself only temporarily in circumstances where the subsidiary group is, perhaps because of particular socio-economic conditions, incapable of functioning normally. This second aspect of subsidiarity involves the state intervening—but temporarily and in limited fashion—to secure the goods of the partial community, but only so long as the partial community is incapable of achieving its ends. Hence the state's intervention should aim at helping the subsidiary group regain the capacity to function for itself.

Part of the reason for the explict articulation of the principle of subsidiarity was the tendency in communism to extend state ownership of the means of production to the supervision or the elimination of various intermediary groups in the society (in Russia for example, state control of religion, of worker's organizations, elimination of all but one political party); and the tendency in Fascism to claim totalitarian jurisdiction (as Mussolini said, "Everything for the state; nothing against the state; nothing outside the state.").[313] But even for democratic societies, the principle of subsidiarity says that there is a limit to the state's intervention.

It would be hard to think of a more American principle of social structure than subsidiarity. Alexis de Tocqueville had already remarked, a century and a half ago, how characteristically American it was for citizens to form some association to address the problems and needs of their common life. And of course, the "parts" of the United States of America (i.e., the states) preceded the establishment of a national government, and they established that national government as "federal," as constitutionally limited to the powers explicitly delegated to it, reserving the undelegated powers to the states. Over the years, the extent of powers implicit in those explictly delegated to the national government has grown, but no one familiar with our continuing political discourse can be ignorant of the fact that there is a constant concern about the expansion of federal jurisdiction.

It is characteristic of the organization of the American polity, for example, that we have no Ministry of Education such as most other countries do that is responsible for the national system of education. We have a Department of Education in Washington, but it does not establish schools or supervise curricula or charter colleges; that is all done by the state boards of education. And even state boards of education do not establish all the schools: private and parochial schools must meet standards, but they can be established by individuals and groups, as can colleges. (There were over one hundred Catholic colleges in existence before the Civil War.)

4. A third area of the Church's teaching, which can be viewed as related to subsidiarity, is that of religious liberty, a topic on which the influence of the Church in America has been decisive. Here there has been a development over the last century in that teaching as it adapted its principles to two contrary historical developments: the growth of liberal democracies on the one hand and the spread of totalitarian and authoritarian (particularly Communist) regimes on the other.[314]

From the time of Leo XIII (and before), the Church held that the ideal or normative relation between Church and state would be one in which the Catholic Church was publicly acknowledged as the true church. Members of other churches or religions would not be obliged to join the Church, but their forms of worship would not have the same public status. Of course there were in fact few countries in which that status was actually accorded to the Catholic Church, but it was deemed the optimal situation.

As totalitarian regimes spread around the world, appropriating a religious establishment for their own ends and persecuting all other religious bodies, the critical question became simply the right or freedom of believers to express their beliefs in public practices.[315] At the same time, American theologians (like John Courtney Murray) were reflecting on the American First Amendment tradition that prohibited any establishment of religion, and arguing that the normative situation should be one in which the state did not have either the right or the responsibility to pass judgment on the status of religions and religious bodies. Rather, Murray and others argued, the state's responsibility should be juridical, limited to protecting the right of individuals (and groups of individuals) to follow their own religious beliefs and to express those in practices. The state should favor religion only by favoring the freedom of religious exercise. Religion—and morality—should be the responsibility of society, not of the state.

These concerns came together in the *Declaration on Religious Freedom* of the Second Vatican Council, of which Murray was a major architect. But many at the Council had reservations about totally separating freedom (of religious exercise) from truth. The issue comes into view in a clause inserted into the final draft of the *Declaration*: "Government, therefore, ought indeed to take account of the religious life of the people and show it favor, since the function of government is to make provision for the common welfare."[316] How should one understand "show it favor" and "the common welfare"? If those clauses are understood in the context of the juridical conception of the role of the state, i.e., that it shows favor and promotes the common welfare (*bonum commune*) only by protecting the freedom of religious exercise, then it also protects the right not to be religious, and so adopts a position of neutrality on whether its citizens are religious or not, and even what it means to be "religious."

This political separation of freedom from truth, the elevation of freedom above the rightness or wrongness of what is chosen, is a concern of Pope John Paul II, who has addressed it as a problem on many occasions.[317] It is a problem intrinsic to liberal democratic theory, i.e., the conception of democracy stemming from John Locke and the social contract theorists. According to this influential theory, we are not born "parts," responsible *ab ovo* to the community that nourishes and forms us from birth, but rather we are born free, owing nothing in justice to others except what we have ourselves agreed to or contracted for. And any reasonable contract will be one which retains for us the maximum amount of that freedom of self-determination that we possess from birth.

This is an issue crucial to our political and moral life together, and one which does not seem destined for an early resolution.

5. The last topic to be addressed is that of solidarity.[318] This is a term that emerges late in the century of social teaching being examined, and has two distinct sources and applications. It refers to human solidarity, and so sets itself against the kind of individualism just referred to, characteristic of liberal democratic society. It implies that we are all somehow one (*e pluribus unum*, as the American maxim has it), whether we think about it or not, and that we should become aware of that solidarity and acknowledge it in our lives.

The two distinct applications of the term come into view if one asks who "we" are in the preceding sentence. In the political-economic context of the social teaching of the Church, the community with which we are in solidarity is our country, our political society—and that means that we have certain definite relations with all the members of our nation, no matter how rich or poor, no matter how far away from us they live, no matter how young or old. We have moral and legal responsibilities to them because we are all members, citizens, of the same body politic, sharing a way of life, sharing values, sharing a history. We strive, with them, after a common good, and we owe them a share in whatever good life we are capable of achieving. The poor and the sick and the children, in Arizona or Montana or Georgia, have a just claim on the taxes that I pay, because they are Americans. Solidarity means caring.

But we can also think of solidarity as bonding human beings, wherever they may be—as members not (yet) of one body politic, but as members of the human race, as persons like me. Such a unity is not merely biological or anthropological, but human and moral. Foreigners, people who are not fellow-citizens, are not like non-persons. Human solidarity is what underlies the protests in America, for example, against the sweatshop conditions of manufacturers in other lands from whom we find ourselves buying shoes and clothes. It is the commercial transactions that brings such exploited people into our field of awareness. Popes from John XXIII to John Paul II have directed our attention to the status of underdeveloped nations, and raised the question of whether some poor nations are not exploited by wealthier nations, just as Leo XIII and Pius XI had earlier raised the analogous question about workers being exploited by capital. Paul VI, speaking of the economic relations between the rich and poor nations, said:

> The teaching of Leo XIII in *Rerum novarum* is still valid: if the positions of the contracting parties are too unequal, the consent of the parties does not suffice to guarantee the justice of their contract, and the rule of free agreement remains subservient to the demands of the natural law.[319]

So, solidarity can refer to either the solidarity of relations of one people in one body politic, or to human solidarity, a solidarity transcending national borders and bonding together human beings into one family, the human family. And one cannot run those two aspects of solidarity together as if there were no distinction between them. Particular political communities, nations, are realities grounded in human nature, however contingent or arbitrary some historical aspects of their borders may be.

The two distinct sources of the teaching about solidarity are reason and revelation: the universal nature of human beings and the moral law deriving from that (as in the quotation from Paul VI above), on the one hand, and the teaching of Jesus and the Church that every human person is a unique image of God, is our neighbor, whom we are called to love as we love ourselves.[320] The revelation of the basis of the paradoxal uniqueness and solidarity of human persons, in our having been created in the image and likeness of God, converges with our understanding of the natural solidarity of the human species, the human family, but it transmutes the character of that natural solidarity.

However, the natural basis of solidarity, in our common membership in the American body politic, and in the human nature we share with all human beings, has a certain inbuilt tension deriving from the differences between these two forms of solidarity. There is, first of all, the difference between the membership in one body politic and the commonality of sharing one human nature. For membership in the body politic is a reality of our lives, grounded in the fact that man is by nature a political animal, as Aristotle noted long ago. We do feel a kinship, a political fellowship, a concern for other Americans that we don't commonly have for non-Americans in the same way. There is a human family, a common good for the human race, but there is no world-wide body politic that embodies that commonality. Though there are human fathers and "Founding Fathers" of our country, the only Father of the human family is the Father of our Lord Jesus Christ.

There is no world government, and even if there were, without a world-wide body politic to bring us toward living together, to make us one—morally and politically—it is difficult to engender the sense of solidarity with, responsibility for, those on the other side of the earth. True, we are growing together in a fashion through the increasing interdependence of our economies; but as Jacques Maritain remarked long ago, that kind of interdependence without a body politic is more likely to produce conflict and injustice than solidarity.

The sense of responsibility to those in other lands is not wholly absent, as is shown by the generosity of many Americans touched by the suffering there due to famines and wars and disease, and by the perception that it is wrong to exploit those in other lands who produce goods for the American market. But generosity is not the same as moral responsibility, and changing perceptions do not provide a stable foundation for ethical dispositions.

This may be part of the reason why, as has been remarked by many, Pope John Paul II has emphasized the theological foundation of human solidarity much more than did John XXIII and Paul VI. Even within democratic political societies, let alone between political societies, as John Paul has noted, it is becoming harder to argue for actions directed toward justice and the common good on moral grounds.[321] But the social teaching of the Church cannot cease to call Catholics and all human beings to the moral vision of the human family:

Solidarity therefore must play its part in the realization of this divine plan, both on the level of individuals [within a body politic] and on the level of national and international society. The "evil mechanisms" and "structures of sin" of which we have spoken can be overcome only through the exercise of the *human and Christian solidarity* to which the Church calls us... [322]

Notes

1 Schuck, Michael J.: *That They Be One: The social teaching of the papal encyclicals,* 1740-1989. (1991, Georgetown Univ Press). pp 1-43.
2 ibid., p 31
3 ibid., p 31
4 ibid., pp 180-188
5 ibid., p 192
6 ibid., p 192
7 Coleman, John A. S.J. (Ed.): *One Hundred Years of Catholic Social Thought.* (1991, Orbis Books, Maryknoll, N.Y.). p 3.
8 John Paul, II, Pope (*Laborem Exercens,* 1981) paragraph 1.
9 When the question is raised as to what the social doctrine of the church is or does it even exist, it usually takes the form of the sense of a catholic ideal "model" deduced from *a priori* philosophical and theological principles, as as an ideal system of organization which is presented as a third way between communism and socialism. Would it then be legitimate for the official Magisterium of the Church to impose it on all the church in every detail and in every circumstance? This question was sharply posed by Fr. Chenu in his small booklet: *La "doctrine sociale" de l'Eglise comme idealogie* (Paris, Edition du Cerf, 1979). Fr. Chenu says we should avoid any "sanctified" hierarchial structures, particularly in the social order, and that we ought to substitute an abstract social doctrine, which comes from authority, but which is capable of local adaptation which would respond to local needs. Fr. Chenu's position was widely accepted in some areas but hotly discussed in Rome. It is suggested that he lacks nuances, that he makes excessive and sometimes inexact remarks. If one reads page 49 and 51 in his pamphlet, you will see that he quotes Pope John XXIII in *Pacem in Terris* (pp 159-160) to support his claim, but he leaves off the last two sentences where Pope John XXIII continues to speak, as did his predecessors, of a "Social Doctrine of the Church" and the authority of the Magisterium in all domains. (See Roger Aubert: "Les grand thèmes de l'enseignement social des papes de Léon XIII à Paul VI," *La Foi et le temps* (Tournai), T. 22 (1992), pp 242-279. See pp 270, 271, 273-274.
10 Desrochers, John: *The Social Teaching of the Church.* (1982, Bangelore, pp 783). pp 376-434.
11 See above Paul VI's *Octogesimo Adveniens,* paragraph 4, p. 12.
12 Boileau, David: *Cardinal Mercier: A Memoir* (1997, Peeters Publishing Co., Leuven, pp 417.)
13 Coleman, op. cit., pp 13-23.
14 Calvez, Jean-Yoes and Perrin, Jacques: *The Church and Social Justice* (1991, Henry Regnery Co.). pp 151-152.

15 Baum, Gregory: *The Priority of Labor* (1982, Paulist Press, New York). p 3.

16 *Laborem Exercens*, paragraph 14.

17 Baum, op. cit., p 87.

18 Terkel, Studs: *Working* (1972, Avon). p. xiii.

19 Coleman, op. cit., p 39.

20 ibid., pp 39-40.

21 ibid., pp 190.

22 Henriot, P., de Berri, E., Schultheis, M. (Eds.): *Catholic Social Teaching: Our Best Kept Secret*, (New York, 1988).

23 U. Nothelle-Wildfeurer, *"Duplex ordo cognitionis," zur systematischen Grundlegung einer katholischen Soziallehre im Anspruch von Philosophie und Theologie*, 1991, 855 pgs.

24 *Catechism of the Catholic Church* (1994, United States Catholic Conference) paragraphs 487-505; John Paul II, *The Splendor of Truth*, 1993, paragraphs 35-64; John Paul II, *Letter to Families*, 1994, paragraphs 7-10, 14.

25 cf. Manfred Spieker, Das Subsidiaritätsprinzip. Anthropologische Vorraussetzungen und politische Konsequenzen, in Die neue Ordnung 48 (1994) 22-34.

26 cf. From the abundant amount of literature about the subsidiarity principle see: Oswald von Nell-Breuning, *Baugesetze der Gesellschaft*, 2 Aufl. Freiburg 1990.

27 cf. The review of two books about European integration of Hans D. Barbier in the Frankfurter Allgemeine Zeitung of 11.1.1993: "the subsidiarity principle changes the postulate of the efficiency in rules for the division of labor between different administrative levels."

28 *Das Parteienspektrum in Polen. Aus den Programmen politischer Gruppierungen*, in: *Ost-Europa Archiv*, 41. (1991), A 569 vv.; Frantiszek Kampka, *Katholische Soziallehre in Polen—Erfahrungen und Perspektiven*, in: *Jahrbuch für Christliche Sozialwissenschaften* 33. Bd. (1992), 155 vv.

29 Documents of the African bishops' conferences are often published in German in the periodical *Weltkirche*, published since 1981 by Adveniat, Misereor and Missio in Munich. It concerns documents from Africa, Asia, and Latin-America.

30 cf. Due to the abundance of information, published on the occasion of the centenary celebration of *Rerum novarum: Une terre pour tous les hommes. La destination universelle des biens, Actes du colloque international organisé par le Conseil pontifical "Justice et paix," du 13 au 15 mai 1991*, Paris, 1992; in Italian: *La destinazione universale dei beni*, in *La Società. Studi, ricerche, documentazione sulla dottrina sociale della Chiesa*, quaderno 1/1992; *L'enseignement social chrétien. Les nouveaux défis. Actes du colloque "Cent ans d'enseignement social chrétien, 1891-1991,"* red. Nicolas Michel, Université de Fribourg, Suisse, Fribourg 1992; *Doctrina social de la iglesia y realidad socio-económica en el Centenario de la "Rerum novarum,"* XIII Simposio internacional de la teología de la Universidad

de Navarra, red. Teodoro Lopez e.a., Navarra, Pamplona 1991; Congreso: *Mexico a un siglo de Rerum novarum*, ed. IMODOSOC, Mexico city 1991; *Catholic Social Teaching en-route in Africa*, red. Obiora Iké, Enugu, Nigeria 1991; Manfred Spieker, *Vom katholischen Soziallehre zu den Transformationspprocessen in Polen und in der ehemaligen DDR*; *Cent ans de Catholicisme social en Alsace. De l'encyclique Rerum novarum (1891) à la fin du XXe siècle*, red. Raymond Mengus, Strasbourg 1991.

31 Leonardo Boff, *Aus dem Tal der Tränen ins Gelobte Land. Der Weg der Kirche mit den Unterdrückten*, Düsseldorf, 1982, 18; id. *Zärtlichkeit und Kraft. Franz vom Assisi mit den Augen der Armen gesehen*, Düsseldorf, 1983, 125. See the critique on this of M. Spieker, "Politik und Oekonomie in der Theologie der Befreiung," in *Gottesreich und Revolution*, red. Rupert Hofmann, Münster, 1987, 93 vv.

32 Hugo Assmann, Frank J. Hinkelammert, *Götze Markt*, Düsseldorf 1992; L. Boff, *Der Markt und die Religion der Ware*, Concilium 28 (1992) 195 vv.

33 *Pacem in terris*, 123; *Populorum progressio*, 77; *Sollicitudo rei socialis*, 44; *Centesimus annus*, 28.

34 cf. also Michel Novak, *Der Geist des demokratischen Kapitalismus*, Frankfurt 1992.

35 cf. M. Spieker, *Katholische Soziallehre und Civil Society. Der Beitrag der katholischen Soziallehre zu den Transformationsprozessen in Mittel- und Osteuropa* in *Vom Sozialismus zum demokratischen Rechtsstaat*, red. M. Spieker, l.c. 127 vv.

36 *Osservatore Romano* (German weekly edition) from May 28, 1993.

37 cf. Hans Joachim Höhn, "Katholische Soziallehre heute—Positionen und Perspektiven," in *Theologische Revue* 89 (1993) col. 89 vv.

38 Ursula Nothelle-Wildfeuer, *Vom Naturrecht zum Evangelium? Ein Beitrag zur neueren Diskussion um die Erkenntnistheorie der katholischen Soziallehre im Ausgang von Johannes Paul II*, in Jahrbuch für Christliche Sozialwissenschaften 32 (1991) 43 vv.

39 cf. Matthias Möhring-Hesse, *Politik aus dem Glauben und christliche Gesellschaftsethik*, in Jahrbuch für Christliche Sozialwissenschaften Bd. 32 (1991) 65 vv.

40 *Barmherzigkeit oder Gerechtigkeit? Zum Spannungsfeld von christlicher Sozialarbeit und christlicher Soziallehre*, ed. Norbert Glatzel/Heinrich Pompey, Freiburg 1991.

41 Hans Maier, "'*Rerum novarum*' und die katholische Soziallehre 1891-1991," in *Internationale Katholische Zeitschrift Communio* 20 (1991) 359; also in *Osservatore Romano* (German weekly edition) of June 28, 1991, pg. 6 and in the documentation *Une terre pour tous les hommes*, l.c. pg. 122.

42 Among the assistance organizations of the German Catholics there are also numerous assistance organizations in other countries and with other religions.

43 It should be noted that what is being criticized here is not McCormick's position. The position McCormick is reporting on (as De Jonghe re-

ports) is that of the Jesuit editors of *Civiltà Cattolica*. McCormick is simply reporting their position. He, as do many moral theologians, agrees with this position. Also, most theologians with expertise in Catholic social thought would come down on the side of the other whom Professor De Jonghe critizes. Also, no one holds that any encyclical was written in ignorance of social reality. (Editor's comment)

44 *Guidelines for the study and teaching of the Church's social doctrine in the formation of priests*, Congregation for the Catholic Education, Dec. 30, 1988, in *L'Osservatore Romano*, Weekly Edition, no. 32, July 8, 1989 and no. 33, Aug. 14, 1989 (from here on mentioned as *Guidelines*; Jean-Paul II, *La splendeur de la vérité*, 1993, no. 99 to no. 101; *Catéchisme de l'Eglise Catholique*, 1992, no. 2401 to no. 2463.

45 *Guidelines*, no. 3 to and including no. 5.

46 L. De Raeymaeker, *Inleiding tot de wijsbegeerte*, 1948, 28-35; H. Meyer, C. Schoonbrood, O.F.M., *De vrijheid van de filosofie en de encycliek Humani generis*, 1957, 47-48; *Æterni patris*, 1879, no. 6 to no. 24.

47 See as well Pius XII, *Pentecostal Message*, 1941. Important is the commentary by J.Y. Calvez in "Eglise et société économique," *L'enseignement social des papes de Léon XIII à Pie II* (1978-1958) [sic], 1959, 76-77; O. Lottin, *Morale fondamentale*, 1954, 117-122; John Paul II, *Veritatis splendor*, 1993, no. 43 and no. 44.

48 *Guidelines*, no. 9; *Gaudium et spes*, no. 63; *recta ratio* was given in the Dutch translation of *Gaudium et spes* (uitg. Katholiek Archief) as "menselijk zuiver geweten." In French as "droite raison"; in German as "rechte Vernunft"; in English as "right reason."

49 *Guidelines*, no. 14.

50 Jozef Ratzinger, "Naturrecht, Evangelium and Ideologie in der katholischen Soziallehre. Katholische Erwartungen zum Thema," in *Christlicher Glaube and Ideologie*, red. Klaus von Bismarch—Walter Dircks, 1964, 24-30, cited by W. Weber, *Kirchliche Soziallehre in Person und Gemeinschaft, Aufsätze and Vorträge der christlichen Soziallehre*; A. Rauscher, "Die moderne katholische Soziallehre, Entwicklungstendenzen, Problemfelder, Herausforderunger," in *Christliche Gesellschaftslehre*, 1989, 12-20; N. Greinacher, "Katholische Soziallehre, Theologie der Befreiung," in *Hundert Jahre katholische Soziallehre. Bilanz and Ausblick*, 1991, 198-201; A.M. Knoll, *Katholische Kirche und scholastisches Naturrecht*, 1962, 141.

51 Charles Curran, Richard McCormick (edit.), *Readings in Moral Theology, nr. 5: Official Social Teaching*: New York, 1986, from here on cited as Readings.

52 O. von Nell-Breuning, *Gesellschaftslehre*, in *Zur christlichen Gesellschaftslehre. Beiträge zu einem Wörterbuch der Politik*, 1947, Heft 1, 2-10, 25-26; *Christliche Soziallehre* in *Stimmen der Zeit*, pg. 173, 1963-64, Heft 3, 208, cited by W. Weber in W. Weber, *Person in Gesellschaft*, 1978, 21; G. Gundlach, *Katholische Soziallehre*, in *Staatslexikon*, Bd. 4, 1959, 914, cited by W. Weber, op.cit., 1978, 21. See also, Johannes

Messner, *Das naturrecht. Handbuch der Gesellschaftsethik, Staatsethik und Wirtschaftsethik*, 1960, 115-116, also cited by W. Weber, op.cit., 1978, 21.

53 J. Coleman, *Development of the Church's Social Teaching*, in *Readings*, 176, 186-87.

54 Richard A. McCormick, S.J., "*Laborem exercens* and Social Morality," in *Theological Studies*, 1982, in *Readings*, 226-27. One can find an analogous chronological arrangement and considerations of equal value in A. De Wolf, "Economische rechtvaardigheid voor allen en de inductieve benadering van het Kerkelijk sociaal economisch spreken," in *Economie en rechtvaardigheid*, red., J. Verstraeten, 1989, 36-38.

55 Charles E. Curran, *The changing anthropological basis of Catholic social ethics*, in *Readings*, 190-202 (referring to *Octogesima adveniens*, nr. 4); Richard McCormick, art. cit., 1986, 227.

56 NOTE: Charles Curran never states his position as interpreted here. "In fact, all the way through I have pointed out that *Mater et magistra* and *Pacem in terris* actually have continued the tradition of dealing primarily on a natural law basis and talking only about creation." In fact, in his judgment "the change to a more scriptural and Christological approach came with the Pastoral Constitution on the Church in the Modern World." Curran points out in Chapter 1 on the Human Person that "it considers creation but then brings in sin and finally ends with Christ the new man." In fact, he has actually criticized this approach for being too optimistic. "You will note in that first chapter there is no reference to the final eschaton. The fullness of Christ will only be present at the end of time. Chapter 3 on human activity does bring in that eschatological dimension which is missing in the first two chapters of the Pastoral Constitution."—Letter to the editor from Fr. Curran.

57 *Pacem in terris*, 1963; see the introduction V to XVIII in the translation of *Ecclesia docens*; J. Bryan Hehir, "Continuity and Change," in *The Social Teaching of the Church*, in I, 245. C.J. Pinto de Oliveira, "Evangile et droits de l'homme," in *Jean Paul et les droits de l'homme*, 1980, 55-82. See especially, J. Punt, "Die Menschenrechte und die moderne katholische Soziallehre," in J. Punt, *Die Idee der Menschenrechte, ihre geschichtliche Entwicklung und ihre Rezeption durch die Moderne katholische Sozialverkündigung*, 1987, 173-247.

58 See J. Maritain, *Man and the State*, 1951, 95-107.

59 Charles Curran, art. cit. in *Readings*, 198-202. (NOTE: Curran's point has been that there has been a distinct shift to a more historically conscious approach that began in the 1960's and reached its zenith with *Octogesima adveniens*. "I also think that John Paul II has pulled back somewhat from the approach of Paul VI. In this regard, I would call your attention to an article by Mary Elsbernd in *Theological Studies*, Vol. 56, 1995, beginning on page 39.")—Letter to the editor from Fr. Curran.

60 J. Maritain, *La loi naturelle ou loi non écrite*, 1950, 1986, 119-141; W. Weber, "Naturrecht mit werdendem Inhalt," in *Person in Gesellschaft*,

1978, 115-129; R.A. Armstrong, "Primary and Secondary Precepts," in *Thomistic Natural Law Teaching*, 1966, 86-102, 143-185.

61 R.A. McCormick, S.J., "*Laborem exercens and Social Morality*," in *Theological Studies*, 1982, in *Readings*, 223-226; *De corporatieve gedachte bij de katholieke sociologen in de 19de eeuw*, red., F. Van Goethem, 1942 (2), 294; G.B. Donnelly, "The Pope and the Corporation," *America*, March 11 and 2, 1933, in which the author refers to the just appeared pioneering work of A.K. Berle and G.C. Means, *The Modern Corporation and Private Property*, as source for evidence in favor of the doctrine of *Quadragesimo anno*.

62 NOTE: The third point of criticism of Curran deals with some problems that might be connected with induction. Again he is willing to recognize some of these as problems. However, he also sees induction based on human experience especially involving the experience of the poor and the oppressed. Therefore, an inductive method must do much more than give good statistical data as the author claims on the following pages.

63 Professor Dr. C. Van Gestel, *Commentaar en tekst van de encycliek van Johannes XXIII "Mater et magistra"*, 1962, 21-22.

64 *Guidelines*, nr. 10; *Gaudium et spes*, nr. 36, 52, 62; M.D. Chenu, *De Kerk in de wereld van deze tijd. Schema 13*, 167, 74.

65 See with respect to this, P. Sorokin, *Tendances et déboires de la sociologie américaine*, 1959, 401; J. Goudsbloem, *Balans van de sociologie*, 1974, 240; A.W. Gouldner, *The Coming Crisis of Western Sociology*, 1970, 528; Paul VI, *Octogesimo anno*, 38-39, 40.

66 Congrégation pour la doctrine de la foi, *Instruction sur quelques aspects de la théologie de la libération*, 1984, 17-18 (nr. 4-5), nr. 10, nr. 20; *Guidelines*, nr. 68-69.

67 J. Monnerot, *Les faits sociaux ne sont pas des choses*, 1946, 61-74.

68 P. Winch, *The idea of a social science and its relation to philosophy*, 1970, 18-20, 86-91.

69 E. Nagel, "Der Einfluss von Wertorientierungen auf die Sozialforschung," in *Werturteilsreit*, red., E. Topitsch, H. Albert, 1971, 237-261; T.W. Adorno, et al., *The Positivist Dispute in German Sociology*, 1976, 307; Th. de Boer, A.J.F. Köbben, *Waarden en wetenschap*, 1974, 399.

70 F.H. Tenbruck, *Die unbewaltigen Sozialwissenschaften oder die Abschaffung des Menschen*, 1984, 230-243.

71 *Centesimus annus*, 1991, nr. 39.

72 Leo XIII, *Diuturnum*, July 29, 1881, edition *Ecclesia docens*, nr. 6; *Immortale Dei*, November 1, 1885, edit. Marmy, nr. 11 and footnotes.

73 *Pacem in terris*, edition *Ecclesia docens*, Part 1, A., nr. 1 up to and including nr. 8 and B., nr. 1 up to and including nr. 7; Part 2, nr. 10.

74 N. Monzel, *Die katholische Kirche in der Sozialgeschichte*, 1980, 307.

75 Ernst Benz, "Der Mensch in christlicher Sicht," in: *Neue Anthropologie*, vol. 6, red. Hans Georg Gadamer/Paul Vogler, Stuttgart 1975, 373-428, 374.

76 Walter Kasper, "Das theologische Wesen des Menschen," in *Unser Wissen vom Menschen. Möglichkeiten und Grenzen antropologischer Erkentnisse*, red. W. Kasper, Düsseldorf 1977, 95-116, 105.

77 Anton Rauscher, *Personalität, Subsidiarität*, Cologne 1975, 9.

78 op. cit., cf. Walter Kasper, p. 110.

79 op. cit., Ernst Benz, p. 388.

80 op. cit., Walter Kasper, p. 114.

81 Hans Freyer, *Theorie des gegenwärtigen Zeitalters*, Stuttgart 1955, 67.

82 Nikolaus Monzel, *Solidarität und Selbstverantwortung*, München 1959, 51.

83 cf. Josef Punt, "Die Idee der Menschenrechte. Ihre geschichtliche Entwicklung und ihre Rezeption durch die moderne katholische Sozialverkündung" (*Abhandlungen zur Sozialethik*, red. Anton Rauscher und Lothar Roos, Bd. 26), Paderborn u.a. 1987; Lothar Roos, "Demokratie, Demokratisierung und Menschenrechte in den Dokumenten der Katholischen Soziallehre", in *Demokratie, Menschenrechte und politische Ordnung*, red. Bernhard Fraling et al. (Latijns Amerika und die Katholische Soziallehre. Ein lateinamerikanisch-deutsches Dialogprogramm. Teil 3), Mainz 1993, 19-74.

84 cf. Gerhard Schmidtchen, *Ethik und Protest. Moralbilder und Wertkonflikte junger Menschen*, with commentary of Lothar Roos and Manfred Seitz, Opladen 1992, 210-219.

85 "Marxsche Ideologie musste scheitern. Kolakowski beim deutschen Philosophen-Kongress," in *Deutche Tagespost* 114 of Sept. 23, 1993, page 10.

86 cf. Heinrich Pesch S.J., *Lehrbuch der Nationalökonomie, Erster Band: Grundlegung*, Freiburg i. Br. 3 u. 4 (the first printing appeared in 1904) p. 28 vv.: §4 has as title: *Der Mensch Herr der Welt inmitten der Gesellschaft*. In this part Pesch develops the principle of solidarity.

87 With particular emphasis Gustav Gundlach has pointed out that one should take into account both the "intrinsic structure" of social life, and the "exterior development" and the necessity of "being organized": *Die Ordnung der menschlichen Gesellschaft*, 2 Bde., Cologne 1964, passim; especially: I, 78 et seq., p. 218 e.v.

88 Heinrich Pesch speaks of the "three fundamental pillars of social organization." These are the family, the state, and the institution of private property, *op. cit.*, p. 163-243.

89 The considerations in this part come from the article of the author: "Ehe und Familie in unserer Gesellschaft," in *Sendung und Dienst im bischöflichen Amt: Festschrift der Katholisch-Theologischen Fakultät der Universität Augsbutg für Josef Stimpfle zum 75. Geburtstag*, red. Anton Ziegenaus, St. Ottilien 1991, p. 197-218.

90 Josef Höffner has extensively treated marriage and family and their meaning for society in the framework of his book *Christliche Gesellschaftslehre* (Kevelaer 1975, p. 79-120). Against all attempts to undermine the concepts marriage and family as fundamental values and institutions of or-

ganization through the formulation of the problem, Höffner holds firm to the "timeless valid structure of the family" as natural community of parents with their children.

91 The following considerations are derived from the not yet published manuscript *Das Eigentum im Dienst des arbeitendem Menschen*, that will appear soon in Russian.

92 Joseph Höffner, *Soziale Gerechtigkeit und soziale Liebe*, Saarbrücken 1935, 9.

cf. *Ethica Nicomachaea*, 1129 b 15 vv.

93 cf. Waldemar Zimmermann, "Das 'Soziale' im geschichtlichen Sinn- und Begriffswandel," in: *Studien zur Soziologie, Festgabe für Leopold von Wiese*, hg. von, L.H. Ad. Gesck, Jürgen Kempski und Hanna Meuter, Bd. 1., Mainz 1945, 173-191.

94 For the reference to Aristotle in this paragraph, see *Politics* I, 2; 1253a1-b1.

95 cf. Aristotle, *Nicomachean Ethics*, 1129 a 30.

96 cf., ibid., 1129 a 30.

97 cf., ibid., 1129 b 25 vv.

98 cf., ibid., 1129 a 34.

99 cf., ibid., 1130 a 5 e. vv.

100 cf., ibid., 1129 b 25 vv.

101 cf., ibid., 1130 a 32 vv. and b 15.

102 cf., ibid., 1131 b 28.

103 cf., ibid., 1131 b 25. English translator's note: I have used the term "rectificatory justice" here based on Ross' English translation of Aristotle. However, the term in the Dutch text is the same that is subsequently used for "iustitia commutativa," which is here transliterated as "commutative justice."

104 cf., ibid., 1132 b 21.

105 cf., ibid., 1131 a 13.

106 ibid., 1130 b 30 e.v.v.

107 cf., ibid., 1131 a 20 e.v.v.

108 ibid., 1131 b 30.

109 ibid., 1132 a 1.

110 ibid., 1132 a 4 vv.

111 cf. for this more extensively Rolf Kramer, *Soziale Gerechtigkeit-Inhalt und Grenzen* Berlin 1992, 29-39.

112 Thomas Aquinas, *Summa Theologiae*, I-II 90 a 3.

113 *Summa Theologiae* II-II 58 a 5.

114 ibid., II-II 59 a 5.

115 cf., ibid., II-II 58 a 6. Articles 5 and 6 treat first the question whether and to what extent justice is to be regarded as a general virtue.

116 cf., ibid., II-II 58 a 6 ad 4. "That this being directed [to the common good] is a virtue, in other words something attained by the natural will capacity and not comprised completely of innate disposition, was not a problem for Thomas, because according to his teaching, humans, due to

their natural urge, only strive after their own well-being, but still experience restraint with respect to the common good. Where continual restraint must be overcome, a separate virtue is demanded." (Arthur F. Utz, *Sozialethik*, pg. 1, Heidelberg 1958, 201).

117 cf., ibid., II-II 58 a 6.

118 cf., ibid., II-II 57-79; *Recht und Gerechtigkeit*, commentary of Arthur F. Utz (=The German Thomas Edition, pg. 18), Heidelberg-Graz 1953, 461 (so also in: Thomas Aquinas, *Recht und Gerechtigkeit, Theologische Summae*, II-II, questions 57-79. Subsequent edition of part 18 of the German Thomas edition. New translation of Josef F. Groner, comments, as well as the completely revised and completed commentary of Arthur G. Utz, Bonn 1987, 312; cited from here on out as Utz, *Nachfolgefassung*).

119 cf. *Summa Theologiae* II-II 61 a 1. (See English translator's note, footnote #103.)

120 cf., ibid.

121 cf., ibid.

122 cf., ibid., I-II 90 a 3.

123 For a full explanation see Arthur F. Utz, *Sozialethik*, Bd 1, 103-176; Bernd Kettern, *Sozialethik und Gemeinwohl. Die Begründung einer realistischen Sozialethik bei Arthur F. Utz*, Berlin 1992, 118-132.

124 "Aristotle, by his schema, held Thomas back from systematically identifying, at least partially, the justice of the common good and that of the distributive." (Utz, *Nachfolgefassung*, 449).

125 cf., ibid., 449 v. The philosophical analysis of Thomas's shortcoming: Thomas does not start from the concrete human, but rather from *natura humana*, which imposes its standards as absolute norm on each human action: the common good is the general good of human nature.

126 cf. Utz, *Sozialethik*, pg 1 208-214; vf. Höffner, *Soziale Gerechtigkeit und soziale Liebe*, 41-65.

127 Luigi Taparelli, *Saggio teoretico di Diritto naturale appogiato sul fatto*, Palermo 1840-1843, pg. 1, nr. 354 v.

128 Utz, *Sozialethik*, Bd. 1, 215.

129 cf. Taparelli, *Saggio teoretico*, Nr. 363.

130 cf. Höffner, *Soziale Gerechtigkeit und soziale Liebe*, 9 v.

131 For the individual authors cf. the citations in Höffner, *Soziale Gerechtigkeit und Liebe*, 11-22 and Utz, *Sozialethik*, Bd. 1, 220-226.

132 *AAS* (1903/1904), 515: "publicus iustitae socialis assertor."

133 *Bulletin des oeuvres des cercles*, 1922, IV, 3.

134 *AAS* 15 (1923), 354 v.

135 cf. Arthur F. Utz/Brigitta Gräfin von Galen. *Die katholische Sozialdoktrin in ihrer geschichtlichen Entfaltung. Eine Sammlumg päpstlicher Dokumente vom 15. Jahrhundert bis in die Gegenwart*, 4 parts, Aken 1976: the roman numerals mean the groups according to subject; the arabic numbers the subchapters, here: XIX 47.

136 cf. Utz/Galen IV 184.

137 cf., ibid., IV 173.

138 cf., ibid., IV 118.
139 cf., ibid., IV 127 and 135.
140 cf. Parallelisms of justice, justice of the common good, and social justice (Utz/Galen IV v., 118, 135, 157, 173, 184); cf. also the encyclical of Pius XI *Studiorum ducem* of June 29, 1923, in which the pope treats an identification of the legal justice of Thomas and social justice: Thomas formulated the correct principles about legal or social justice (*AAS* 15 (1923), 322).
141 Utz, *Sozialethik*, Bd. 1, 220; cf. Utz/Galen IV 135 and 148.
142 cf. Utz/Galen IV 184.
143 Utz, *Nachfolgefassung*, 454.
144 cf. Utz/Galen IV 135
145 cf., ibid., II 108
146 cf., ibid., II 129-132
147 Utz/Galen XV 63. Paul VI formulated a similar call in a papal letter *Hemos sabido* to Cardinal Antonio Caggiano, Archbishop of Buenos Aires, and to the archbishops and bishops of the Argentinian republic (12 April 1964; Utz/Galen XVII 135): "You must demand unions and social institutions for the protection of the legitimate interests of the workers. With that social justice shall be turned into practice."
148 cf. Arthur F. Utz/Josef F. Groner, *Aufbau und Entfaltung des gesellschaftlichen Lebens. Soziale Summe Pius XII*, 3 parts, Freiburg/Schweiz 1954 vv. (Utz/Groner is cited here with citation of the Arabic numbers in the margin, here: 585)
149 cf. Utz/Groner 3390
150 cf. Utz/Groner 4361 and 4465-4471 (the call to a return of the workers exposed to social revolutionary dangers to the "warm manger of Christ" causes a rather curious mixed metaphor of curial prose). In a letter of Paul VI to the 25th meeting of the Social Weeks in Spain (March 7 1966; Utz/Galen XX, 22) social justice is regarded as suitable means for the prevention of class conflict. Reform processes that are determined by social justice did not allow the society to become the stage for class conflict. The application of Christian principles assumes communal efforts for the spiritual, material, and human perfection of all. Instruments are, for example, wages, job and work, and tax politics and policy, "with which one can bring a more humane world of justice and love closer." The instruction of the Congregation for Sacred doctrine *Libertatis conscientia* (1986) repeats in nr. 77 the conviction that the effort for social justice does not legitimize class conflict; social justice is only to be reached via dialogue. The Church encourages the establishment of unions, like trade unions, that make an effort for the protection of rights and legitimate interests of the employees and for social justice. Nr. 78 reads: "The fight against injustice makes sense only if this strives for the establishment of a social and political order that complies with the requisites for social justice."

151 cf. Utz/Groner 6245. A few years later a letter from Secretary of State
Cardinal A. G. Cicognani to Cardinal G. Siri, the president of the Social
Weeks in Italy (September 5, 1965; Utz/Galen XXII 68), reads: "The
more Catholics make an effort to fulfill the free social connections and
their different functions from a uniform vision on the modern political
community, the more according to His Holiness the forming of a modern civil and political consciousness is guaranteed that complies with
the Christian social tradition and the more complete actualization of
virtues of social justice and love [will result]. Indeed these virtues demand precisely the active and conscious participation in communal life
on all levels and condemn the all too often occurring position of negative criticisms, of mistrust, of disinterest, and of refusal to carry joint
responsibility in the political community."

152 Utz/Galen IV 268

153 cf. Utz/Galen IV 352-379. "A new aspect is treated in a letter from
Secretary of State Cardinal A. G. Cicognani to Bishop González Moralejo
as a result of the 21st Social Week of the Catholics in Spain (September
19, 1962): for the papal Secretary of State the problems of the economy
seem to be solved only if one studies the principles of social justice. One
must be prepared to make contributions, if one could bring justice into
being because of that (This means that when privileges are abandoned
and the feudal style of life takes place, a land reform is considered necessary)."

154 Utz/Galen IV 639. This chapter from *Gaudium et spes* is repeated in a
letter to the 25th session of the Social Weeks in Spain (March 7, 1966;
Utz/Galen XX 17).

155 Utz/Galen IV 503.

156 ibid., IV 520.

157 Utz/Galen VI 104. In nr. 90 of the Instruction of the Congregation for
the Sacred Doctrine *Libertatis conscientia* (1986) the duty to solidarity is
emphasized especially for developing countries. Social justice must be
served by a correct testing of trade relations between North and South
and through the promoting of a more humane world for all, a world in
which each can give and receive and in which the progress of one is not
a hinderance to the development of the other (there is reference to *Mater
et Magistra* and *Populorum Progressio*, as well as to a speech of John Paul
II to the Corps Diplomatique on January 11, 1986, in: *L'Osservatore
Romano* of January 12, 1986,4-5).

158 Utz/Galen XV 24.

159 cf. Gustav Gundlach, art. "Solidarismus," in *Staatslexikon der
Görresgesellschaft*, Bd. 4, Freiburg i Br. 51931, col. 1616.

160 cf. The explanations of the pope in a speech to the participants of the
main gathering on the occasion of the 50-year anniversary of the International Labor Organization (I.L.O.) in Geneva (June 10, 1969). After
he showed great appreciation for the efforts of the organization for social justice (Utz/Galen XX 35) and for the upbuilding of social justice as

a moral and humanitarian idea (*idem.* 41), he calls to mind that the effort for social justice, including efforts for a peaceful and just settlement of work conflicts, serves the general peace (ibid. 32 enumerates protagonists of social justice in Switzerland).

161 Utz/Galen IV 880.

162 ibid., IV 892.

163 cf. For the ideas of this chapter, I am thankful to the suggestions of an article of Karl Homann: Karl Homann, "Demokratie und soziale Gerechtigkeit," in Bernhard Fraling/Manfred Mols/Felipe E. Macgregor (Hg.), *Demokratie, Mensenrechte und politische Ordnung* (=Peter Hünermann/Juan Carlos Scannone (Hg.), *Lateinamerika und die Katholische Soziallehre. Ein lateinamerikanisches Dialogprogramm*, Bd. 3) Mainz 1993, 75-98.

164 Friedrich August von Hayek, *Recht, Gesetzgebung und Freiheit. Eine neue Darstellung der liberalen Prinzipen der Gerechtigkeit und der politischen Oekonomie*, Bd. 2, Landsberg am Lech 1980, 112.

165 With this idea, Hayek distances himself from Max Weber's conception of order, especially Friedrich August von Hayek, *Freiburger Studien*, Tübingen 1969, 165 vv. cf. Hardy Bouillon, *Ordnung, Evolution und Erkenntnis. Hayeks Sozialphilosophie und ihre erkenntnistheoretische Grundlage*, Tübingen 1991.

166 cf. Hayek, *Freiburger Studien*, 119-121.

167 cf. C.B. Macpherson, *The Political Theory of Possessive Individualism*, Oxford 1962. Concerning Macpherson's conviction about the background of the "possessive individualism," see John Dunn, *The Political Thought of John Locke*, Cambridge, 1969.

168 *Doctrine de Saint-Simon*. Paris 1924, p. 378.

169 *Hist. Wörterbuch der Philosophie*, Bd. 4, 290.

170 cf. Alan Macfarlane, *The Origins of English Individualism*, Oxford 1978.

171 E. Mounier, *Oeuvres complètes*, vol. 3, p. 452.

172 *Centesimus annus*, n. 47.

173 Suarez, *De legibus*, I, 2, 5

174 cf. J. Finnis, *Natural Law and Natural Rights*, Oxford 1980, 206 e. vv.

175 *Leviathan*, I, ch. 14: "The Right of Nature, which writers commonly call *Jus Naturale*, is the Liberty each man has, to use his own power, as he wills himself, for the preservation of his own nature, that is to say, of his own life, and consequently, of doing anything which in his own judgment and reason, he shall conceive to be the aptest means thereunto."

176 *Rudiments*, ch. 1, part 2.

177 cf. W. L. Newman, *The Politics of Aristotle*, I, Oxford 1887, pg. 166.

178 *Polit.* III 4, 1278b19-23

179 ibid., 1283b40-42.

180 ibid., 1268b31.

181 *Doctrina politica de Santo Thomàs*, Salamanca, 1992.

182 I 60, 5 ad 5, III 46, 2 (God is the supreme and common good of all the Universe), *Quodl.* I, q. 4, a. 3 (God is the common good of all the Universe and of all its parts).

183 *Exposito in librum Job*, c. 7.

184 II-II 26, 3: "because each part naturally loves the common good of the whole more than its own particular good."

185 *Q. d. de spiritualibus creaturis*, q. un., a. 8 ad 5.

186 III 63, 3.

187 I 93, 2 ad 3: "The Universe is more perfect in goodness than the intellectual creature as regards extension and diffusion; but intensively and collectively the likeness to the Divine goodness is found rather in the intellectual creature, which has a capaciaty for the highest good."

188 I 49, 3.

189 cf. *De potentia* q. 6, a. 1 ad 8.

190 I 93, 2 ad 3: "Part is not rightly divided against the whole, but only against another part."

191 II-II 129, 6 ad 1.

192 I 96, 4.

193 cf. *Summa contra gentiles*, III 134: "Moreover there should be mutual friendship among men, in accord with which they assist each other either in spiritual or earthly functions."

194 *Gemeinschaft und Einzelmensch. Eine sozialmetaphysische Untersuchung, bearbeitet nach den Grundsätzen des hl. Thomas von Aquin*, Salzburg-Leipzig, 1935, 217.

195 I-II 96, 1: "Its good is procured by many actions."

196 I-II 109, 3: "Now it is manifest that the good of the part is for the good of the whole; hence everything, by its natural appetite and love, loves its own proper good on account of the common good of the whole universe, which is God . . . . But in the state of corrupt nature man falls short of this in the appetite of his rational will, which, unless it is cured by God's grace, follows its private good, on account of the corruption of nature." cf. II-II 26, 3 and 4.

197 *O.c.*, 251 e. vv.

198 One finds in Thomas's statement a particularly large number of texts. It goes back to Aristotle, *Eth. Nic.* 1094b9-10. cf. *In III Sent.*, d. 32, q. 1, a. 5; I-II 111, 5; II-II 47, 10; 88, 11; CG I 41; III 17. 69. 145.

199 *Contra Gentiles*, I 86; II-II 58, 9 ad 3.

200 II-II 58, 5 (DTA).

201 I-II 96, 3.

202 *CG* I 86; cf. II-II 58, 9 and 3.

203 I-II 92, 1 and 3.

204 I-II 92, 1 ad 3 ("The good of any part is considered in comparison with the whole. Man must be well proportionate to the common good.").

205 I-II 21, 4 ad 3: "Man is not ordained to the body politic, according to all that he is and has, but all that is, and can, and has, must be referred to

God. " Conversely, II-II 65, 1: "The whole of man is directed as to his and to the whole of the community of which he is a part. "

206 II-II 152, 4 ad 3: "The common good takes precedence over the private good, if it be of the same genus. "

207 As, in general, the ultimate goal and the perfection of humans.

208 *Der Begriff des Gemeinwohls bei Thomas von Aquin. Ein Beitrag zum Problem des Personalismus,* Heidelberg 1954.

209 "L'individu et le groupe dans la scolastique du 13e siècle," in *Revue néo-scolastique de philosophie* 22 (1920) 341-357.

210 *Gemeinschaft und Einzelmensch,* Salzburg/Leipzig 1935.

211 *O.c.,* p. 28.

212 *De la primauté du bien commun contre les Personnalistes,* Québec/Montréal 1943; "In Defense of St. Thomas Aquino. A Reply to Father Eschmann's Attack on the Primacy of the Common Good", in *Laval théologique,* 1945, 1-103.

213 *La notion thomiste du bien commun,* Paris 1932.

214 *Personne et societé. Théories actuelles et essai doctrinal,* Gembloux 1939.

215 *Sociaal-wijsgerige opstellen,* Tilburg 1948.

216 *Liberalismus, Sozialismus und christliche Gesellschaftsordnung,* Freiburg 1900, p. 133.

217 "Personalismus," in *Wörterbuch der Politik,* Heft V, 352.

218 G. Gundlach, "Gemeinwohl" in *Staatslexikon der Görresgesellschaft,* Bd. III3, Freiburg 1959, 737 e. vv. cf. Johannes Schwarte, *Gustav Gundlach S.J., massgeblicher Repräsentant der katholischer Soziallehre während der Pontifikate Pius' XI und Pius' XII,* München/Paderborn/Wenen 1975, 464 e. vv.

219 *Deutsche Thomasausgabe,* Bd. 18 Graz/Heidelberg 1953, 564-571.

220 *De regimine principum,* I, c. 14; I-II 95, 1; *De virtutibus,* q. un., a. 1. 7.

221 II-II 152, 4 ad 3; *De virtutibus,* a. 9.

222 *DTA,* B. 18, 565.

223 II-II 58, 5.

224 II-II 58, 7 ad 2: "The common good of the realm and the particular good of the individual differ not only in respect of the *many* and the *few*, but also under a formal aspect. For the aspect of the *common* good differs from the aspect of the *individual* good, even as the aspect of the *whole* differs from that of the *part*. "

225 *O.c.,* 569.

226 A. F. Utz, *Bibliographie der Sozialethik,* Bd. V 305.

227 *Free Persons and the Common Good,* New York/London 1988, p. 80 evv.

228 *Fundamentals of Christian Sociology,* 1962.

229 S. Alasdair MacIntyre, *After Virtue, A Study in Moral Theory,* London 1981, 238-245.

230 J. J. Rousseau, *Du contrat social,* bk. 2, ch. 3.

231 *Diuturnum,* nrs. 1-3, 5, 15, 17, editie *Ecclesia docens,* 1939.

232 *Immortale Dei*, pp. 24-28, 36, 55-56, in *Actes de Léon* XIII, Paris 1939, bd. II.

233 *Sapientiae Christianae*, nrs. 3, 7, 8-9, 12, 33, 40, 54, ed. *Ecclesia docens*, 1940. Here also is a referece to the *Summa theologiae*, II, II, 47, 12.

234 *Rerum novarum*, nrs. 25-26, 29, ed. Urbi et orbi, Dutch text, 1938.

235 *Quadragesimo anno*, nrs. 85, 95, ed. Urbi et orbi, Dutch text, 1938.

236 *Divini redemptoris*, nrs. 32, 51 in Magenest, *Le discours social de l'Eglise*, pp. 200, 207.

237 *Mit brennender Sorge* and *Non abbiamo bisogno*, in Marmy, *La communauté humaine selon l'esprit chrétien*, 1948, 2nd ed., 133-146 and 115-145.

238 *Summi pontificatus*, in Marmy, op. cit. 1194-1195.

239 Radio message, Pentecostal message of June 1, 1941, in A. F. Utz and J. F. Groner, op. cit., nr. 591.

240 Radio message *Con sempre nuova freschezza*, Christmas message of December 24, 1942, in F. A. Utz- J. F. Groner, op. cit., nr. 276.

241 Radio message *Con sempre nuova freschezza*, Christmas message of December 24, 1942, in F. A. Utz- J. F. Groner, op. cit., nr 276.

242 J. Y. Calvez, *Eglise et societé économique*, dl. 1, 1958, p. 157.

243 *Gaudium et spes*, ed. Catholic archives, *Constitutions and Decrees of the Second Vatican Council*, z.d., nr. 74.

244 *Catéchisme de l'Eglise Catholique*, 1992, 676 pages. We refer to the numbering of the paragraphs in this publication.

245 *Justitia in mundo*, November 30, 1971, in D. Maugenest, op. cit., 569-593.

246 We refer in the text to the numbered paragraphs of the French edition, *Cathéchisme de l'Eglise Catholique*, 1992, Paris, 676 pages.

247 cf. L. Janssens, *Personne et société, théories actuelles et essai doctrinal*, 1939, pgs. 5-119.

248 Dom Odon Lottin, *Morale fondamentale*, 1954, 546 pages. (Lottin gives, on page 189, a summary of the most prominent pulications with relation to the discussion being carried out. One can find a similar summary in L. Janssens, op. cit., pgs 177-178).

249 O. Lottin, op. cit., p. 199.

250 Lottin refers to his *Psychologie et morale au XIIe, et XIIIe siècle*, vol 2, 1948, pgs 11-26.

251 Aristotle, *Nicomadean Ethics*, in *The Works of Aristotle*, ed. W. D. Ross, vol. IX, bk. 9, 1179-1181.

252 Aristotle, *Politica* in *The Works of Aristotle*, ed. W. D. Ross, vol. X, bk. 7, ch. 16, 20-35.

253 Lottin cites different passages from the commentaries of Thomas Aquinas on the *Ethica* and the *Politica* of Aristotle regarding this material, cf. *Morale fondamentale*, pg 193.

254 Thomas Aquinas, *Summa theologiae*, I. II, 90, 2. Thomas refers here to the *Politics* of Aristotle (*Politics*, I, 1), where he writes about the political commonwealth as the highest society in the sense of the most encom-

passing compared to the family and the individual. Thomas also speaks in this context about a "perfect" community.

255 Lottin cites *De regimine principum*, lib. I, 1 and *Summa theologiae*, I. II, 60, 3, ad 2; 81, 8 ad 1; 113, 1.

256 *Summa theologiae*, I. II, 91, 4.

257 ibid., 93-95 and 98, 1.

258 O. Lottin, op.cit., pg. 199, with reference to *Summa theologiae*, I. II, 21, 4 ad 3.

259 *Summa theologiae*, II. II, 64, 2; 64, 5; 64, 6; 65, 1.

260 O. von Nell-Breuning, *Reorganization of Social Economy, the Social Encyclical Developed and Explained*, 1939, ed., pg. 207, footnote 4.

261 J. Maritain, *The Person and the Common Good*, 1985, fourth edition, pg. 58.

262 O. Lottin, op. cit. p. 191-192. The author refers to *Contra gentiles*, III, CXII.

263 *Summa contra gentiles*, III, CXIII.

264 ibid., III, CXIV.

265 ibid., III, CXV up to and including CXVII.

266 ibid., III, XVII.

267 ibid., III, XVIII.

268 *Summa theologiae*, I, 47, 1; I, 47, 2; I, 47, 2, ad 1; I, 103, 2.

269 ibid., I, 50, 3 í, 50, 4, ad 3. This hierarchy of perfections was worked out by Thomas influenced by the Neoplatonic vision of pseudo-Dionysius the Areopagite.

270 ibid., I, 73, 1, corp.

271 Professor Dr. Magister Angelinus, O.F.M. cap., *Wijsgerige gemeenschapsleer*, 1948, chapter 5, "Communal well-being and particular well-being," 238-272, puts this in a rather simple language and with a great sense of tradition.

272 *Guidelines for the study and teaching of the Church's social doctrine in the formation of priests*, document of the Congregation for Catholic education, *Osservatore Romano* (English edition), 1989, n. 32, 3-10; n. 33, 3-10, cited subsequently as *Guidelines*.

273 ibid., n. 40, n. 41.

274 *Gaudium et spes*, (1965), n. 15; n. 31; n. 68; *Octogesmia adveniens* (1971), n. 22; n. 24; *Sollicitudo rei socialis* (1987), n. 45; *Libertatis conscientia* (1986), n. 86. See also W. Palaver, "Die Diskrepanz von Wort und Tat in der katholischen Soziallehre am Beispiel von Kirche und Demokratie," in *Hundert Jahre katholische Soziallehre*, 1991, 49.

275 John XXIII, *Pacem in terris* (1963), n. 70; n. 74-78.

276 Paul VI, *Octogesima adveniens* (1971), n. 74-78.

277 *Guidelines*, Appendix 1, IV, n. 4.

278 John Paul II, *Sollicitudo rei socialis* (1987), n. 44, 3.

279 John XXIII, *Mater et magistra* (1961), 91-96.

280 *Gaudium et spes*, 1965, n. 14.

281 John Paul II, *Laborem exercens*, 1987, n. 14.
282 *Libertatis conscientia*, n. 86. The document refers to *Gaudium et spes*, 1965, n. 68 and *Laborem exercens*, 1987, n. 14.
283 *National Conference of Catholic Bishops. Pastoral Letter on Catholic Social Teaching and the U. S. Economy*, 1986, chapter IV, n. 295 to n. 325.
284 John Paul II, *Centesimus annus*, 1991, n. 35.
285 ibid., n. 43. The text refers in footnote 85 to *Laborem exercens* n. 15, where it states that humans, in no matter which economic system, must always remain conscious of their own value and work, for this is for their own good.
286 *Quadragesimo anno*, 1931, n. 65.
287 ibid, n. 76-87.
288 *Discorsi e radiomessaggio di Pio XII*, VI, 1944-1945, 124 vv.
289 Cited by J. Villain S. J. in *L'enseignement social de l'Eglise*, tome III, p. 65.
290 ibid., pp. 66-67.
291 ibid., 75-76.
292 Fr. O. von Nell-Breuning, S. J., *Mitbestimmung*, 1950, 19-23.
293 O. von Nell-Breuning, "Mitbestimmung des Arbeiters," in *Wirtschaft und Gesellschaft Heute*, II: Zeitfragen, 1957, 106-127. Here it is about an article that originally was published in *Stimmen der Zeit* 146 (1950), H. 10, 286-295.
294 *Quadragesimo anno*, 1931, n. 45; n. 63-74. See also E. De Jonghe, "Het vraagstuk van het medebeheer," in *De Gids op Maatschappelijk Gebied*, 1952, 7, 555-581; G. Ripert, *Aspects juridistiques du capitalisme moderne*, 1946, 49-123.
295 See P.J.A.M. Steenkamp, *De gedachte van bedrijfsorganisatie in protestants christelijke kring*, 1952, 200; J. Ponsioen and G.M.J. Veldkamp, *Vraagstukken der hedendaagse samenleving*, 1955, p. 419; A. Philip, *La démocratie industrielle*, 1955, 300; F.J.H. Van der Ven, *Arbeidsrechtelijke en sociale opstellen*, 1945, 156-169; W. Banning, *Moderne maatschappijproblemen*, 1957, 154-169.
296 Y.-Y. Calvez and Y. Perrin, *Eglise et société économique: l'enseignement social des papes, de Léon XIII à Pie XII (1878-1958)*, 362-378.
297 "Über das Lohnverhältnis hinaus," in *Festschrift für Wilhelm Herschel zum 85. Geburtstag*, 1982, 303-319.
298 G. Schaub, *Arbeitsrecht. Handbuch*, 1972, Buch XVI Betriebsverfassung, 210-211, pp. 1562-1564; 215, pp. 1582-1598; Buch XVIII Die Unternehmensverfassung, 255, pp. 1845-1846; 256, pp. 1846-1852.
299 R. Blanpain, *Codex Arbeidsrecht*, 1991-1992, 863-925. Concerning Holland we consulted M.G. Rood, *Wet op de ondernemingsraden* (to supplement 14, March 1990).
300 Commission for the European Communities, *Statuut van de Europese Vennootschap*, supplement 5/89, p. 74. The social partners, namely the European employees and the employers' organization, should momentarily begin talks to come to a recommendation for a plan for a recom-

mendation of the European Commission concerning European employees councils. cf. *De Financieel Economische Tijd* of Nov. 24, 1993.

301 Catholic social teaching is not merely a social philosophy taught by the Church: "there can be no genuine solution of the 'social question' apart from the Gospel." John Paul II, *Centesimus Annus #5*.

302 The Social Action Department of NCWC (National Catholic Welfare Conference), the organization of the American bishops, was founded in 1919.

303 A competent and comprehensive history of these developments is David J. O'Brien, *American Catholics and Social Reform: the New Deal Years* (New York: Oxford University Press, 1968)

304 This is the classical term constantly used by the papal documents, which derives from Greek and Roman political philosophy and from the theological tradition: *bonum commune*. In the other essays in this volume it is translated as "general well-being," but in America the traditional translation "common good" is standard. It occurs in Aristotle's *Politics* (1268b31) as *koinon agathon*.

305 The kind of group in view here is one in which the whole of life is shared, in contrast to groups constituted for particular goals: voluntary associations, unions, baseball teams, etc. In these cases too there may be a good sought that can only be sought by a group, but that good does not encompass or lay claim to the allegiance deserved by natural groups (family and state) that seek goods essential to human life, and that live together, share a way of life.

306 This is the traditional name, although it is misleading because the second and third species of justice are also generally spelled out in laws.

307 *Rerum novarum* in E. Gilson, ed. *The Church Speaks to the Modern World* (New York: Doubleday, 1954) p. 222.

308 ibid, p. 229. Paul VI in *Populorum progressio*, many years later, cites the same principle in addressing the relation between developed and underdeveloped countries: "The teaching of Leo XIII in *Rerum novarum* is still valid: if the positions of the contracting parties are too unequal, the consent of the parties does not suffice to guarantee the justice of their contract, and the rule of free agreement remains subservient to the demands of the natural law." Op. cit. #59.

309 ibid, p. 206.

310 Francis J. Haas, *The Wages and Hours of American Labor* (New York: Paulist Press, 1937). Already in 1931, cf. his "Leo XII and Collective Bargaining" in *America*, XLV (May 23, 1931). Haas was named to the National Labor Relations Board after its establishment by the Wagner Act in 1935.

311 He headed the Social Action department of NCWC and wrote more than a dozen books, beginning already in the twenties, championing social justice for labor. With respect to the New Deal, cf. his "Roosevelt on Social Justice" in Review of Politics, VII (July, 1945).

312 cf. *Quadragesimo anno*, #79-80.

313 Aristotle remarks that it is characteristic of tyranny to forbid or discourage any associations of the people other than those controlled by the state: the more individualism, the less danger to the tyranny. *Politics* V:11.

314 Basically, the distinction between totalitarian and authoritarian envisaged here is that the former is based on an ideology that brooks no rivals, tolerates no appeal to a (moral or religious or scientific) standard opposed to the ideology, while authoritarian regimes are based simply on a monopoly of the means of force.

315 Declaration on Religious Liberty (*Dignitatis humanae*) #15: " …there are forms of government under which…the public authorities themselves strive to deter the citizens from professing their religion and make life particularly difficult and dangerous for religious bodies."

316 Op. cit. #3.

317 "Freedom attains its full development only by accepting the truth." *Centesimus annus* #46.

318 On "solidarity", cf. *Centesimus Annus* #10. One of the topics that appears several times in these essays is that of worker participation, through councils or boards, in the decisions taken by the managers or boards of directors of corporations. This topic is not addressed here because it has commanded very little attention on the American scene (note that it is different from the role of workers in a worker-owned company, or one in which the workers are major stockholders, such as United Airlines). Part of the reason for the lack of attention is a skeptical view about how meaningful such councils have been in other countries where they have appeared, e.g., the *Mitbestimmung* of the German Worker's Councils.

319 Paul VI, *Populorum progressio*, #59.

320 E.g., John Paul II, *Sollicitudo rei socialis*, #40.

321 *Centesimus annus* #47 speaks of a kind of "crisis within democracies themselves, which seem at times to have lost the ability to make decisions aimed at the common good."

322 *Sollicitudo rei socialis* #40, my emphasis.

Biographies

Professor David A. Boileau received his doctrate from the Institute of Philosophy in Leuven (1961). He is former Dean of St. John's Seminary in Little Rock, Arkansas. He teaches ethics at Loyola University in New Orleans, has directed the Institute of Human Relations at Loyola University, the Louisiana Committee for the Humanities and Human Services for the International Brotherhood of Teamsters. He is president of the North American Association of Alumni and Alumnae of Louvain's Institute of Philosophy.

Professor Fred Crosson received his doctrate in philosophy from Notre Dame University in Indiana. From 1956 to 1958 he was Belgian American Foundation Fellow at the Institute of Philosophy in Leuven. From 1968-1975 he was Dean of the College of Arts and Letters at Notre Dame and is currently Cavanaugh Professor of Humanities at Notre Dame. He is the author of several books on philosophy and some forty articles.

Professor Dr. E. De Jonghe was an emeritus professor in the social philosophy and the history of political thought in the Catholic University of Leuven and instructor in the social doctrine of the church in Rolduc.

Professor Dr. L. Elders is a professor of metaphysics and the natural theology in the Institute for Philosophy and Theology in Rolduc of the diocese of Roermond.

Dr. B. Kettern is a member of the editorial staff of "Die Neue Ordnung" and employee in the Sozial Wissenschaftliches Intitut in Walbersberg.

Professor Dr. A. Rauscher is a professor in the social teaching of the Church in the Catholic faculty of theology at Augsberg University and he is Director of the Katholisch-Sozlal Wissenschaftliches Zentralstelle te Mönchengladbach.

Professor Dr. L. Roos is a professor of the Social Doctrine of the Church in the Catholic Faculty for Theology of the University of Bonn.

Professor Dr. M. Spieker is a professor of the social doctrine of the Church in the University of Osnabrück. He is also chairman of the International Federation for Christian Social Teaching.

Professor Dr. J. Verstraeten is a professor of the social doctrine of the Church in the Catholic University of Leuven.

Index